Financing Sustainability

This publication is a co-production between

Duisenberg school of finance

SEO Economic Research

commissioned by

Holland Financial Centre

VU University Press
De Boelelaan 1105
1081 HV Amsterdam
The Netherlands

info@vu-uitgeverij.nl
www.vuuitgeverij.nl

Design cover: Total Identity, Amsterdam
Type setting: JAPES, Amsterdam (Jaap Prummel)

ISBN 978 90 8659 559 4
NUR 780, 794

Financing Sustainability

Insights for Investors, Corporate Executives, and Policymakers

M. Kerste

N. Rosenboom

B.J. Sikken

J. Weda

VU University Press, Amsterdam

Table of Contents

Foreword

The transition of the global economy from a reliance on fossil resources to renewable resources requires an enormous amount of financing. Studies done in Europe estimate that an additional 550 billion pounds is required for the transition in the UK and 100 billion euros in the Netherlands between now and 2020. Extrapolate this globally, and the amounts become astronomical.

Financing this transition represents both a challenge and an opportunity for the financial sector. An opportunity, because financing sustainability offers new possibilities for growth. In addition, it can also be an effective way for financial institutions to demonstrate their positive contribution to society in the aftermath of the financial crisis.

A challenge, because financing the sustainable energy transition is often associated with a unique combination of risk factors. First, the earnings capacity of 'Clean Tech' investments is closely tied to the volatile prices of fossil commodities. Second, public opinion of what is sustainable and what's not constantly changes. Third, relevant legislation, subsidies and fiscal treatment are highly volatile. And finally, the technologies themselves are evolving at a rapid pace.

To sum up, great opportunities but also associated material financial risks, as is often the case with great opportunities. Thankfully, we do not have to start from scratch. We've been making these investments on a comparatively small scale for about 20 years, so we do have some experience. And the academic community has been conducting extensive research as well. Over the past few years, scientific research has contributed significantly to a better understanding of both the opportunities and risks related to financing sustainability.

With this book, which brings together the latest academic insights in a way that investors, corporate executives, and policymakers can use on a day-to-day basis, we hope to add our own positive contribution.

Sjoerd van Keulen
Chairman Holland Financial Centre

Acknowledgements

This book has been developed based on an extensive literature research. The authors therefore thank the many academics, thought leaders, and practitioners on whose research this publication has been developed.

In addition, the authors would like to express special thanks to Noreena Hertz, Professor of Globalisation, Sustainability and Finance at Duisenberg school of finance, for providing intellectual guidance to the research process.

Also special thanks to Michael Schouten, Teaching Fellow, Duisenberg school of finance, for pro-actively initiating the development of this publication.

In addition, the authors express their gratitude to Gerard van Baar, Managing Director, Centre for Finance & Sustainability, Holland Financial Centre, and Robin Fransman, Deputy Director, Holland Financial Centre, for their continuous support and stimulating advice.

Finally, the authors thank the members of the Finance & Sustainability Advisory Board at Duisenberg school of finance (Rob Bauer, Pieter Duisenberg, George Molenkamp, Dirk Schoenmaker) for their support and valuable feedback.

Amsterdam, June 2011

Marco Kerste
Nicole Rosenboom
Bernd Jan Sikken
Jarst Weda

Introduction and Overview

The Role of Finance in Accelerating the Transition towards a Sustainable Economy and Society

Finance plays a critical role in accelerating the transition towards a more sustainable economy and society. For example, significant additional investments in clean energy infrastructure are needed to meet the growing energy demands and to address the threat of climate change. New financial instruments like green bonds and index-linked carbon bonds may help spur the transition towards a low-carbon economy. Sustainable investment approaches have the potential not only to stimulate sustainable business practices, but also to generate better risk-adjusted financial returns.

Going forward, sustainability[1] – as a societal challenge, an inspirational vision, a business opportunity, and/or a way of thinking – will affect almost every profession in the financial industry. Investment managers, for example, increasingly need to take environmental and social factors into account in their investment and ownership decisions. Most insurers already anticipate extreme weather events due to climate change – such as windstorms and flooding – in their underwriting business. At the same time, climate change and the emergence of low-carbon technologies provide insurers with many new business opportunities, e.g. in the form of cover for renewable energy projects and insurance for carbon market trades. Bankers can stimulate sustainable development in a profitable way through, for example, clean energy finance, green mortgages, and pay-as-you-drive insurance. Finally, policymakers can stimulate sustainable development through clear, stable and predictable policies, and enabling/supporting innovative finance mechanisms that leverage the power of public-private partnerships.

In short, just like finance is key to sustainability, sustainability is key to finance.

The Scope of This Book

This book focuses on four specific topics in the finance & sustainability domain:

1. Financing the transition towards sustainable energy;
2. Carbon trading;

1. Whilst the term "sustainability" is being used to mean different things by different parties, this book uses the term "sustainability" in the context of the World Commission on Environment and Development (1987) definition of sustainable development. This commission (also known as the Brundtland commission) defines sustainable development as "development that meets the needs of the present without compromising the ability of future generations to meet their own needs".

3. Sustainable investing;
4. Innovations in financing environmental and social sustainability, e.g. green bonds, index-linked carbon bonds, payment for environmental services, peer-to-peer lending.

The first three topics have been selected for two main reasons: (1) their potential impact in terms of accelerating the transition towards a sustainable economy and society, (2) the maturity of the academic literature in that domain.

The fourth topic was added as the enormous challenge to build a sustainable economy and society can most likely not be met only with the existing solutions and actions. Innovative financial instruments, both publicly and privately initiated, will most likely play a key role going forward.

This book provides an overview of key insights from the academic literature. To broaden the perspective, publications from leading international organizations and think tanks have also been considered. The literature review took place in the period March to August 2010. Later publications – with a few exceptions – have therefore not been covered. The aim of the literature review in this book is to provide a broad understanding of the current academic debate on each topic, explicitly accepting that it is not possible to explore every aspect of the academic literature on each individual subject.

In this introduction, an overview of some key insights is provided for each of the four topics.

1. Financing the Transition to Sustainable Energy

Investments in sustainable energy are critical

The world is facing an enormous challenge in the transition towards a more substantial role for sustainable energy (SE) as compared to traditional energy sources. Demand for energy is continuously increasing due to economic and population growth, a demand which cannot be met by conventional energy alone in the long run. At the same time climate change, and also the need for energy security, is putting significant pressure on finding alternatives for fossil fuels.

This challenge has a strong financial element to it: the transition to sustainable energy is only possible if significant investment flows are directed towards the sustainable energy sector. Calculations of required investments vary considerably depending on operational definitions and the reduction targets underlying the calculation – stronger reduction targets obviously require higher investments.

Notwithstanding the differences, calculations from various trustworthy sources – like the Stern Review, UNFCCC, IPCC and IEA – point to a massive lack of investment flows compared with what is needed. As a reference, the Stern Review calculated required investments of US$540 billion per year starting in 2005, while global investments amounted to circa US$145 billion in 2009 and are expected to reach an annual US$500 billion only in 2030. The Stern Review presses for immediate investment, in order to avoid adaptation costs.

Investments in sustainable energy face a harsh combination of risks

As with any other investment decision, risk and return play a vital role in the funding of sustainable energy initiatives. Although the risk with SE investments is generally assessed as high, it seems that it is the *combination* of relevant risk above all that forms a barrier. Risks of specific importance to the SE sector are:

- Policy and regulatory risk: the development of SE projects is regulated and supported by governments in many ways, making financial attractiveness dependent on clear, stable and predictable public policy;
- Technological risk: SE projects are often characterized by technological and innovative solutions, with uncertainty on R&D costs, term-to-maturity, lack of capacity storage options, and whether solutions will prove fit for the intended use;
- Market uptake: the success of SE projects is often uncertain due to the development of fossil fuel prices (i.e., low price of fossil fuels decreases the attractiveness of SE), the innovative and technological character of many SE products and a lack of individual willingness to pay for end-products or advantages ('externalities'); and
- Resource risk (like the availability of wind).

At the same time, the academic assessment of financial attractiveness is inconclusive. Methodologies like the levelized cost approach and the net cost approach, using for instance the McKinsey abatement cost curve, provide interesting insights but have an important drawback: differences in risk between technologies are not taken into account. Therefore, neither approach fully reflects the investment case faced by decision-makers. Simply focusing on the actual risk-adjusted return of sustainable energy companies, by comparing financial multiples (valuation) between traditional and sustainable energy firms, has not yet led to satisfactory results either. The lack of publicly listed companies in the sustainable energy sector could be one reason for this. The diversity within the sector and the lack of experience-based financial data in many parts of the industry are other probable explanations. The research that has been done points to potential attractive returns but most of all to the need for further research in this area.

Specific barriers – like scale and regulatory barriers – prevent a massive uptake in sustainable energy investments

Although none of them is without flaws, the methodologies to assess financial attractiveness discussed in this book point to potentially viable sustainable energy investments. At the same time, the current investment flows are deemed insufficient. The literature defines sector characteristics posing barriers to sustainable energy investments. Key barriers include:

- Informational barriers: for example, as the sector is relatively young, there is limited quantitative data available on investment results. This makes it hard for investors to build and assess the financial business case. In addition, informational barriers exist in the research and development phase, where asymmetric information between investors and entrepreneurs/technicians might prevent projects from being funded;
- Scale barriers: attracting funding might be difficult when large investments are needed upfront, especially when combined with long lead times, as is the case with offshore wind and building energy efficiency;
- Market barriers: sustainable energy sources compete with fossil fuels. As such, a relatively low price of fossil fuels might prevent the uptake of sustainable energy; and
- Regulatory barriers: for example, termination of subsidies during the lifetime of a project or unexpected changes in industry standards have serious repercussions for financial attractiveness.

Both the private and public sector play an important role in overcoming these barriers and, thereby, stimulating the uptake in sustainable energy investments

Barriers can be decreased in many ways, and this can be spurred by private and/or public initiatives.

An initial option is to focus on managing risks. The specific risk challenges that SE investors face provide ample commercial opportunities for private insurers. In fact, numerous insurance products focused on SE risks have been introduced in recent years, like performance risk insurance through wind power derivatives, energy savings insurance and energy savings contracts.

From a policy perspective, many instruments exist. Often quoted policy instruments and/or recommendations include:

- Combine emission trading markets with ambitious and coherent national reduction targets;
- Implement or raise energy efficiency standards;
- Ensure consistency and reliability in public policy;
- Implement regulation on governance and transparency towards climate risks;
- Provide direct government support to R&D investments, with a specific focus on carbon capture and storage;
- Phase out subsidies for fossil fuels.

Focus should also be on innovative financial instruments...

Focusing on traditional funding sources and risk management as well as existing public policy instruments alone will not suffice. The enormous challenge ahead asks for innovative ways to increase funding by both the private (financial) sector and governmental institutions. Examples include specific climate change funds, index-linked carbon bonds and (supra)national green banks. The latter was proposed in the UK recently, and could facilitate centralizing the many dispersed government initiatives to boost SE funding as well as increase the independence of public support from the political arena. Many innovative ideas have been suggested, and future research should focus on success factors – in terms of both the process from idea to realization and the impact on funding of SE investments.

... and on specific solutions for developing countries

Future energy use will be greatly affected by the development of non-industrialized countries. Climate funding needs in developing countries are immense, and a prerequisite for successful global climate change. At the same time, developing countries face specific risks and barriers – in addition to those also encountered in developed countries. Examples include unstable and immature political, legal and tax systems, small scale, lack of technical knowledge, and poorly developed financial markets.

As the Official Development Assistance (ODA) from governments in developed countries is insufficient – and is expected to remain so – success depends on increased funding from the private sector.

The Clean Development Mechanism, which is part of the Kyoto Protocol and facilitates companies in developed countries fulfilling carbon emission reduction targets by investing in projects in developing countries, contributes to catalyzing investments but is not expected to cover total funding needs.

Many point to the Public Finance Mechanism (PFM) – financial commitments by the public sector – as an alternative to catalyze private sector investments. In particular, PFMs should be focused on catalyzing investments by institutional investors, by far the largest potential source of private funding. Recent discussions have concentrated on specific funds to attract institutional investors, like challenge funds and cornerstone funds. Further research is necessary in this field.

2. Carbon Trading

The idea of using market-based mechanisms to address negative externalities effectively and efficiently has been around for a long time

The conceptual underpinnings for carbon trading began with Pigou (1920), who pointed to the benefits of taxing companies for the negative externality emanating from pollution. Forty years later, Coase (1960) noted the reciprocal nature of harmful effects and referred to trade as an efficient and effective market-based mechanism to regulate these effects. Other economists later applied his insights specifically to environmental problems.

Notwithstanding some earlier activities, it was only with the Kyoto Protocol, signed in 1997 by 37 industrialized countries and the European Community, that carbon trading really became an economic force to take into account. Carbon trading occurs on compliance markets and voluntary markets.

Voluntary carbon markets are primarily driven by ethical, public relations, and/ or pre-compliance motives

The academic literature points out two reasons why economic agents are active on voluntary carbon markets. The first involve public relations and ethical motives. Offsetting emissions by buying credits that represent an emission reduction elsewhere might signal a sustainable image (relevant mainly for companies). Pre-compliance is the second motive for voluntary trade, and refers to trade pending future regulation – e.g. because it is expected that certain voluntary rights might eventually become part of a compliance market. Trade volumes on voluntary markets are considerably more modest than those on compliance markets. Still, these markets have shown fierce growth in recent years.

Compliance carbon markets are based on regulation

Compliance markets mostly refer to cap-and-trade schemes. In a cap-and-trade scheme governments set a limit (or cap) on the permitted level of greenhouse gas (GHG) emissions, and allocate emission allowances in accordance with this cap. By granting an increasingly insufficient number of emission allowances, these permits are growing in value and, vice versa, emissions entail growing private costs. In this way negative externalities are priced. A progressively lower cap entices companies to cut its emissions, invest in cleaner technology, or buy sufficient allowances to compensate the gap between allowed emissions (i.e. granted emission rights) and actual emissions levels.

The Kyoto Protocol is the backbone of most compliance markets

The Protocol provides for three trade mechanisms. Participants can:

- trade in allowed emissions for each country under the Protocol (so-called Assigned Amount Units, or AAUs);
- earn credits by investing in emission reduction projects in other member countries (the Joint Implementation mechanism, or JI); and/or
- earn credits by investing in emission reduction projects in developing countries (the Clean Development Mechanism, or CDM).

After ratifying the Kyoto Protocol, the EU implemented the EU Emission Trading Scheme (EU ETS), which has become the largest carbon trading market in the world. EU ETS is currently in its second phase, which ends after 2012. Despite uncertainty surrounding post-2012 global reduction targets, i.e. successor of the Kyoto Protocol, the EU has already decided on a third, 8-year trading period (2013-2020, phase III).

A single global price for carbon is not yet in sight, because there is no global carbon market and no political consensus and supporting infrastructure

Still, market-linking through project-based and other mechanisms encourages arbitrage, and this should reveal a global carbon price range. The primary drivers of carbon prices are – at least in the long term – the number of credits created, the expected demand from industry, and the ease of closing any shortfall between supply and demand using the technology and investments available during the relevant commitment period.

Assessing the success of emissions trading is highly complicated due to the impact of 'external factors' on emission levels

One of the main objectives of carbon trading is to reduce GHG emissions. Its success, and more specifically the success of its underlying mechanisms, is therefore most often measured in terms of resulting emission reduction or – as a surrogate for this – the volume of emission rights traded.

Assessing effectiveness is, however, highly complicated because the impact of carbon trading has to be isolated from other policy measures, economic developments and potential over-allocation, the latter providing opportunities to comply with obligations without having to reduce emissions.

Many view phase I of the EU ETS as a success, having laid the groundwork for the biggest emission trading scheme in the world. However, effectiveness in terms of reducing emissions has so far been limited. Lenient cap levels in phase I (2005-2007) and over-allocation due partly to economic recession in phase II (2008-2012) have failed to impose real restrictions, and emissions actually increased. Stricter caps in phase III (2013-2020), along with less free allocation of emission rights (phasing out 'grandfathering' of emission rights), are expected to result in a 'short' position, however.

Policy uncertainty creates an additional risk factor for investment decisions

Public policy impacts the pricing of carbon emissions. Clear public policy is therefore a precondition for the effective functioning of carbon markets. In the past few years, though, the business sector has received mixed messages from politicians around the world. For example, the outcome of Copenhagen has resulted in "a significant step backwards" for prospects of international carbon markets (Blyth, 2010).

Still, it is important to note that climate policy risk will not impact all business investment cases in the same way. IEA (2007), for example, indicates that (i) policy risk is greater for investment decisions made close to a potential policy change, that (ii) policy risk is more pronounced if climate policy is a dominant economic driver, and that (iii) risk premiums depend on the technology being considered, the market context and the exact climate change policy mechanism under consideration.

3. Sustainable Investing

Most empirical studies indicate that integrating sustainability principles into business strategies can enhance corporate financial performance

In the academic literature, many different definitions of Corporate Social Responsibility (CSR) exist. In this book, it is defined as a combination of:

- good corporate governance: protecting shareholders' interests;
- environmental efficiency: protecting environmental stakeholders' interests; and
- good stakeholder relations: protecting the interests of stakeholders other than shareholders and environmental stakeholders, including those of employees and the local community.

Notwithstanding the empirical challenges of determining the financial bottom line of CSR, most empirical studies indicate that CSR can enhance corporate financial performance, regardless of which aspect of corporate responsibility the study focuses on – corporate governance, environmental performance or stakeholder relations.

The 'value drivers' that support the business case for CSR include operational efficiency opportunities, increased brand value and reputation, better risk management, attracting and retaining talented employees, and pre-empting regulatory intervention.

Most empirical studies indicate that including environmental, social, and governance (ESG) information into investment decisions has at least the potential to generate better risk-adjusted financial returns

Empirical research on the economic rationale for Socially Responsible Investment (SRI)[2] generally focuses on the question of whether SRI funds provide better returns than comparable conventional funds. Three meta-studies are discussed in this book, compromising 47 academic studies[3] in total. Two main conclusions can be drawn. First, many academic studies produce statistically insignificant results. This may indicate that, overall, no clear differences exist between the performance of SRI funds compared to conventional funds. Or it may indicate that more refined research methodologies are needed to measure potential differences. Second, independent of the degree of significance of the statistical results, most studies indicate a positive or neutral-positive link between ESG factors and investment performance. This supports the hypothesis that including ESG factors in investment decisions has the

2. In this book, SRI is considered as a generic term for investment approaches that incorporate ESG issues into fund management. It covers, for example, ethical investing, impact investing, and sustainable investing. Sustainable investing, the main focus in this book, is defined as an investment approach that integrates long-term ESG criteria into investment and ownership decision-making with the objective of generating superior risk-adjusted financial returns.

3. It is important to note that most of these studies focus on SRI funds in general and not specifically on sustainable investments (a sub-category of SRI).

potential to enhance investment performance. This hypothesis is also confirmed by a number of recent academic studies which use refined econometric techniques (multi-factor models). In general, these studies reach a positive verdict on the question of whether SRI funds outperform conventional funds.

More and more investors are looking at ways to integrate sustainability information into investment and ownership decisions with the objective of generating superior risk-adjusted financial returns

Since its launch in April 2006, almost 900 asset owners, investment managers, and professional services organizations[4] have signed the UN-backed Principles of Responsible Investment (PRI). These principles aim to integrate consideration of ESG issues into investment decision-making and ownership practices, and thereby improve long-term returns.

Today, many asset owners and asset managers no longer focus on the question of whether sustainability considerations lead to better risk-adjusted investment returns, but rather on how to improve the investment performance through a sustainability focus.

Sustainable investing is not yet a mainstream approach; significant barriers exist

Various key barriers are currently inhibiting the transition towards sustainable investing as a mainstream investment approach. A study from the World Economic Forum (2011), based on a survey among investor and corporate executives, highlights the following key barriers:

- For investors, e.g. restrictions in conventional valuation models, lack of ESG expertise;
- For corporations, e.g. insufficient integration of sustainability factors into core business strategies, lack of a formal approach in setting ESG targets and holding senior staff accountable;
- For investor-corporation interaction, e.g. lack of clarity on which ESG factors are financially material and over which time frame; and
- At the system-wide level , e.g. disproportionate focus on short-term performance and issues with a near-term impact.

Overcoming these key barriers requires efforts from investors, corporations, and other key stakeholders in the investment value chain

The study from the World Economic Forum (2011) highlights various strategic options for asset owners, asset managers, corporations, and other key stakeholders to

4. Status in May 2011.

overcome these key barriers and thereby help accelerate the transition towards sustainable investing. For example:

- Where appropriate, linking incentives in the investment value chain more towards superior risk-adjusted financial performance over the long term;
- Buy- and sell-side analysts working with corporate executives to determine key performance indicators for financially material ESG factors at the sector level, and asset owners using their mandates to asset managers to encourage the analysis of these factors.

4. Innovations in Financing Environmental and Social Sustainability

Innovative financing focuses on a 'non-traditional' use of financial instruments that aim to generate additional funds for development and/or improves the effectiveness of existing funds for development

Innovative financing is often used in the context of the Millennium Development Goals, being aimed at finding alternative sources to finance their achievement. During the International Conference on Financing for Development in 2002, the international community explicitly recognized the value of exploring innovative sources of finance.

Being a relatively young academic discipline, Innovative Finance (IF) lacks an internationally agreed definition. The three main elements generally included are: (i) IF refers to the 'non-traditional' use of financial instruments; (ii) IF generates additional funds for development; and/or (iii) IF improves the effectiveness of existing funds for development.

Most literature on IF focuses on official flows to developing countries aimed at improving poverty, health and/or the environment. In this book a slightly enlarged scope is used: Innovative Finance, as defined by the three elements above, aims at providing funds to developing and developed countries for 'social and environmental development' by means of official flows and purely private mechanisms.

Many innovative finance instruments have a relatively short history, which makes it difficult to analyze their effectiveness

Most IF instruments have not been implemented for long, or are even still in their design phase. Assessment of the experience so far is still in its infancy. Lacking an academic consensus on how to assess IF instruments, this book defines a general framework to describe and analyze them. The framework comprises five steps, in which the following characteristics of the instruments are described:

1. Underlying problem and objectives
2. Structure of the instrument
3. Place of the instrument in the IF landscape
4. Business case assessment (before implementation)
5. Impact and lessons learned (after implementation)

This framework is used to assess a sample of IF instruments.

Examples of innovative finance instruments include: green bonds, index-linked carbon bonds, payment for environmental services, peer-to-peer lending

Green bonds (GB) are aimed at increasing funding resources for low-carbon investments by creating a financial instrument that appeals to the debt market, especially institutional investors, and at increasing low-carbon investments by decreasing debt risk premiums for this type of project and activity. Green bonds are advocated by many institutions, and several have been issued in the last five years. Still, the funds generated are relatively small compared with the required investment flows.

Index-linked carbon bonds (ILCB) are aimed at increasing low-carbon investments by providing a hedge for investors facing regulatory risks. ILCBs are government-issued bonds, with interest payments linked to the outcome (measurable) of public policy. ILCBs in their simplest form link the return of the bond to the actual GHG emissions of the issuing country against published targets, with higher GHG emissions resulting in a higher interest rate to be paid by the issuing country. As the return of the bond is linked to the extent governments keep their promises on low-carbon policies – e.g. the promise to decrease GHG emissions to a certain level – an ILCB offers the opportunity for an investor to mitigate regulatory risks. In practical terms: an investor buys a government bond – the ILCB – and invests in a low-carbon project of choice. The financial return of the low-carbon project will depend on the government keeping its promise on, for example, the level of feed-in tariffs for renewable energy. If the government fails to do so, the return of the project will decrease, but the interest received on the bond will increase. Although ILCBs are not used as yet, they offer an interesting opportunity to decrease regulatory risk, one of the key barriers for investments in sustainable energy.

Payments for Environmental Services (PES) try to correct the market failure of split incentives between landowners and the beneficiaries of ecosystem services. For example, deforestation might be in the interest of a landowner, but the loss of environmental services – such as carbon sequestration and storage, biodiversity protection, watershed protection, and landscape/scenic beauty – is to the detriment of the many beneficiaries. PES schemes seek to reconcile conflicting interests through compensation. They are intended "to support positive environmental externalities through the transfer of financial resources from beneficiaries of certain environmental services to those who provide these services or are fiduciaries of environmental resources" (Mayrand & Paquin, 2004). The goal of PES programs is to make privately unprofitable but socially desirable practices profitable to individual land users, thus causing them to adopt them (Engel et al., 2008).

Another example of innovative finance instruments is Peer-to-Peer (P2P) lending. P2P lending is an alternative credit market that allows individual borrowers and lenders to engage in credit transactions without traditional banking intermediaries while they aggregate small amounts of money provided by a number of individual lenders to create moderately sized, uncollateralized loans to individual borrowers. Web-based P2P lending markets have grown excessively, with e.g. the well-known P2P company Prosper having provided funding amounting to $179 million between 2006 and 2009 and Kiva, a not-for-profit P2P finance company, $60 million between 2007 and 2009.

In the following chapters, a literature overview is provided on each of the four topics. Chapter 1 concerns financing the transition towards sustainable energy; Chapter 2 insights into carbon trading; and Chapter 3 sustainable investing. Innovations in financing environmental and social sustainability (e.g. green bonds, index-linked carbon bonds, payment for environmental services, peer-to-peer lending) are described in chapter 4.

1. Financing the Transition to Sustainable Energy

Chapter Overview

1.1 Introduction

In the long term, economic growth and population growth will inevitably put pressure on the availability of conventional energy. At the same time, climate change and the need for energy security imply mirrored dynamics, but with the same result: the need to find alternatives for fossil fuels. The transition from conventional towards sustainable energy (SE) sources requires significant investments. As yet, however, the flows going to the SE sector are far from sufficient. This chapter highlights the leading literature and empirical research on 'financing the transition to sustainable energy'. It first describes the environmental and corresponding investment challenge. Then the attractiveness of SE investments is discussed, defining risks and barriers standing in the way of the required magnitude of funding. Acknowledging that the current level of funding is clearly insufficient to meet the challenge of climate change, Section 1.4 provides insight into the instruments – both private and public – to increase funding. The last section focuses on developing countries, whose role is essential but most challenging in fighting climate change.

1.2 Sustainable Energy

1.2.1 Sustainable Energy: Saving the Future

Defining sustainable energy

Sustainable Energy (SE) is the provision of energy such that it meets the needs of the present without compromising the ability of future generations to meet their own needs.[1] It has two key components: renewable energy technology (RET or RE) and energy efficiency (EE).[2] Power-generating RETs include wind power (onshore and offshore), solar power (photovoltaic and thermal electricity generation), geothermal power, small-scale hydropower, ocean/tidal power, municipal solid waste-to-energy and biomass (Figure 1). Liquid biofuels include first-generation (sugar-based) and second-generation (cellulosic, algal, etc.). Although nuclear energy and large-scale hydropower meet the aforementioned definition of SE, they are generally not regarded as such.[3]

Figure 1 Renewable Energy Technologies

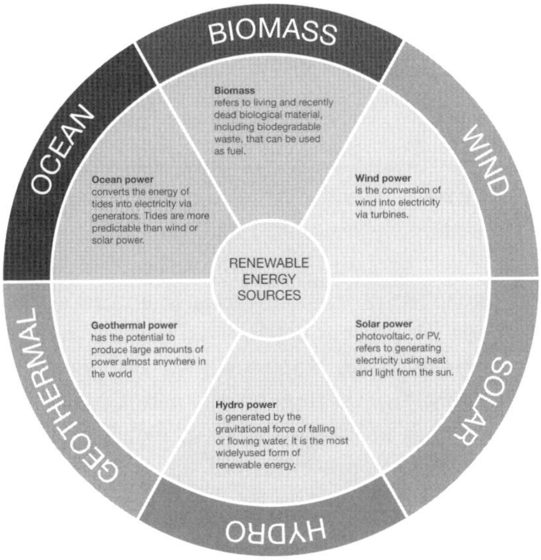

Source: PwC (2009, p. 15)

1. Renewable Energy & Energy Efficiency Partnership (REEEP) and Tester (2005, p. xix).

2. Sustainable energy overlaps with the term 'clean technology' or 'cleantech', which was popularized in large part through the work of the Cleantech Group. It is a broader concept and consists of 11 segments. Cleantech includes, among others, energy storage, energy infrastructure, transportation, water (waste water), materials, recycling and agriculture.

3. Large hydro can have severe negative environmental consequences (WEF, 2010, p. 56). Nuclear power in its current form has many concerns regarding costs, safety, waste disposal and proliferation (WEF, 2010, p. 26).

Improving energy efficiency represents the largest, most cost-effective and immediately available way to mitigate greenhouse gas emissions (WEF, 2009b, p. 8). The International Energy Agency (IEA, 2009) reckons that energy efficiency gains account for more than half of the abatement potential in its "450 Scenario".[4] Other research hints at comparable potential (Efiong, 2007; Project Catalyst, 2009). With total investments of US$170 billion in existing technologies (water heating, heating and cooling, lighting and appliances), total annual energy savings of roughly US$900 billion a year could be achieved (Farrell & Remes, 2008, p. 1).

The energy and climate challenge ahead

The global population has grown from 2.5 billion in 1950 to 6.5 billion in 2005 and is expected to expand a further 2.5 billion to over 9 billion people in 2050. This is the equivalent of two Chinas, with its current population of 1.3 billion. Already there has been a strong surge of resource/energy prices in line with GDP growth in emerging economies (e.g., Brazil, Russia, India and China), indicating that population growth without corresponding increases in the energy supply will result in considerable cost increases. Some projections indicate that by 2030, total energy consumption could reach almost twice its 1980 level. Accommodating this demand with the 'traditional' energy supply seems impossible. In other words, renewable energy sources are first and foremost essential to provide the minimum requirements for sustaining human life (Mizuguchi & Monoe, 2009, pp. 4-7; PwC, 2009, p. 10).

Along with economic growth and corresponding consumption and production requirements, the second major factor contributing to the need for sustainable energy is climate change. The Intergovernmental Panel on Climate Change (IPCC) argues that "most of the observed increase in global average temperatures since the mid-20th century is likely due to the observed increase in anthropogenic GHG concentrations" (IPCC, 2007, p. 10). To prevent detrimental climate change, the IPCC reasons that deep emission cuts are required. Many scientists and policymakers, including the United Nations Framework Convention on Climate Change (UNFCCC) and the European Union, believe that holding the rise in global mean temperatures below two degrees Celsius compared to pre-industrial times is essential (Enkvist, Nauclér, & Rosander, 2007; McKinsey & Company, 2009; Müller, 2008).

A third driver behind RET is security of energy supply, i.e., increasing fuel independence (M. Thompson, Elford, Glover, Prouty, & Quealy, 2007). Energy supply is "secure" if it is adequate, affordable and reliable. Security risks include the incapacity of an electricity infrastructure system to meet growing load demand; the threat of an attack on the centralized production, transmission and distribution grids or pipelines; or global oil and gas supply restrictions due to political actions, or even just volatile prices. For example, the EU's dependency on a foreign supply of fossil fuels is likely

4. The number 450 refers to stabilizing the atmospheric concentration of CO_2e at 450 parts per million.

to increase over time.[5] Increasing shares of RETs could reduce any temporary interruption of fossil fuels due to disputes with oil (transport) providers.

Energy use will continue to rise progressively with global economic and population growth. To keep up with energy demand and simultaneously stabilize the atmospheric concentrations of CO_2 equivalents[6] at levels the scientific community deems safe, sustainable energy sources are vital. This requires immediate action. From an environmental point of view, a single year of delaying abatement could cause 1.8 $GtCO_2e$ of additional emissions globally.[7] In case of delay, emissions would grow according to the business-as-usual scenario. During a year of delay, high-carbon infrastructure with long lifetimes (e.g., coal-fired power plants) would be built in order to meet economic growth requirements and to replace depreciated assets. In addition to forgone abatement of 1.8 $GtCO_2e$, the new high-carbon infrastructure causes a lock-in effect and commits the world to 25 $GtCO_2e$ of cumulative emissions over the following 14 years.[8] Based on these calculations, delaying abatement by 10 years, from 2010 to 2020, causes a reduction of 40% of the potential abatement, results in a cumulative lost abatement opportunity of 280 $GtCO_2e$ by 2030 (comparable to 25 times the combined emission of the US and China in 2005), and a massive lock-in effect (McKinsey & Company, 2009, p. 46).

1.2.2 *Funding Sustainable Energy*

The investment challenge

To meet energy demand and prevent climate change, investment in sustainable energy is of critical importance.[9] Numerous institutions and authors have calculated the investments required for abatement:

- Sir Nicholas Stern estimated the annual global investment needed to avoid the worst impacts of climate change to be around 1% of global GDP each year provided that action is started immediately. At the time, global GDP was circa US$54 trillion. Therefore, the global investment estimates in the *Stern Review* amount to circa US$540 billion annually (Cameron & Blood, 2009, p. 6; Stern et al., 2006). Four pathways to lower GHG emissions are set out in the *Stern Review*: reducing

5. Currently 85% of the EU's oil is imported. Almost all oil will be imported by 2030, by which time 85% of gas and 60% of coal will also be imported.

6. The global warming impact of other GHG is measured in terms of equivalency to the impact of carbon dioxide (CO_2) via global warming potentials.

7. The figures and conclusions on delaying abatement discussed in the remainder of this section are based on McKinsey & Company (2009).

8. 14 years is the average effective lifetime of high-carbon infrastructure. However, the range is broad: coal-fired power plants have a lifespan of 40 to 50 years, many industrial plants 20 to 30 years, and vehicles typically 10 to 20 years (McKinsey & Company, 2009, p. 47)

9. Here, the focus is on the road towards sustainable energy. In terms of responding investments, this means the focus is on prevention (referred to as 'mitigation') and not on anticipative measures to alleviate the adverse impacts of climate change (referred to as 'adaptation').

demand for emissions-intensive goods and services, increasing energy efficiency, action on non-energy emissions (e.g., avoiding deforestation), and switching to lower-carbon technologies for power, heat and transport. Stern admits that a portfolio of technologies will be required, since "[i]t is highly unlikely that any single technology will deliver all the necessary emission savings, because all technologies are subject to constraints of some kind, and because of the wide range of activities and sectors that generate greenhouse-gas emissions" (Stern et al., 2006, p. xiv);

- The UN estimated that US$200 to 210 billion worth of additional investment and financial flows would be necessary in 2030 to return global GHG emissions to current levels. This figure is divided between 7 sectors – energy supply, industry, buildings, transportation, waste, agriculture and forestry – and technology R&D[10] (UNFCCC, 2007);
- To realize the abatement potential as calculated by McKinsey & Company, global incremental investments (i.e., investments above and beyond business-as-usual) of €320 billion annually for the period 2011-2015 would be required, increasing to €810 billion for the period 2026-2030, of which roughly 60% is needed in the transport and buildings sectors.[11] These figures correspond to 5 to 6% of projected global investments in fixed assets in the business-as-usual scenario in the respective periods (McKinsey & Company, 2009, pp. 40-41);
- The International Energy Agency (IEA), in its "450 Scenario", describes another way of meeting the world's energy needs while restricting emissions to a level consistent with a 2°C temperature increase. It estimates that this scenario would require a total investment of US$38 trillion between now and 2030, equivalent to 2% of global gross domestic product (GDP). This is US$10.5 trillion more than required under the business-as-usual scenario. The largest chunk of additional investment, around 45% (US$4.7 trillion), is needed in transport, followed by buildings (US$2.5 trillion), power plants (US$1.7 trillion), industry (US$1.1 trillion) and (second-generation) biofuels production (IEA, 2009; WEF, 2010);[12]
- The Intergovernmental Panel on Climate Change (IPCC) reckons that the costs of cutting GHG emissions by 50% by 2050 could be in the range of 1 to 3% of global GDP (IPCC, 2007; The World Bank, 2010).

Clearly, the calculations of investments required for abatement differ substantially. These differences in outcomes are partly due to the operational definitions used by the respective institutions. For example, some institutions calculate the funds needed to cover the incremental costs of a low-carbon project over its lifetime (mitigation costs), while others calculate the additional financing requirement created as a result of the project (incremental investment needs). The latter can be up to 3 times higher

10. Detailed information on the (additional) financial requirement per sector can be found in chapter four of UNFCCC (2007, pp. 35-95).

11. See Exhibit 4.2.1 in McKinsey & Company (2009, p. 42) for a detailed breakdown of both figures.

12. In this business-as-usual or "Reference Scenario", a global mean temperature increase of 6°C per 2030 is estimated.

than the former.[13] In addition, mitigation costs increase steeply with the stringency of emission reduction targets and with the certainty of reaching them. The policy choices assumed by the institutions greatly influence the outcome of their calculations.

Although sources differ in their calculation methods and results, it is evident that current investment flows are insufficient to meet funding requirements. Total global annual investment in sustainable energy amounted to US$145 billion in 2009. It looks set to rise to US$200 billion in 2010, and to continue growing beyond that, to US$500 billion per 2030 (WEF, 2010).[14] This leaves, regardless of which model or source is used for funding requirements, a gap between the funding flowing into sustainable energy and what is needed to reach global climate goals.

An important elaboration of this assertion is the question of where this gap originates. Merely identifying the discrepancy between current investment flows and the funding requirements to meet global climate goals leaves this question unanswered. There are various options:

- a gap between the funding needs to meet government commitments (e.g., EU agreements) and available finance;
- a gap between available finance and the funding needs of existing SE projects;
- a gap between available finance and the number of SE projects, i.e., are there enough creative inventors and courageous entrepreneurs in energy, compared to other sectors?

This question is underexposed in current policy reports and the academic literature.[15] It seems that the general assumption is that available finance (i.e., capital supply) is insufficient compared to funding needs (i.e., capital demand). Whether this concerns a discrepancy between climate ambitions and funding (the first gap) or a discrepancy between the funding needs of existing projects and the available finance (the second gap) is often left an open question.

13. Many clean investments have high up-front capital costs, followed later by savings in operating costs. Therefore, the incremental financing requirements tend to be higher than the lifetime costs reported in mitigation models (The World Bank, 2010).

14. For an update of these figures, reference is made to WEF (2011).

15. Some of the few examples include Wustenhagen & Teppo (2006, pp. 9-10), who hint at a possible shortage of entrepreneurs in the SE sector, and UNEP (2009, p.14), who point to a "shortage of deal flow" as a constraint against institutional investors being active in low-carbon investments. UNEP (2009, p.19), however, further defines this as "a shortage of sufficiently commercially attractive, easily executable deals" with one of the prime reasons being that projects are too small. In the view of the writers of this book, this underlines the importance of one of the barriers for funding (lack of scale) and does not reflect a lack of projects.

Funding sources

SE investments can be funded by either equity or debt.[16] *Equity* means selling a stake in the project or company, providing (partial) right of ownership, control and a stake in residual earnings. Typical equity providers for SE investments are venture capital firms (VC), private equity firms (PE), infrastructure funds[17] and pension funds. Alternatively, companies or project developers might make an initial public offering (IPO) or issue additional shares, raising capital on the stock market from a wide range of investors.

With *debt finance*, funds are borrowed for a specified period under certain terms and conditions including an interest rate and loan repayment schedule. Mezzanine finance is a hybrid type of lending with a risk-return profile between equity and loans. Repayments are scheduled behind senior debt, resulting in higher risk. Providers of mezzanine therefore demand a higher interest rate compared with senior debt. Still, risk and return are lower than that of equity capital. Typical providers of debt to SE investments are banks.

The various providers of funds have different risk-return profiles, resulting in a focus on different types of investment projects in different parts of the technology life cycle. VC, for example, accept relatively high risks but demand high returns. They are therefore an important funding source for start-ups which usually have a high-risk profile. Table 1 summarizes the various funding sources, the type of investment they typically focus on in view of risks and an indication of levels of return.

Table 1 Typical funding sources of sustainable energy investments

Source	Equity				Equity/debt	Debt
	Venture capital	Private equity	Infrastructure funds	Pension funds	Banks – mezzanine	Banks – senior debt
Typical investment characteristics	Start-ups, new technology, prototypes	Pre-IPO companies, demonstrator technology	Proven technology, private companies	Proven technology	Demonstrator/ proven technology, new companies	Proven technology, established companies
Expected Return*	IRR: > 50%	IRR: 35%	IRR: 15%	IRR: 15%	LIBOR+700 bps	LIBOR+300 bps

Source: adapted from UNEP, SEFI, NEF, & Chatman House (2009); * returns are purely indicative and reflect market conditions per June 2009; IRR = Internal Rate of Return; LIBOR = London Interbank Offered Rate

16. A third option is internal funding. The focus here is on external funding.
17. Funds drawn from a range of institutional investors and pension funds, targeting infrastructural projects like roads and power-generating utilities (long duration, steady and low-risk cash flows).

Figure 2 gives examples of different types of SE, categorized according to the stage of development of the technology and the type of financing that private capital markets typically commit in each stage.

Figure 2 Sustainable energy by stage of maturity and private funding sources

Stage of Technology Development	Early R&D, Proof of Concept	Demonstration & Scale-Up	Commercial Roll-Out	Diffusion & Maturity
Examles of Sustainable Energy Technologies	• Advanced battery chemistries • Algal biofuels • Artificial photosynthesis • Fuel cells (automotive) • Hydrogen storage • Integrated biorefineries • Material science • Next-generation solar • Osmotic power • Synthetic genomics	• Carbon Capture & Storage • Cellulosic biofuels • Enhanced geothermal power • Floating offshore wind • Fuel cells (distributed generation) • Grid-scale power storage • Marine (wave, tide) • Plug-in hybrids • Solar Thermal Electricity Generation • Smart grid	• Biodigestors • Coal-bed methane • Fuel Cells (UPS) • Heat pumps • Hybrids • Industrial energy efficiency • LED lighting • Offshore wind • Solar photovoltaics • Small-scale hydro • Smart meters	• Building insulation • Bicycles • Compact Fluorescent Lights • Condensing boilers • Large-scale hydro • Municipal solid waste • Onshore wind • Public transport • Sugar-cane based ethanol • Traditional geothermal power • Waste methane capture

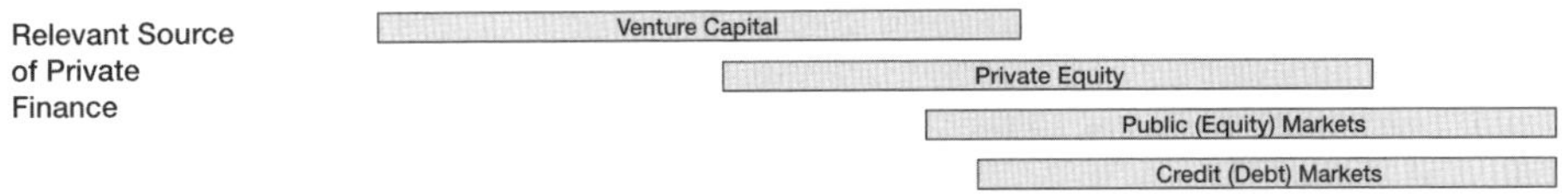

Source: WEF (2010, p. 35)

Funding can be based on a specific project (project finance) or on the company starting the project (corporate finance or on-balance sheet finance). Available funds for project finance deals depend on the cash flow the project is expected to generate and the specific risk profile of the project. With corporate finance, the company receiving the funds decides which part is used for which projects. In that case there is no (or a limited) link between availability of funding and the project characteristics; investors provide the company with funding based on the risk-return profile of the company. Not all SE investments will have the luxury to choose between the two financing models, mainly depending on the scale of the project or company. For investments "ranging from several tens to hundreds of millions of euros, the project initiator often has not enough capital available to finance the project on its balance sheet, and therefore project finance is used" (de Jager et al., 2008). Especially larger companies investing in SE can choose between the two models and will do so based on which one provides the cheapest funding.[18]

18. Attractiveness also depends on fiscal regimes and public support schemes.

1.3 Business Case for Funding of Sustainable Energy Investments

1.3.1 *Introduction*

Understanding capital flows to sustainable energy sectors requires insight into investment decisions. City of London et al. (2009) puts the importance of this point as follows, “whilst it is clear that business has a critical role to play in financing, developing and deploying low carbon solutions, it is important to understand that investors … need to make returns on this investment”. Financial attractiveness being key, a generally accepted way of understanding investment and funding decisions is the discounted cash flow methodology.[19] By discounting all future cash flows (CF) to one moment, treating investments as negative cash flows, the net present value (NPV) of an investment is calculated.[20] The cash flows are discounted by means of the weighted average cost of capital (WACC), reflecting the return demanded by the providers of debt and equity.

$$NPV = \sum_{t=0}^{N} \frac{CF(t)}{(1+WACC)^t}$$

Projects with a NPV greater than zero are economically viable, because the return on the investment is then expected to be higher than the required return by investors. Financial attractiveness is therefore determined by expected return (i.e., future cash flows) and required return. The latter is directly linked to risk: investors demand higher return, and thus a higher WACC, for investments with higher risk.

1.3.2 *Risks*

Investment decisions require an in-depth analysis of risks potentially impacting success and profitability. Risk assessment typically includes analyzing a number of risk areas, identifying the risks that are of importance for the investment under consideration as well as their expected impact.[21] The following general risk areas are considered:

- Project-level risk: risks specific to the selected project, e.g., lead time risk (i.e., estimating time and costs involved in the planning stage), construction risk, technological risk (i.e., will the technology work, be fit for the purpose, etc.), environmental risk, and operation and management risk;

---

19. Biermans et al. (2009) conclude that SE investments have to obtain their funding from the same capital markets as any other investment. This implies that financial attractiveness is a key variable in decisions on funding SE investments, as it is for other investments.

20. This ‘moment’ is generally the start of the investment life cycle.

21. This assessment is used as an input to determine the required return, i.e., the WACC in the NPV formula, with a higher (non-diversifiable) risk profile resulting in a higher WACC. For a more detailed discussion on WACC calculation see for instance Brealey & Myers (2003).

- Economic and financial risk: adverse changes in financial/economic factors like interest rates, currency exchange rates and inflation;
- Market risk: market-specific risks, like resource risk (referring to the availability, quality and price of, e.g., raw materials, funding and human resources), competitive environment and market adoption risks (i.e., the demand for a new product);
- Country and political risk: country-specific economic and political risks,[22] like government (in)stability and the status and maturity of the legal system, including a solid basis for security over assets, policy and regulatory risk (i.e., adverse changes in policy and regulations);
- Force majeure risk: risk of natural catastrophes.

Building on Justice (UNEP et al., 2009), Ecofys (de Jager et al., 2008), Sjöö (2008), Meijer, Hekkert, & Koppenjan (2007), Wustenhagen & Teppo (2004; 2006) and SEFI & Marsh (2005), the following risks are of specific importance for SE investments:

Policy and regulatory risk

Regulatory risk is often assessed as one of the main risks of SE investments. Governments tend to support the deployment of sustainable energy in many ways, while also regulating relevant procedures and impacting the competitive environment (e.g., fossil fuel subsidies). Regulation and policy instruments include licensing procedures, subsidies, tax-based incentives, portfolio standards, liberalization of the electricity market, emission regulation – just to name a few. Success and profitability are often heavily, and directly, influenced by public policy, implying that adverse deviations from expected policy regimes pose a serious risk.

To get a grip on this risk and assess its possible impact, investors will analyze the "duration of the regime, its legal basis, its ability to be amended, a country's track record of continually adjusting or replacing legislation, and the impact of a change of political party in government" (UNEP et al., 2009). Another, more direct, instrument is lobbying for particular forms of regulation.

Unclear, unstable and unpredictable public policy can hamper the development of sustainable energy. Policymakers should take this into account. At the same time, the length of regulation certainty cannot be expected to be infinite. Defining the minimum length of regulation required for investors to build a solid business case could prove helpful for policymakers, especially for instruments directly impacting investment return like feed-in tariffs. This will obviously depend on the planning and financing horizon, but also on the dependency of public policy over the lifetime of a project (this will most often decrease). The only source found on this subject is SEFI & Marsh (2005), which roughly estimates 10 years would be sufficient for onshore wind, while offshore wind would require 15 years due to its longer planning and financing horizon.

22. Part of political risks refers to policies on a supranational level, e.g., EU legislation.

Technological risk

Technology is generally an important element in SE investments. Exploiting the potential of renewable energy sources in an economically efficient way, as well as increasing the efficiency of current energy use, often calls for (innovative) technological solutions. The development of these technologies is risky because it is not certain what the R&D costs will turn out to be, how long it will take for the technology to become mature, whether the technology will work, and whether it will prove fit for its intended use.

Resource risk

Resource risk can refer to the availability of the resource as such, like is the case with wind. But also when resources are generally available, SE projects might have to compete for them with others. An interesting ethical example is the use of corn as fuel or as food (Sjöö, 2008). Wustenhagen & Teppo (2006) point to human capital as a potential resource risk. The SE sector, being relatively young, is highly dependent on entrepreneurial skills. Investors might fear that the sector attracts idealists rather than entrepreneurs, making them vulnerable to poor management of their investment.

Market adoption risk

As with any 'new' industry, SE investments face uncertainties in the market uptake. The innovative and technological character of many SE solutions makes it even harder to predict consumer interest. Market adoption further depends on SE-specific regulation (e.g., product standards like energy classes) and the role of utility companies (e.g., connection of small-scale energy projects to the electricity grid).

Prices of fossil fuels influence the competitive environment and impact market uptake. Assumptions about the development of fossil fuels will therefore be part of the business case. If actual prices are lower than expected, the relative attractiveness of SE sources will decline, resulting in a lower return on investment.

The benefits of SE technologies are for a large part not private but societal in nature. Although society at large would be expected to attribute value to these benefits, this is not reflected in an individual willingness to pay. Many times, market adoption for SE investments therefore depends on making someone pay for these externalities (e.g., via carbon emission trading).

Table 2 provides an overview of the main risks for SE investments per risk area.

Table 2 Main risks of sustainable energy investments

Risk area	General description of risk area	Main SE risks
Project-level risk	Risks specific to the selected project: - lead time risk (i.e., estimating time and costs involved in the planning stage), - construction risk, - technological risk (i.e., will the technology work, be fit for the purpose, etc.), - environmental risk and - operation and management risk	- Technological risk - Lead time risk
Economic and financial risk	Adverse changes in financial/economic factors, like: - interest rates, - currency exchange rates, - inflation	- Not of specific importance
Market risk	Market-specific risks: - resource risk (referring to availability, quality and price of, e.g., raw materials, funding and human resources), - competitive environment (i.e., characteristics and actions of competitors, impacting competitive position of the firm/project/product), - market adoption risks (i.e., the demand for a new product)	- Resource risk - Development of fossil fuel prices - Market adoption risk
Country and political risk	Country-specific economic and political risks, like: - government (in)stability, - status and maturity of the legal system including a solid basis for security over assets, - policy and regulatory risk (i.e., adverse changes in policy and regulations)	- Policy and regulatory risk
Force majeure risk	Risk of natural catastrophes	- Not of specific importance

Source: SEO Economic Research, based on de Jager et al., (2008), Meijer et al. (2007), SEFI & Marsh (2005), Sjöö (2008), UNEP et al. (2009); Wustenhagen & Teppo (2006)

1.3.3 *Financial Attractiveness*

Financial attractiveness is determined by the combination of risk and return. Comparing the financial attractiveness of investment opportunities is usually based on public stock market figures providing insight into financial ratios on profitability compared to, e.g., company market value, shares outstanding or funding obligations. If individual companies are not publicly quoted, experience with other companies (publicly quoted) in the sector is combined with company-specific data.[23] The literature on the attractiveness of SE investments, however, is not often based on financial ratio analysis. Below, the methodologies which are used instead – the levelized cost approach and the net cost approach – are discussed first; thereafter the literature on the financial ratio analysis, which *is* available.

Levelized cost approach

Much of the research on the development of alternatives to fossil fuels has focused on comparative costs (Houghton & Cruden, 2009). Being an important lever in competitiveness and market uptake, relative costs would provide a good indication of the financial attractiveness. A way to compare cost levels is the concept of *levelized cost.* The levelized cost represents the present value of the total cost of building and operating a generating plant over its economic life, converted to equal annual payments.[24]

Lazard (2008, p. 2) uses the concept of levelized cost to assess the comparative financial attractiveness of renewable energy technologies based on US cost figures. The authors conclude that certain renewable energy technologies are already cost-competitive compared with conventional generation technologies, even before factoring in environmental and other externalities (like potential carbon emission costs) or the fast-increasing construction and fuel costs affecting conventional generation technologies.[25] This is illustrated in Figure 3.

Figure 3 classifies levelized costs ($/MWh) per sector, divided into sustainable energy types ("alternative energy") and non-sustainable types ("conventional energy"). Each sector comprises a variety of technologies, and therefore ranges of levelized costs are presented.[26]

Lazard's exercise is a good example of an in-depth levelized cost analysis. Other examples include NEA, IEA, & OECD (2005), CUPC (2008) and WEF (2010). Results of levelized cost analyses vary significantly, however, across existing studies due to underlying assumptions, e.g., fuel price projections and employment of different discount rates (Van Kooten & Timilsina, 2009, p. 11). A general consensus on the most suitable assumptions does not seem to have been reached yet. A general drawback of the levelized cost approach is that externalities are not included, and therefore the costs do not reflect the total costs to society.

---

23. Most often, a NPV calculation approach underlies the analyses.
24. Definition taken from IEA's 'Energy Glossary'.
25. Costs do not include transmission costs to connect electricity grids, which could be substantial for wind power, especially where wind farms are remotely sited (e.g., offshore or mountainous regions). Costs are levelized in real dollars (i.e., adjusted to remove the impact of inflation).
26. Levelized costs of solar thermal, for example, vary from US$90 to US$145 per MWh, with 'solar tower' representing the lower boundary and 'solar trough' representing the upper boundary.

Figure 3 Levelized cost of energy comparison (2008 US$)[27]

Source: Lazard (2008, p. 2)

The levelized costs are determined as a price level which would facilitate a fixed return for all technologies, net of the costs of the specific technology.[28] As such, it implies that trade-offs between technologies are based on their costs, with low-cost technologies attracting capital flows. Houghton and Cruden (2009) argue that such a "cost optimization approach" has important shortcomings, most importantly it does not reflect all key variables for investment decisions. The authors prefer an "investment-led approach", analyzing the development of (commercial) capital flows based on the maximization of investor value in which costs is only one of many variables. Indeed, two important variables of great interest to investors are missing in the levelized cost approach: upside opportunity of investments in SE technology – i.e., (energy) savings – and differentiation of risk between technologies.[29] The first issue is tackled within the net cost approach, which takes the upside opportunity into account and is discussed next. The second issue merits additional explanation.

The type and magnitude of risk differs between technologies. As an example in advocating the 'investment-led' approach, Houghton & Cruden (2009) argue taking price volatility into account when assessing attractiveness. This is important because price volatility, and thus risk, is high for commodities like fossil fuels, but low for manufactured goods like hydrogen. Krohn et al. (2009) raise a similar point. They state that levelized costs calculations normally underestimate the cost of conventional fuels because their dependency on volatile oil and gas prices increases risk and would

27. Reflects production tax credit, investment tax credit, and accelerated asset depreciation as applicable. Assumes 2008 dollars, 60% debt at 7% interest rate, 40% equity at 12% cost, 20-year economic life, 40% tax rate, and 5-20 year tax life. Assumes coal price of US$2.50 per MMBtu and natural gas price of US$8.00 per MMBtu.

28. In corporate finance terminology, Lazard determined "the levelized cost of energy, on a US$/MWh basis, that would provide an after-tax IRR to equity holders equal to an assumed cost of equity capital".

29. By using a uniform cost of capital (WACC) for all technologies, differences in required return in view of differences in risk are not taken into account.

justify a higher cost of capital. They conclude that applying the same discount rate for all technologies results in favouring conventional fuels.[30] Additional research is needed to calculate the effect of differentiated discount rates per technology on the financial attractiveness of SE technologies.

Abatement cost curve: net cost approach

An abatement cost curve identifies a global cost curve of GHG abatement opportunities[31] beyond business as usual. One of the key elements underlying the analysis is the focus on net costs, i.e., all costs of an abatement measure, including investment costs, net of monetized (energy) savings. Although the exercise is most importantly intended to show the potential for CO_2 reduction, the abatement cost curve also shows relative financial attractiveness: the lower the net costs, the higher the financial attractiveness. McKinsey & Company (2009) provides an update of earlier work on the abatement cost curve (see Figure 4).[32]

Figure 4 shows that all energy efficiency measures have a net positive financial profile, as do some renewable energy measures like small hydro and first-generation biofuels. McKinsey concludes, "there are about 11 $GtCO_2e$ per year of abatement opportunities in 2030 … where the energy savings actually outweigh the upfront investments, so that these opportunities carry a net economic benefit over their lifetime". Evidently, one would expect measures with a net positive cash flow profile to result in a vast number of investment activities. This is especially true for energy efficiency. Whereas the investment equation of other energy investments is often less clear, it seems undisputed that many energy-efficiency investment opportunities provide a positive net cash flow. Investment flows, however, are relatively low (Efiong, 2007). Apparently, the business case for energy efficiency faces other barriers (see Section 1.3.4).

Notwithstanding the insights the abatement cost curve provides, some important drawbacks remain. First, as with the levelized net costs approach, differences in risk between technologies are not taken into account.[33] Moreover, costs are *before* taxes, tariffs and subsidies. This approach "serves as useful starting point for policy makers [but] does not reflect the economic investment case faced by those making decisions about whether to capture these opportunities" (McKinsey & Company, 2009, p. 40).

---

30. The authors refer to Awerbuch as an important source of inspiration. Early in 2000, Awerbuch concluded, "[t]he divergence between valuation theory and practice is perhaps nowhere greater than in energy planning, where outmoded accounting concepts and engineering approaches, long since discarded in manufacturing and other industries, still provide the sole basis for decision-making (Awerbuch, 2000, p. 1032).

31. "Potential to reduce emissions of GHGs" (McKinsey, 2009)

32. Vattenfall (2007) includes a comparable exercise, identifying a global cost curve of GHG abatement opportunities beyond business as usual.

33. McKinsey uses a uniform interest rate of 4% to calculate capital costs.

Figure 4 Global GHG abatement cost curve beyond business-as-usual (2030)

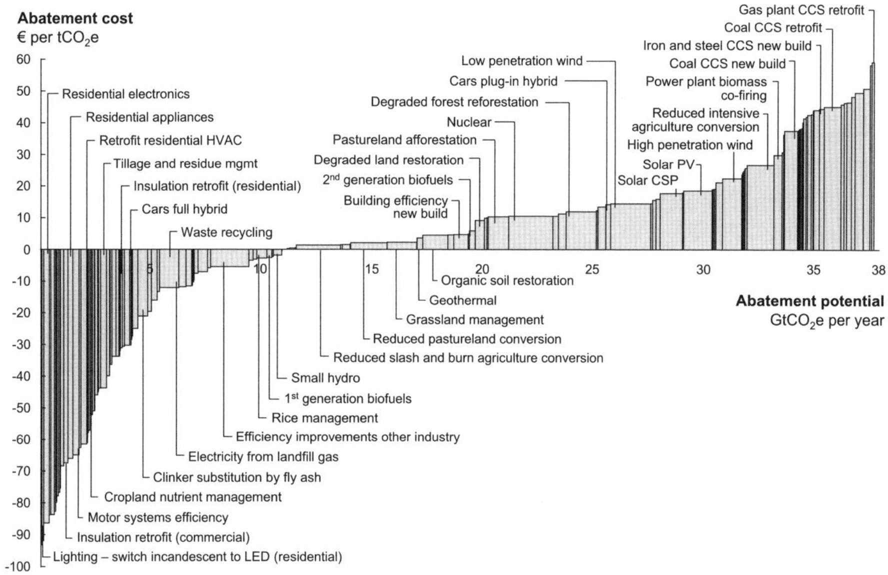

Note: The curve presents an estimate of the maximum potential of all technical GHG abatement measures below €60 per tCO_2e if each lever was pursued aggressively. It is not a forecast of what role different abatement measures and technologies will play.
Source: Global GHG Abatement Cost Curve v2.0

Source: McKinsey & Company (2009)

Actual performance of SE investments: market approach

A seemingly logical way of assessing the financial attractiveness of SE investments is tracking their actual risk-adjusted returns based on available market information.

WEF (2009a) shows that high volatility (i.e., risk) of publicly quoted Clean Energy companies is combined with consistently high returns, "making them an attractive investment proposition on a risk-adjusted basis" (WEF, 2009a, p. 19).[34] The data sample includes publicly quoted "leading clean energy companies", implying a possible bias towards the more profitable (and large) companies. In a more detailed attempt to shed light on the risk-return profile of publicly quoted SE companies, Houghton & Cruden (2009) compare financial multiples reflecting risk and/or return between fuel cell providers, alternative energy technology providers, traditional utilities and the oil&gas industry. They found valuation differentials that do not match with weak returns of the fuel cell companies and an imperfect relationship between risk and return, implying a need for further research.

Based on research by NEF, WEF (2009a) points to exceptional internal rates of return by venture capital and private equity investments in SE of 60% in the period

34. Data is based on the WilderHill New Energy Global Innovation Index (NEX), which tracks the performance of some 80 to 90 leading clean energy companies.

1997-2008/H1, but this is based on a relatively low number of exits and primarily caused by a small number of big successes. Wustenhagen & Teppo (2006) execute a high-level analysis of VC returns, concluding that there might be attractive returns, but mainly point at ample scope for further research. Kenney (2009) still regards the Wustenhagen paper as the exception to the lack of academic interest in the field of greentech VC investment. He concludes that notwithstanding the recent focus on investment by VC companies in sustainable energy, "... understanding of Greentech VC investment is still limited", pointing to the need for more empirical research on actual returns of energy VC.

Focusing on the differences in risk return and valuation multiples between traditional and renewable energy firms and the background of these differences – what Houghton & Cruden (2009) call the "investment-led approach" – could provide interesting insights into SE investment decisions.[35] Academic research, however, has not yet thoroughly tackled this subject. The lack of publicly quoted companies in the SE sector could be one reason for this. The diversity within the sector and the lack of experience-based financial data in many parts of the industry are other possible reasons.

1.3.4 Barriers to Funding of Sustainable Energy Investments

Both the levelized cost approach and McKinsey's abatement cost curve indicate a potential for financially viable investments in SE, stimulating the latter to question: "[i]f there are such attractive abatement opportunities, why then have consumers and entrepreneurs not already captured them?"[36] This seems all the more puzzling as both the public's and politicians' awareness and acknowledgement of the necessity of a transfer to sustainable energy have grown substantially (PwC, 2009; Stack, Balbach, Epstein, & Hanggi, 2007).

Neither the levelized cost approach nor the net cost approach, however, take all relevant investment elements into account. Most importantly, the impact of risk – by means of a differentiated required rate of return – is not accounted for. Although the described risk categories in section 1.3.2 are encountered within other industries as well, SE sector characteristics imply that the risk of many SE investments is perceived as high. Biermans, Grand, Kerste, & Weda (2009) conclude it is especially the set of

35. Alternatively, the actual performance of specific sustainable investment types could be analyzed as long as it is possible to identify a related 'traditional' alternative. An interesting example is the research on green buildings by Eichholtz et al. (for instance Eichholtz, Kok, & Quigley (2009); and Eichholtz, Kok, & Quigley (2010). They compare the rents on green buildings (i.e. "certified" as such by independent rating agencies) with otherwise identical office buildings and find higher rents for the former category.

36. Reasons that may be relevant but not taken into account by the McKinsey analysis are: sunk costs and consumer preferences which might not always be in line with low-carbon ideology.

risk characteristics combined in this one industry that poses a barrier to investments.[37]

SE investments do not meet funding requirements (see Section 1.2.2). Apparently, sector characteristics pose barriers to investments. As explained, risk and return are unmistakably essential in this regard. Below, the potential barriers preventing funding of SE investments as described in the literature are summarized and categorized in informational barriers, scale barriers, market barriers and regulatory barriers. All barriers influence (perceived) risk and return one way or the other, thereby impacting the financial attractiveness.

Overview of barriers

Informational barriers

Evidently, investors need to understand what they are investing in and what financial benefits they can expect. This is true for both professional investors and consumers. Due to regulatory, innovative and technical characteristics, SE investments are often complex in nature (SEFI & Marsh, 2005). UNEP & MISI (2009) conclude "[c]onsumers, lenders, developers, utility companies, and planners, both in developed and developing countries, often lack adequate information about clean energy". This is especially true for potential savings offered by energy-efficiency alternatives (McKinsey & Company, 2009; Plinke, 2008; WEF, 2010).

In addition, the sector is relatively young, resulting in a lack of experience with and quantitative data on investment results. This makes it hard for investors to build and assess the financial business case. Informational barriers are especially important in the research and development phase, where asymmetric information between investors and entrepreneurs/technicians might prevent projects being funded.[38]

The informational barriers also imply that investors, if interested in a deal, face higher transaction costs (negotiating, consulting with experts, monitoring agreements, finding partners), evidently reducing returns.

Scale barriers

Attracting funding might be difficult when high investments are needed upfront, especially when combined with long lead times. Uncertainty and the importance of risks grow when the amount at stake is high and it takes a long time before success is

37. The authors have executed a high-level check of various barriers/risk characteristics shared with other industries, like telecom, ICT and pharmacy. None of these sectors share the combination (and magnitude) of risks encountered by SE. It would still be worthwhile to look at those comparable other sectors to see what can be learned. This is hardly done in the research and papers reviewed in this book. One of the few exceptions is Wustenhagen & Teppo (2006).

38. This is one of the reasons why public funding is so important in the R&D phase.

proven. SE solutions are in many cases capital intensive, as is the case with offshore wind and building energy efficiency, and have long lead times.[39] This clashes with investors' short time horizons (Cameron & Blood, 2009).[40] But also with short payback periods required by consumers, like with most energy-efficiency investments consumers face (McKinsey & Company, 2009).[41] In conclusion, capital intensity combined with long lead times is regarded as an important barrier for SE investments (Plinke, 2008; Wustenhagen & Teppo, 2006).

Although the sector is characterized by high upfront investments and capital intensity, many projects are relatively small compared to investments in fossil fuel power-generation plants.[42] This results in high transaction costs – permits, planning costs, assembling finance – relative to, e.g., kW capacity (UNEP & MISI, 2009). SEFI & Marsh (2005) conclude, "[a]ttracting the financial interest of international lenders and insurers generally requires a minimum project size of €10 million [t]ime and time again, the small scale of a potential project has prevented an otherwise viable deal".

Besides size of investments, also the relative size of energy savings might pose a barrier.[43] The opportunities of these savings are often overlooked because, in many industries, energy costs only reflect a relatively small part of total costs (Plinke, 2008). In this regard, McKinsey & Company (2009) also points to the challenge that many savings opportunities are small on an individual level – the level at which investment decisions are made – while related energy savings are high on aggregated (societal) level, as is the case with low-energy lighting.[44]

Market barriers

Sustainable energy sources compete with fossil fuels. As such, a relatively low price of fossil fuels might prevent the uptake of sustainable energy. PwC (2009) expects a continuous rise in fossil fuel prices, because the remaining fossil fuel sources are ex-

39. Offshore wind farms, for example, have turnkey investment costs of 1,200 to 1,850 Euros per kW, compared to 800-1,100 €/kW for onshore wind farms (Junginger, Faaij, & Turkenburg, 2004, p. 100).

40. Relatively certain profits in the short term will be favoured over reaping (uncertain) long-term benefits based on high upfront investments.

41. Specifically for energy efficiency in buildings, the time to replace existing building stock (30 to 50 years) is an important barrier as retrofitting a building is more expensive than implementing energy efficiency when building in the first place (WEF, 2010).

42. For complete clarity: upfront investments and capital intensity are assessed compared to total investments of a specific project or total cash flow profile. That they are assessed 'high' for SE investments should thus be seen in relative terms and does not imply that investments are high in absolute terms. In addition, especially in the case of on-balance funding, investors often look at the company executing the project instead of only at the project itself. It is easier and cheaper to assess the financial power of one large corporate than of a number of small companies. SE projects are in many cases developed by small companies.

43. This mainly refers to energy efficiency investments.

44. Needless to say there are also examples of substantial savings opportunities on an individual level, e.g., within a shipping fleet.

pected to be in areas that are more difficult to reach. More generally, Pindyck (2007) simply points to depletion as a reason for rising fossil fuel prices. At the same time, the costs of SE are expected to decline in view of increasing economies of scale. Pindyck (2007) concludes that there is "reason to think" price differences may decline over the next fifty years. For now, the demand of SE has not yet grown to sufficient levels for production to achieve sufficient economies of scale (UNEP & MISI, 2009), preventing SE solutions from being competitive compared with conventional fuels (PwC, 2009; UNEP et al., 2009). The relatively low price level and the uncertainty regarding future price development of fossil fuels are therefore still seen as a barrier.[45]

Although reductions have been made in the past few decades, fossil fuels are still heavily subsidized (Jefferson, 2008; SEFI & Marsh, 2005). The World Bank and IEA have estimated that global annual subsidies for fossil fuels are in the range of US$100-200 billion (UNEP & MISI, 2009).[46] Subsidizing fossil fuels results in an inequitable market structure, allowing fossil fuels to be sold at artificially low prices, providing non-market incentives in favor of fossil fuels and reducing the competitive power of SE solutions.[47]

The road to a society based on sustainable energy instead of fossil fuels is regarded more and more as critical to meet the growing demand for energy and prevent adverse climate change. The latter is largely attributed to GHG emission, caused by the use of fossil fuels. Hence, fossil fuels put a grave cost on society, and the solution is to be found in deployment of sustainable energy. At first sight, this would simply cause everybody to stop using fossil fuels and turn to sustainable energy. However, neither costs to society of fossil fuels nor benefits of sustainable energy are included in prices. If costs (benefits) of conventional (sustainable) energy would be factored into prices, the return of investments in these technologies would be lower (higher). Because this is not the case, these so-called 'externalities' prevent a level playing field between conventional fuels and SE (Stack et al., 2007; UNEP & MISI, 2009; Wustenhagen & Teppo, 2006).

Market organization can fail to align incentives properly. An important example is the so-called split incentive or agency issue posing a barrier for energy-efficiency investments in the building sector (Efiong, 2007; McKinsey & Company, 2009; Owen, 2006). If a building owner invests in energy efficiency, normally the tenant's energy

45. Work by various groups (e.g., (Lazard, 2008; McKinsey & Company, 2009; Vattenfall, 2007)) concludes that there are seemingly many SE opportunities with competitive cost structures. As explained in section CR: §1.3.3, there are certain drawbacks to these analyses. Still, it seems safe to say relatively high costs alone is not a showstopper for all SE investments.

46. For a detailed discussion on fossil fuel subsidies and an overview of energy subsidies on the country and energy source level, see Victor (2009).

47. The same could be said of subsidizing sustainable energy. However, many of the barriers described here result from market imperfections, providing a stimulus for government interference with SE solutions. This hardly seems the case for fossil fuels. Moreover, it seems at least fair to say that providing a competitive edge for fossil fuels is rather out of line with the general public policy to promote sustainable energy.

bill will decrease. The building owner will therefore not necessarily benefit from his investment and will thus have a limited incentive to invest.[48]

Regulatory barriers

The barriers mentioned above all have a considerable impact on the cash flow of SE investments, in many cases preventing an attractive business case. (UNEP et al., 2009) describe the necessity of public policy as follows: "[r]enewable energy is most typically attractive in a policy-driven market. This is because it is often only marginally competitive, if at all, compared with conventional power on a standalone basis". Combined with the importance attached to a shift to SE by politicians and the public alike, government interference in the sector is high.[49]

As described in section 1.3.2, policy intervention results in policy and regulatory risk. Risk of, e.g., termination of subsidies during the lifetime of a project or unexpected changes in industry standards have serious repercussions for financial attractiveness (Kann, 2009; SEFI & Marsh, 2005; Wustenhagen & Teppo, 2006).[50] According to Jefferson (2008), policies are often based on short-term and unrealistic targets and exaggerated claims of CO_2 reduction, resulting in misdirected subsidy systems and unnecessary support of mature technologies. Incorrect design of public policy and lack of clarity are potential barriers as well (Holmes & Mabey, 2009; Jefferson, 2008)

Financial crisis

The financial crisis is often seen as an important barrier preventing SE investments in the recent past. Although the SE sector was certainly not the only sector reaping the sour fruits of the crisis, it was hit relatively hard. The reason for this lies in its characteristics. The financial crisis caused a decrease in the supply of capital. The little capital available was only provided to low-risk investments – especially by banks whose business model turned towards traditional core-business. To obtain finance, investments would have to be small, short term and have predictable returns. As discussed above, SE investments do not fit this profile, being more often than not capital intensive, long term and high-risk. In addition, the sharp decrease in oil prices did not do any good to the economics of SE investments (Biermans et al., 2009; PwC, 2009; WEF, 2009a).

Luckily, the impact was not as great as expected. Whereas IEA still anticipated a decrease of 20% over 2009 in November of that year, when the dust cleared clean energy investments had only dropped by 6.5% in 2009. The unexpected recovery was

48. The same is true for energy efficiency investments by construction companies, resulting in benefits for homeowners instead of the construction companies.

49. Section CR: §1.4.2 deals with the role of public policy in lowering barriers to SE investments.

50. In terms of net present value this means risky cash flows, resulting in a high discount rate and thus a low NPV.

caused by rapid growth in China, general recovery of financial markets and the inclusion of a green stimulus policy in the government reaction to the crisis (WEF, 2010).

Box 1 Business case: Better Place, successful in obtaining funding

Risks and barriers prevent many SE projects from being funded. It is interesting to analyze projects which are funded notwithstanding these challenges. One example is Better Place.

Better Place was started in 2007 by Shai Agassi. He saw electric vehicles (EV) as the solution to decrease oil dependency and had a solution for the major challenge faced by the industry. Although electric vehicles are generally seen as highly promising, the industry had not really found a solution for its biggest frustration: quick recharging. Whereas it is not a problem to have a long recharge time when doing this overnight at home or during work hours, this is not an option when traveling for longer distances. The best option in the market at the time – the Tesla Roadster – was able to drive 250 miles, after which a recharge of two hours or more was required. Agassi's solution combines the traditional idea of charging spots with a novelty: robotized battery-swap stations that change batteries – rather than recharge them – within minutes. His vision entails a worldwide structure of both options, thereby providing the infrastructure to make electric cars a cheap and accessible alternative to traditional vehicles. Money would be made by buying electricity (green) in bulk and reselling it to customers much the same way as in the mobile phone industry – based on unlimited miles, a maximum number of miles each month, or pay as you go.

In terms of obtaining funding, Better Place has been a success. By April 2009 it had already raised US$400 million worth of venture capital and other private funding. The total initial investment was US$200 million, with the Ofer family – partly via Israel Corp. – having a majority stake. Other investors include VantagePoint Venture Partners, Morgan Stanley, and Esarbee Investments Canada. In 2010 a further US$350 million was raised by a consortium led by HSBC, the latter gaining 10% share ownership.

Being a start-up with an innovative/R&D character, venture capital and private funding are the most logical sources of funding. This is also the phase in the life cycle where the risks and barriers are most profound. The Better Place business case provides an interesting example as it has clearly been able to overcome these challenges. Some key factors for its success are the following:

- Clear earning model: the concept is clear on how and when money will be made once the infrastructure is implemented. In addition, the earning model – although based on a system unprecedented in the car industry – has proven successful in the mobile phone industry. These elements – clarity and proven success – are important to attract investors at the start-up and R&D phase;

- Immediate consumer advantage: although EV results in a reduction of energy-cost per mile of driving, upfront investment for consumers is high due to battery costs. This is a key barrier for consumer take-on. Deutsche Bank (2008, p.12) concludes that Better Place provides a "business model in which it will own the battery and sell the consumer "miles" at a lower cost than the equivalent cost of gasoline in each country (this is the only model that we know of in which the consumer can immediately benefit from lower fuel costs, without incremental upfront cost in the vehicle)".
- Alternatives: EV is becoming more interesting compared to its alternatives. Besides the oil price volatility, the limits of further efficiency gains in traditional energy use of cars are in sight, making it a more compelling alternative for car producers;
- Combining environmental concerns and innovation with industry beliefs and business logic: starting from a known – though still innovative – technology (EV) which is generally regarded as promising in decreasing oil dependence and focusing on the main element preventing it from becoming practically – and thus financially – interesting.

Source: SEO Economic Research, based on Deutsche Bank (2008), Roth (2008) and C. Thompson (2009)[51]

Barriers and risks per stage of the life cycle

With each stage of maturity of the technology life cycle, an investment will encounter new risks and barriers. Knowing which risks and barriers are relevant during which part of the life cycle helps to design (policy) solutions to overcome obstacles.[52]

Generally speaking, there are two important finance gaps during the technological life cycle. At the time technologies move out of the R&D phase towards demonstration and deployment, risks are high because of increasing scale – and thus production costs – while demand is still low and uptake uncertain. The increased scale implies a need for funding beyond internal and public sources usually characterizing R&D investments. Venture capital would be the most logical next step, but venture capital firms might still assess risks as too high or scale as too small (although increasing) for transaction costs. This 'valley of death' often prevents innovations from getting deployed (UNEP, SEFI, & New Energy Finance, 2008).[53]

Going from deployment, via diffusion, to commercial maturity, venture capitalists typically exit projects. Project developers need to attract new and/or additional fund-

51. See also: 'Better Place wins $350 m. investment', Israel 21c (26-1-2010), (www.israel21c.org). 'Ofer to invest $30 mln in electric car deal', Reuters (27-12-2007), (www.reuters.com) 'Q&A: Agassi's Better Place idea–brilliant or nuts?', CNET News (23-4-2009), (news.cnet.com)
52. See Section CR: §1.2.2 for an overview of SE technologies per stage of the life cycle.
53. For more on the valley of death, see for instance Auerswald & Branscomb (2003) and Beard, Ford, Koutsky, & Spiwak (2009).

ing for increasing investments. This is often difficult because projects are too small to go to the stock market but are still too risky for banks to step in due to the low track record and lack of securing assets. This is called the 'debt-equity gap'. Biermans et al. (2009) conclude that both the valley of death and the debt-equity gap are more pronounced for SE investments due to their unattractive risk-return profile.

For effective policymaking, an overview of risks and barriers per stage of the life cycle is required. Table 3 provides such an overview based on UNFCCC (2009).[54]

Table 3 Financing barriers for sustainable energy investments per stage of the technical life cycle

Stage of technological maturity	Risks / Funding barriers
Research & Development	– Concept not proven yet, resulting in insufficient rate of return – Spill-over effects, preventing reaping of full potential benefits – Lack of good technical information, resulting in high risk
R&D, Demonstration	– Lack of technological track record, resulting in high risk
R&D, Demonstration, Deployment	– High costs and lack of policy to overcome them, leading to low return
R&D, Demonstration, Deployment, Diffusion	– Energy prices and subsidies – Lack of or insufficient carbon prices – High upfront capital costs, including requirement for parallel infrastructure – Lack of market – Split incentives – Lack of labour skills – Lack of regulatory framework and international standards
Commercial nature	– Inefficient regulatory environment – Lack of specific risk assessment/management tools – Lack of appropriate financial packages – Lack of awareness and information – Market imperfection

Source: SEO Economic Research, adapted from UNFCCC (2009)

1.3.5 Attractiveness per Energy Technology

Opinions on the attractiveness of energy technologies – and what will be the 'next best thing' – differ and are constantly updated. Some general observations on a sample of the major SE energy sources are discussed below, primarily based on WEF

54. For a different typology of stages in the life cycle and relevant risk in each stage, see for example (de Jager et al., 2008).

(2010).[55] This is purely meant as a reference, providing a general idea of the latest insight into the rationale for investment streams.

Onshore wind is the most mature technology, able to compete with conventional energy sources without a subsidy. Development is no doubt spurred by feed-in tariffs and tax credits (e.g., in Germany, Spain and the US). **Offshore wind** is a logical step after onshore wind. It provides enormous potential but is still relatively unexploited. Challenges include grid connection, long lead times, high capital expenditure and low margin on offshore wind turbines compared to onshore turbines. In December 2009, various European countries signed the 'North Seas Countries' Offshore Grid Initiative', planning to develop a European offshore wind grid in the North and Irish seas. Notwithstanding dramatic cost reduction in 2009, **solar photovoltaics** (PV) remains one of the most expensive RE technologies. Its potential is not expected to be exploited for several years. The PV market is mainly driven by policy incentives. **Biomass** held up well in 2009. It is based on a range of feedstocks like wood and is driven by public policy, e.g., renewable portfolio standards (RPS) in some US states where other renewable sources are scarce. Its main bottlenecks are long-term availability and price risk of feedstock. **Geothermal** is interesting due to its predictability and is the lowest cost form of RE. It is hindered by long project duration and high capital costs, partly caused by the required (though risky) exploration drilling. **Small hydro**[56] is a mature and well-established RE technology, though a variable source of power. Together with large hydro it accounts for 16% of global power. It is characterized by relatively low risk and small size. Bottlenecks are grid access and environmental and social resistance.

55. WEF (2010) discusses a total of 10 clean energy sectors which are assessed as promising in terms of abatement and cost competitiveness with conventional energy. For explanation of the technologies, see Section CR: §1.2.1. WEF itself adds that the discussed technologies are by no means the only sources. Nor is WEF the only party assessing technologies. Among many others, see for instance Canaccord Adams and the Daiwa Institute of Research.

56. Large hydro is generally not included in SE technologies, see Section CR: §1.2.1.

Table 4 Key data on attractiveness per energy technology

Energy technology	Levelized costs	Current and (potential) scale	Project return
Onshore wind	US$68-109/MWh	140GW (800GW)	10-20%
Offshore wind	US$109-205/MWh	2.4GW (120GW)	Marginal
Solar PV (grid scale and residential)	US$170-450/MWh	21GW (1000GW)	Incentive based
Solar thermal electricity generation (STEG)	US$190-250/MWh	616MW (80GW)	n/a
Biomass incineration/ gasification/ anaerobic digestion (AD)	US$70-148/MWh US$90-170/MWh US$80-189/MWh	45GW (150GW)	±10%
Municipal solid waste-to-energy	US$38-157/MWh	18GW (50GW)	±12%
Geothermal	US$55-83/MWh	10GW (40GW)	12-37%
Small hydro	US$70-120/MWh	92GW (328GW)	8-13%
Sugar-based ethanol	Competitive with oil at around US$45 per barrel	/	8-15%
Next-generation biofuels	Competitive with oil at around US$150 per barrel	/	/
Energy efficiency	Investment potential of US $170 billion with an average internal rate of return (IRR) of 17%	/	/

Source: WEF (2010, pp. 24-25); no information on calculation method of project returns

1.4 How to Increase Funding of Sustainable Energy Investments

As explained, investment decisions are based on the cash flows they generate and the return investors demand based on the relevant risks (i.e., the cost of capital). Due to the high-risk profile and the barriers described in section 1.3, the financial attractiveness of SE investments (or investors' perceptions of the attractiveness) can be too low to attract sufficient funding. In order to increase funding, solutions can be designed to improve cash flows and/or risk profile. Although most attention is focused on government-based solutions (public policy solutions), the private (financial) sector should also be involved in finding solutions to increase attractiveness, or a combination of the two (public-private solutions).

1.4.1 Risk Management

Techniques to identify, quantify and manage risk are well-established in the financial community – and many of them can be effectively applied to SE projects. With a risk management analysis framework in place that assesses controllable project intrinsic volatilities (e.g., energy volume risk, asset performance risk and energy baseline uncertainty risk) and hedgeable project extrinsic volatilities (e.g., energy price risk, labor cost risk and currency risk), energy experts and investment decision-makers can exchange the information they need to expand investment in energy projects (Mills, 2003; Mills, Kromer, Weiss, & Mathew, 2006). An important element in managing risks is the possibility to decrease risks at a pre-defined price by means of financial instruments. Financial risk management instruments (FRMIs) can be provided by private companies or can be part of public finance mechanisms (PFMs). Figure 5 provides an inventory of potential FRMIs related to risks of large- and small-scale RE projects and of carbon-financed projects.[57]

Risk insurance by the private sector

In the field of risk insurance, climate change has a double impact. First, insurance companies will have to adapt their internal risk management to the new environment of increased climate and energy risks. The insurance sector faces material liability exposures to both the causes and consequences of climate change, many of which have already begun to materialize (Ross, Mills, & Hecht, 2007). Some insurers have begun to apply their expertise in risk management towards helping their customers avoid liabilities. Proactive approaches are likely to yield a "win-win-win" situation, in which insurers, policyholders, and third parties affected by climate change-related externalities will all benefit from decreased risk (Ross et al., 2007).

---

57. Further information on instruments and their use can be found in several UNEP/GEF reports (http://www.unep.fr/energy/activities/frm/). Available data on scale of use – necessary to assess to what extent risks in SE investments are insured – is relatively old and focused on specific areas rather than providing a full overview. This information has therefore not been included here.

Figure 5 Renewable energy project risks by project phase and related FRM instruments

Renewable Energy Project Risks	Financial Risk Management Instruments
Risks associated with Large Scale Projects	
Project Development/ Pre-construction Phase	
Concept to implementation	Grants, Contingent Grants (GEF)
Construction Phase	
Construction/ Completion Risk	Insurance – Construction All Risks (CAR/EAR)
Counterparty Risk	Surety bonds - Performance guarantees Liquidation damages
Operating Phase	
Performance Risk	Insurance
Counterparty Risk	Surety bonds - Performance guarantees Liquidation damages
Fuel Supply/Weather resources Risk	Weather Insurance/ Derivatives
Credit Risk	Guarantees Credit derivatives
Generic – All Phases	
Financial Risk	Standard derivative products
Political Risk	Political Risk Insurance MFI Guarantees Export Credit guarantees
Force Majeure Risk	Insurance Catastrophe bonds
Risks associated with small scale projects	
Project Developer	
Development (Credit) Risk	Guarantee Funds
End User	
Risks of physical damage including theft	Insurance
Credit Risk	Guarantees Credit lines
Risks associated with Carbon Financed projects	
Market Risk	Standard derivative products to hedge against price
CER delivery Risk	Insurance – carbon delivery guarantee, permit delivery guarantee

Source: UNEP & GEF (2008)

Second, the intention to prevent climate change, resulting in a vast potential landscape of SE investments, provides commercial opportunities for insurers. The specific risk profile of SE investments poses challenges to companies in covering these risks. Risk insurance instruments could play an important role in diminishing the risks of SE investments. This has caused numerous insurance companies to create new business units targeted at SE projects in recent years (SwissRe, 2009). Examples of commercial opportunities include:

- Energy savings insurance: protecting the installer or owner of an energy-efficiency project from under-achievement of predicted energy savings, e.g., by means of energy savings insurance or real options and derivatives for energy efficiency (Mills et al., 2006, p. 198; SEFI & Marsh, 2005);
- Renewable energy project insurance: covering performance risk for renewable energy systems, e.g., through wind power derivatives;

- Coverage extensions to fill gaps in green building projects: green building can involve new risks during construction and operation compared to conventional buildings (SwissRe, 2009);
- Energy service contracts: a third party (e.g., energy service companies, ESCOs, and energy suppliers) funds the cost of an efficiency improvement and is paid out of the savings, whereby secondary markets in these contracts could evolve as the market matures (WEF, 2010).[58]

Table 5 gives an overview of insurance providers and the sector in which their SE products can be categorized as per 2009. Unsurprisingly, wind energy projects were best served by the insurance market.

Table 5 Inventory of renewable energy and carbon insurance providers[59]

Insurance company	Wind	Solar	Geothermal	Biofuels	Comprehensive	Carbon
ACE						*
AIG	*				*	*
Aon				*		
Axa		*	*			
Caron Re					*	
Chubb					*	
Munich Re		*	*			*
Navigator Group	*					
Renewco	*					
RNK Capital LLC						*
RSA					*	
Sompo Japan Insurance	*	*				
Sovereign GIC	*					
Swiss Re	*					*
Tokio Marine & Nichido	*					
Travelers'	*					
Willis Holding	*					
World Bank			*			*
Zurich						*

Source: Mills (2009)

58. Already used on a larger scale in, e.g., the UK, following the implementation of a white certificate scheme (documents certifying that a certain reduction of energy consumption has been attained). For more background on the economics of ESCs, see for instance Sorrell (2005).

59. Carbon-credit insurance: CDM and carbon-offset projects.

In line with opportunities, recent years have indeed seen numerous insurance products targeted at renewable energy projects and their risks (see Box 2 for two examples). Some authors suggest, however, that most of these products are little more than bundling/repackaging of existing offerings (general (energy) project-related insurance products that are given new, 'green' names), rather than pure innovation to fill coverage gaps or carefully tailor coverage to the unique features of these technologies (Mills, 2009, p. 29).

Box 2 Examples of sustainable energy insurance schemes

Insurance4Renewables
Munich, RSA Insurance Group (RSA), and CarbonRe – with support from the Global Environment Facility (GEF) and the United Nations Environment Programme (UNEP) – have launched a mechanism for insuring renewable energy projects in developing countries. The global renewable energy insurance facility offers standard and customized insurance solutions for renewable energy projects in developing countries.[60] I4R has a special focus on medium and large-scale projects in developing countries and offers, in addition to standard renewable energy insurance, special insurance lines such as country and political risk, third party counter credit and credit insurance covers and consultancy services.

CarbonRe, an insurance broker specializing in clean energy projects, is the appointed broker for access to the facility. Expertise is offered on a broad spectrum of technologies such as wind power, photovoltaics, solar thermal, biomass and biogas systems in every phase of construction and operation. Besides the traditional insurance products for construction, operation and transit, the facility offers innovative covers on a case-by-case basis such as carbon counterparty credit risk insurance, carbon all-risk insurance, carbon delivery guarantee insurance/Kyoto multi-risk policy and lack-of-sun/wind insurance (Global Environment Facility, 2009; UNEP, 2008).

Wind power derivative for large-scale wind farm projects
Paris Re has introduced an index-based weather cover for the wind energy sector. The cover was developed in cooperation with MARSH in the framework of a study commissioned by the United Nations Environment Programme (UNEP) and the Global Environment Facility (GEF). When financing a wind farm project, the index-based product designed by Paris Re and MARSH provides coverage against the most important of all weather risks: the lack of sufficient wind (Paris Re, 2008; UNEP, 2008).

A specific form of SE insurance is *energy-savings insurance* (ESI), which is a formal insurance of predicted energy savings traditionally used to guarantee power reductions in retrofitted buildings. It transfers and spreads risk over a larger pool of

60. http://www.insurance4renewables.com/

energy-efficiency projects and reduces barriers to market entry of smaller energy service firms that lack sufficiently strong balance sheets to self-insure the savings. ESI offers an important macro-level benefit of spreading aggregate risk over a larger pool of energy-efficiency projects than most individual purveyors are likely to have. This is a natural benefit of establishing financial markets for previously unmonetized externalities. Furthermore, the presence of ESI encourages the parties to go beyond standard, tried-and-true measures (e.g., simple lighting retrofits) and thereby achieve more significant levels of energy savings (Mills, 2003; Schleich & Gruber, 2008; E. Vine, Mills, & Chen, 2000; E. L. Vine, 1992). Governmental agencies have been pioneers in the use of ESI and could continue to play a role (Mills, 2003). Commercial insurance companies, like AIG and Lloyds, also offer ESI. These products appear to be most widely practised in Canada and the US, with examples also in Brazil and Malaysia (Mills, 2003). It has many potential applications (e.g., for homeowners, offshore property and aviation), but the current supply includes only a few of them: industrial/energy property, real estate and crop (Mills, 2009, p. 7).

If properly applied, ESI can potentially reduce the net cost of energy-saving projects by reducing the interest rates charged by lenders and by increasing the level of savings through quality control. Notwithstanding its potential – as also recognized by policymakers – demand for ESI is low. This is partly due to the fact that performance-based financial products seem to have fallen out of favor, and because there seems to be a profound lack of recognition on the part of customers that predicted energy savings cannot be taken for granted. In many cases, energy-efficiency projects suffer from a lack of quality control, and underperformance as a result (Mills, 2009, pp. 29-30).

Risk insurance by the public sector

UNEP (2009) points to country-risk and currency-risk cover (both supporting the supply of finance) and low-carbon policy-risk cover (supporting the demand for finance) as the main insurance instruments governments should provide.

Country-Risk Cover

Although there are many low-carbon investment opportunities in the developing world, country risk can prevent these opportunities from being realized. Public bodies guaranteeing this risk have an important role to play in overcoming these problems (UNEP, 2009).

Insurance against country risk is already available at the project level from, among others, the Multilateral Investment Guarantee Agency (MIGA) of the World Bank and national export credit agencies (ECAs), which cover political risks. Furthermore, indirect support (international to national) is provided by WB/IFC partial credit and partial risk guarantees (Neuhoff et al., 2010, p. 17).

ECA support usually takes the form of export credit guarantees or insurance (political and/or commercial risk), investment insurance (political risk insurance only), or direct loans. ECAs can help further break down barriers to financing RE projects. However, most RE projects are relatively new and therefore may not meet standard ECA underwriting criteria, e.g., track history of successful trading. Historically, only a small portion of ECA business supports renewable energy projects and/or the sales of renewable energy technology (UNEP & SEFI, 2004).

Currency-Risk Cover

Financial instruments to hedge exchange rate risks, currency controls, devaluation, etc. are already available for commonly traded currencies, but the private sector appears unwilling to provide the same instruments for currencies traded less frequently. This suggests that there is a gap in the market that the public sector can fill (UNEP, 2009), which is especially important for SE investments in developing countries.

Low-Carbon Policy-Risk Cover

Investors are concerned that policy or regulatory risk will undermine the profitability of low-carbon investments, e.g., the adjustment or removal of a feed-in tariff. One way to mitigate policy risk would be to extend country-risk guarantees to cover specific low-carbon policy risks (e.g., insurance could be provided against governments reneging on statutory grandfathering provisions). Alternatively, financial instruments such as put options might allow the policy risk to be hedged.[61] The provision of instruments of this sort could be expected to require no net subsidy (UNEP, 2009, p. 17; UNEP et al., 2009).

1.4.2 *Public Policy Solutions*

There is no question whatsoever about the importance attributed to public policy as a key instrument in addressing climate change. Amongst many others, McKinsey (2009) concludes, “the transition to a low-carbon economy might be the first global economic transition of this scale to be driven largely by policy”. Although crucial, the role of public policy in stimulating funding of SE investments is not easy. As stated by WEF (2009a), “there will be no one-size-fits-all solution”.

Public policy instruments

There are two principal, market-based policy instruments for climate mitigation and the underlying issue of externalities: carbon taxes and carbon emissions trading, also referred to as cap-and-trade or allowance trading.[62] Carbon taxes and cap-and-trade schemes can be and are used conjointly (Kolk & Pinkse, 2005; Kossoy & Ambrosi,

61. E.g., options could be devised to place a floor on a key policy variable that crucially affects the profitability of low-carbon investment, such as the carbon price (UNEP, 2009).

62. See chapter 2 for a detailed discussion on carbon trading.

2010; Nordhaus, 2007; Pinkse, 2007). In addition, governments can chose from a multitude of non-market-based instruments. Table 6 provides an overview of public policy instruments frequently used in stimulating the deployment of sustainable energy. Instruments directly aimed at mobilizing and leveraging commercial funding are often called public finance mechanisms (PFMs).

Table 6 Policy instruments to promote sustainable energy

Category	Instrument/description
Voluntary agreements	Agreements among governments and businesses to promote/stimulate SE.
Education	Information about SE for target groups.
Policy processes	Special measures to facilitate SE projects, including emission reduction targets, shorter permitting processes and increased grid capacity/ connection.
Trade arrangements	*Quota obligations/renewable portfolio standards (RPS)*: impose a fixed share of renewable energy in the electricity mix of consumers, suppliers or producers. A party that fails his obligation has to pay a penalty.
	Tendering: a government or institution issuing a tender asks project developers to prepare a bid for a certain amount of electricity from a certain technology source. The price is determined based on a market mechanism (bid procedure). Tenders usually include long-term purchase contracts. The main disadvantage is the risk that the price will be set too low, resulting in the project not being materialized. For this reason, tendering has been abolished by several countries actively using this instrument in the past.
	Tradable permits: cap-and-trade systems: participants exceeding their objectives (cap) can sell permits to those not meeting theirs.
Direct financial/ price support	*Production subsidies*: provide a financial incentive for each unit of energy produced over a given period.
	Investment subsidies/Capital grants: provide upfront subsidies based on installed capacity, reducing risk and thus capital costs.
Fiscal incentives	*Tax relief*: a tax exemption linked to installed production capacity, with the same result as an investment subsidy.
	Tax credit: a tax exemption linked to the amount of energy production, increasing profits.
	Flexible/accelerated depreciation schemes: allow writing off of assets faster (or differently) than usually allowed, resulting in maximized tax benefit of depreciation and thus higher net present value.
	Energy and emission taxes: taxing the use of conventional energy sources and/or directly taxing emissions.
Accessibility of finance	*Loans*: governments provide loans directly to projects or companies producing SE, often at lower interest rates.
	Loan guarantees: governments guarantee debt repayment to the lending bank, decreasing risk and thus interest rates and/or debt conditions.
	Carbon finance: facilities that monetize the advanced sale of emissions reductions to finance project investment costs.
Public investment	Government investments or participation in SE projects.

Source: SEO Economic Research based on de Jager et al. (2008), EC (2008), PwC (2009), UNEP & SEFI (2008), WEF (2010)

Figure 6 provides an overview of the use of policy instruments for a number of European countries as per 2009.[63]

Figure 6 Number of policy tools per country

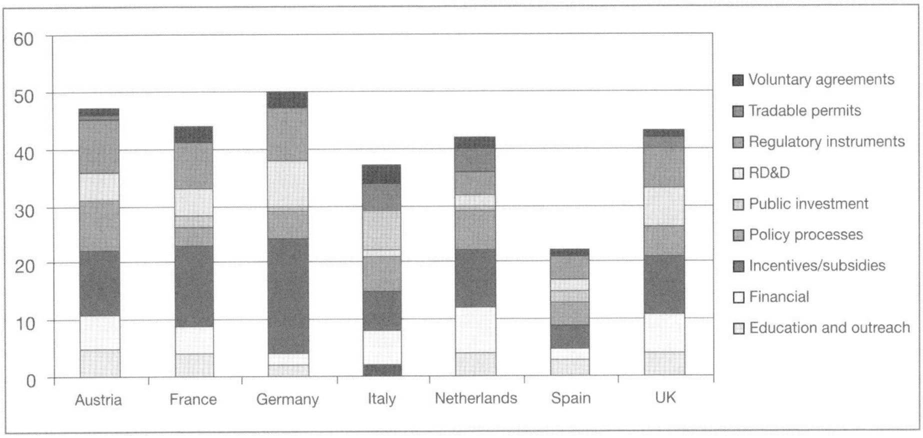

Source: PwC (2009, p. 23)

Selecting public policy solutions to stimulate funding

In determining which public solutions should be used for what SE investments, part of the literature focuses on general solutions for the barriers impacting risk and/or return with which the sector is confronted, while other research focuses on specific countries, funding parties, technologies and/or policy instruments. The latter category provides useful insights into the (proposed) use of a public solution for specific cases like wind project finance in Australia (Kann, 2009) or solar cell promotion in Germany (Frondel, Ritter, & Schmidt, 2008). Here, the focus is on the general framework for selecting policy solutions.

A primary element for selecting appropriate policy instruments is the stage of the life cycle of the relevant SE solution (UNEP & SEFI, 2008; WEF, 2010). As discussed previously, each stage is confronted with specific risks and barriers. In addition, available funding sources depend on the stage in the life cycle as well.

The R&D phase asks for substantial public involvement in order to encourage innovations and the development of new ideas. Before going to the marketplace, projects have to cross the 'valley of death' (see Section 1.3.4, implying policy instruments should be focused on those risks that capital markets cannot take. Towards commercial rollout, SE solutions will have to compete with fossil fuels – a rather challenging battle seen these conventional energy sources are based on years of experience, trust-

63. The policy tools mentioned by PwC do not cover all instruments mentioned in Table 6. This is for a large part due to the greater detail provided in the table.

worthy technologies and incomparable investment flows. Public policy will have to provide economic support during this stage, albeit at exactly the right pace and intensity. The competitiveness of SE technologies should increase towards maturity (and in the end beat fossil fuels). However, policy support will continuously be required at this stage as long as externalities, informational barriers, subsidization of fossil fuels and other barriers remain intact.

Figure 7 summarizes high-level gaps, the typical commercial funding sources and the public finance mechanisms commonly used per stage of the life cycle.

Figure 7 High-level gaps renewable energy technologies

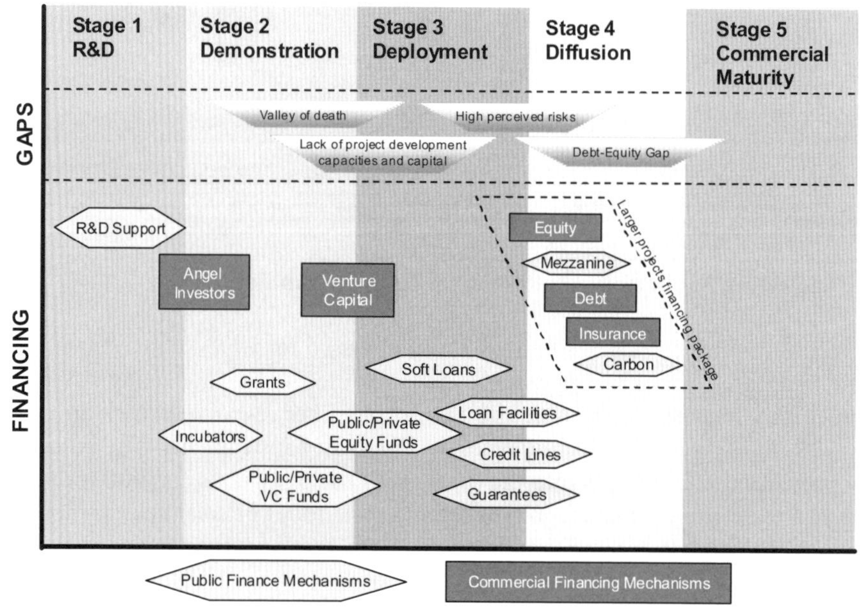

Source: UNEP & SEFI (2008, p. 2)

Table 7 provides a more detailed overview of policy mechanisms, matched to the most appropriate stage of the life cycle.

WEF (2010) includes a detailed assessment of all the instruments in Table 7 based on their scalability, efficiency and multiplier effect[64] as well as their applicability for developed, emerging and/or developing markets.[65]

64. Does each dollar of public money attract follow-on funds from private investors?

65. Scalability and country conditions are also mentioned by UNEP and SEFI (2008) for the evaluation of public finance mechanisms.

Table 7 Policy instruments most suitable for each stage in the life cycle

Stage / *Policy mechanism*	Early R&D	Demonstration & scale-up	Commercial roll-out	Diffusion & maturity
Market		- National/local procurement	- Feed-in tariffs - RPS/Green certificates - Renewable fuel standards	- Best available technology requirement - Utility regulation
Equity finance	- Incubators - National laboratories - Prizes - National/state-funded VC - R&D grants	- Project grants		- Technology transfer funds - Infrastructure funds
Debt finance		- Mezzanine/ subordinated debt - Venture loan guarantees	- Green bonds - Loan guarantees - Senior debt funds	- Export trade credit - Microfinance - Policy risks insurance - ESCO funds
Tax-based	- Capital gains tax waiver - R&D tax credits	- Development zones	- Accelerated depreciation - Investment tax credits - Production tax credits	- Carbon tax
Carbon market				- Domestic carbon cap-and-trade - Project-based carbon credits Carbon funds

Source: SEO Economic Research, based on WEF (2010)

The above studies focus on instruments fit for removing or lowering barriers in each stage of the life cycle, taking into account the commercial funding instruments that are usually used in each stage. Using a different approach, Ecofys (de Jager et al., 2008) links policy instruments directly to their impact on important financial variables used by investors to determine financial attractiveness. The report defines several renewable energy projects (e.g., in the field of wind energy and solar photovoltaic), which are funded based on a project finance scheme. First, the business case is calculated without policy instruments in terms of, e.g., levelized costs.[66] This default scenario is compared with scenarios including specific policy instruments, thus calculating the effect on levelized costs of government loans and interest reduction, government participation, fiscal measures and production support.[67] The change in levelized costs, as a result of introducing policy instruments, is a measure of the effect on financial attractiveness. Although the results are business case specific, and some input assumptions are oversimplified, the analysis certainly shows the importance of proper insight into the effect of policy instruments on risk and project costs. It also draws attention to the vast number of variables to be taken into account when assessing the effect of policy instruments.

A more specific discussion point in the academic literature has been on the choice between quantity-based versus price-based systems.[68] Although theoretical reasoning in the 1990s pointed towards a preference for quantity-based policies, actual experience revealed price-based policies to be more effective. The success of feed-in tariffs was for a large part explained by the lower risks they pose for investors compared to other policy instruments (see for instance Bürer & Wüstenhagen (2009), Dinica (2006)). One example often cited is the success of feed-in tariffs in Germany. Frondel et al. (2008), however, conclude that PV promotion by high feed-in tariffs in Germany has not met climate and employment expectations, while at the same time having drawn funds away from potentially more beneficial investments. Generalized conclusions on preference for types of policy instruments should be prevented, implying the necessity of case-by-case assessment. Moreover, this example points to the potential problem of government failure. Government intervention creates a pool of economic rents, like subsidies, taxes emission rights, etc., which economic parties try to capture by influencing politicians (Helm, 2010). As government mostly has less information on the subjects to be decided on than the private sector does (asymmetric information), it turns to private parties for information, providing a window for influencing decisions. The scale of these activities tends to grow with the economic rents. Helm (2010) concludes, "because climate change is such a large market failure, the scale of the intervention is likely to be correspondingly large, and that *therefore* the scope for government failure is massive, too".[69]

An interesting alternative approach to assess policy effectiveness is to research investors' *perception* of risks (and opportunities) associated with specific energy and cli-

---

66. The concept of levelized costs was explained in section CR: §1.3.3: the levelized cost represents the present value of the total cost of building and operating a generating plant over its economic life, converted to equal annual payments

67. In addition, the effect of reducing regulatory risk by ensuring a long-term commitment of policy schemes is monetized, resulting in reduced levelized costs as high as 10-30%.

68. Quantity-based policies target the amount of relevant units – like the percentage of RE in energy portfolios or allowed emissions – while price-based mechanisms target the price of relevant units – like carbon taxes and feed-in tariffs.

69. The article provides more information on government failure and examples in view of climate change intervention.

mate policies. This field of research is relatively new. In one of the first broad empirical studies, Bürer & Wüstenhagen (2009) questioned 60 private equity investors about which policies they regard as effective. The authors find that although technology-push policies are a prime focus area for many governments, on average market-pull policies are preferred by investors over technology-push policies.[70] Interviews with the investors indicate that a policy mix of both is required to address the different stages of the innovation cycle.

Abatement potential and other policy concerns

Jefferson (2008) claims that stimulating the development of renewable energy technologies by public policy is often done with insufficient regard for their costs, their contribution to electricity generation, transportation fuels' needs, or carbon emission avoidance. He concludes, "[h]igher-cost, less mature renewable energy technologies that have large potential for meeting global energy needs are not getting the support they warrant". The author thus points to an important consideration from a policy perspective: lack of focus on actual abatement potential results in poor energy return on public investment. Besides financial attractiveness, necessary to attract private funding, policymakers should also take impact on climate change ('sustainability return') into account when designing and selecting instruments.

The work of McKinsey & Company (2009) and Vattenfall (2007) provides excellent insights in the sustainability return of SE investments. By linking the abatement potential to net costs per unit of potential CO_2 reduction, they offer starting points for policy prioritization aimed at both financial and sustainability return. Evidently, policy instruments should be focused on those investments providing the highest abatement potential. In addition, the net cost can be regarded as a rough estimation of the potential financial loss/profit of an SE project and therefore as a first indication of the required intensity of policy support in case governments want to stimulate projects: higher net costs imply higher potential losses and therefore higher intensity of policy measures to make investments economically viable, and vice versa. Combined with the stage of the life cycle and investment characteristics, specific policy instruments can be selected.

Another element to be taken into account is the possibility of unintended consequences of policy instruments. An example in this regard, which has received a lot of attention in the literature and media, is the 'Green Paradox'. The Green Paradox states that subsidizing renewable energy reduces the future value of fossil fuels and gives an impetus to exhaust them now, bringing forward the date at which fossil fuels become exhausted with the accompanying adverse impact on climate change (Kem-

70. Instruments to promote innovations in renewable energy can roughly be divided into 'technology-push' and 'market-pull' policies. Examples of the former are public R&D grants for SMEs and investment subsidies; examples of the latter are feed-in tariffs, reduction of fossil fuel subsidies and technology performance standards. See for instance Grubb (2004) and Bürer & Wüstenhagen (2009).

fert, 2009; Sinn, 2008a, 2008b, 2009; Van der Ploeg & Withagen, 2010).[71] The Green Paradox thus links policy incentives for increasing the long-term share of sustainable energy on the one hand to unintended incentives for increased emissions of CO_2 in the short term on the other hand. For instance, Van der Ploeg & Withagen (2010, p. 29) argue that the Green Paradox is dependent on the type of renewable energy, more specifically its costs and 'cleanness', providing additional insights for the selection of policy instruments. Table 8 provides an overview of their taxonomy, concluding that the Green Paradox applies for expensive alternative energy sources which reduce CO_2 emissions to zero, like solar and wind, but not for cheap alternatives like nuclear power.[72]

Table 8 Alternative energy sources to conventional oil and gas

Backstop	Expensive	Cheap
Zero CO_2 emissions	Solar/wind/advanced nuclear *Green Paradox applicable*	Nuclear *Green Paradox not applicable*
Cleaner	CCS coal	–
Bit dirty	–	Coal
Very dirty	Tar sands	–

Source: SEO Economic Research, adapted from Van der Ploeg & Withagen (2010, p. 2)

Although there has been fundamental criticism of the theory underlying the Green Paradox (Hoel, 2010; Kemfert, 2009)[73], it does underline the importance of considering potential, (short-term) adverse effects when designing and selecting policy instruments.

71. The argument is as follows: subsidizing renewable energy such as solar or wind energy leads to lower (future) demand for fossil fuels and a (future) decrease in their consumption. Countries which supply fossil fuels, mainly oil, react by flooding the market with oil, because they assume that in the future oil will be a non-starter. This leads to an increase in supply, and thus further pressure on prices, which will then lead to a higher demand for and use of oil in the short term. An important assumption underlying the analysis is the absence of a tax on CO_2 emissions.

72. For now, it is uncertain whether a green paradox arises in the other combinations in their matrix (e.g., tar sands and carbon capture and storage). However, their framework is an interesting guide for further research.

73. Critics doubt a future lowering of demand for fossil fuels even in the case of an uptake of SE, e.g., in view of the expected rapid growth of economies like China and India. Moreover, they regard it as impossible for the oil supply to be adjusted drastically in the short term in order to 'flood the market'.

Policy recommendations

Based on the many possible ways to select and prioritize public solutions, different policy recommendations can be made. An overview of the main lines of reasoning is provided below:[74]

- Design emissions trading markets. Combine them with ambitious and coherent national emission reduction targets; they are a prerequisite for broad, deep and liquid global carbon markets (Stack et al., 2007; WEF, 2009b);
- Implement and/or raise energy efficiency standards (Jefferson, 2008; McKinsey & Company, 2009; Stack et al., 2007; WEF, 2009b);
  - Many energy-efficiency investments, though financially attractive and providing high abatement opportunities on the aggravated level, do not materialize due to market imperfections. A possible solution would be to align the interests of the large number of consumers and companies who would gain little in absolute terms on an individual basis but much on an aggregated level (see Section 1.3.4 on 'scale barriers'). An effective public policy instrument to achieve this is the use of technical standards and norms (McKinsey & Company, 2009);
  - Regulation of utility companies is now mostly focused on the unit cost of supply aimed at preventing the adverse effects of market power. As such, it does not address climate change although it seems logical to include incentives to improve end-use efficiency where energy products change hands (WEF, 2010);
- Improve consistency and reliability of policy regime and instruments;
- Implement regulation on the governance and transparency of climate risks by companies, because more pronounced disclosure regulations will provide investors with clearer insights into (the hidden) climate risks and opportunities in their portfolios (Cameron & Blood, 2009; Shepherd, 2009; WEF, 2009b);
- Provide direct government support to R&D, because R&D is essential for technology development and decrease of SE costs. In this stage of the life cycle, risks are high, and private funders are hesitant. Direct government support and encouragement instruments should be focused on R&D and technology development, especially of immature technologies with high abatement potential (Jefferson, 2008; McKinsey & Company, 2009; Stack et al., 2007);
  - As coal dependency will remain strong, technologies that capture and store CO_2 emissions are important. Carbon capture and storage (CCS) is still far from commercially interesting and needs government funding to bridge the 'valley of death' (WEF, 2009a, 2009b);
- Phase out subsidies to fossil fuels (e.g., (Jefferson, 2008)).

74. Choices for specific instruments are not included as this requires case-by-case discussion. The recommendations are shared by many authors. Mentioning authors is purely for the sake of background references for the reader.

1.4.3 *Innovative Funding Solutions*[75]

So far, the focus has been on traditional funding sources and risk management as well as existing public policy instruments. However, the enormous challenge ahead and the lack of success in facing this with current action alone imply the need for innovative ways to increase funding. This is not only true for governmental institutions, but also for the private financial sector. As City of London (2009) puts it, "it is essential that ... the financial services sector recognises that reflecting societal concerns is an essential part of its license to operate". Below a number of examples in this area are described, some of which are close to being successful in stimulating funding, while others merit further thought and research:

- Carbon trade: putting a price on CO_2 emissions via cap-and-trade systems provides incentives for abatement investments. Carbon trade is predominantly based on the Kyoto trading mechanism with the EU Emission Trading System (EU ETS) as the biggest carbon market to date[76];
- Carbon bank: as a boost to the Clean Development Mechanism, a financial institution would sell carbon credits at their market (marginal) cost to developed countries – countries would be obliged to buy – while using the proceeds to buy credits from developing countries at a price close to incurred (average) costs. The difference would be used to fund mitigation and adaptation projects in developing countries (see for instance Cameron & Blood (2009), based on the Catalyst Project);
- Global Climate Change Fund: buying emission credits at a floor price, funded by developed countries, supporting the carbon market by increasing investor confidence (Edwards, 2009);
- Green bonds: funds raised specifically for mitigation and adaptation projects. An example of this is the program launched by Swedish Bank SEB and the World Bank, responding to a demand by Scandinavian institutional investors (Cameron & Blood, 2009; Cameron & Holmes, 2009);
- Green Bank: the case for a Green Bank is discussed in detail in Box 3;
- Index-linked carbon bonds: bonds issued by governments, whereby the actual interest payments depend on whether these governments keep environmental promises. E.g., interest payable rises when the verified GHG emissions of the issuing country breach a promised maximum or decrease when feed-in tariffs for SE are higher than a pre-approved level. In this way the bonds provide a hedge instrument against regulatory risk. The idea of index-linked carbon bonds has emerged from discussions with participants in the London Accord community. It was presented to the World Bank in 2009 and discussed with government debt

75. This section provides a snapshot of some promising innovations. For a more comprehensive literature overview on innovative funding solutions, refer to Chapter 4.

76. Although the Kyoto Protocol has been in force since 2005, it seems carbon trading has not reached its full potential in terms of catalyzing SE investment. For a literature review on this subject, see Chapter 2.

offices and treasuries. Further market research on supply and demand is required[77] (City of London et al., 2009);
- Micro-finance: scale is an important barrier to many SE investments. Small projects, most importantly on the household and community levels, could be financed based on micro-credit (Balachandra, Nathan, Salk, & Reddy, 2010);
- Innovative use of existing financial instruments: existing financial instruments could be used in an innovative way to stimulate SE investments. Examples include mortgaging SE technologies – whereby the SE technology is seen as a valuable asset providing funders with a security base – or leasing RE assets. The latter is a flexible form of finance, focused on assets. It could provide great potential to funding of RE investments as these are mostly asset-based. Public policy could stimulate this by means of fiscal incentives and information-sharing (Balachandra et al., 2010)
- Energy-efficiency instruments: energy-efficiency investments are relatively expensive, and their outcome is uncertain. On several accounts, parties like banks, nonprofits, energy services companies and building owners have cooperated to design solutions to guarantee savings and prevent high initial investments. An example is the Clinton Foundation Climate Change Initiative's Energy Efficiency Building Retrofit Program (Cameron & Blood, 2009).

Box 3 Business Case – Green Bank

Government intervention to facilitate funding of climate change investments is a generally accepted necessity. As part of public policy, governments use financial instruments – e.g. grants, insurances, loans, etc. A recent idea to improve institutionalization of these instruments is the establishment of a Green Investment Bank in the UK, as proposed by the Green Investment Bank Commission in June 2010. The idea of a government-owned or -sponsored financial institution focused on a specific area is not new, nor is this concept new to the SE sector. Examples include the Instituto de Crédito Official in Spain, with funding activities focused on renewable energy and energy efficiency amongst other sectors, and KfW Bankengruppe in Germany that supports investments in a range of areas including environmental protection and energy efficiency. In addition, ideas of this kind have also been part of legislation proposals in the US during the last two years – although without success as yet.

The recent proposal in the UK is the most explicit one linking a separate financial institution established by the government on the one hand with required investments for the transition to a low-carbon economy on the other. The Green Investment Bank (GIB) would be established by an Act of Parliament but not be accountable to ministers or Parliament for individual decisions in order to build credibility in the market. Its goal would be threefold: (1) increasing the availability of capital for investments in view of mitigating and adapting to climate

77. According to Onstwedder et al. (2010) anecdotal evidence indicates there is investor appetite.

change; (2) better channeling of existing government resources in this area; (3) bridging to financeable market risk.
The GIB would roughly consist of two interrelated parts: a 'UK Fund for Green Growth', aimed at providing public sector funding and support, and a 'Banking division', aimed at "catalyzing private sector investments to enable Britain's low carbon transition". In terms of funding of activities, three funding types are proposed by the Commission:

- initial bank capitalization to support activities: e.g. via bank bonus taxes, proceeds of sale of government assets and revenues from EU ETS auctions;
- government funding for disbursement of grants: e.g. via incorporating the large number of existing quangos and funds focused on low-carbon investments into the GIB;
- financing for ongoing activities and 'commercial' investments: e.g. via green bonds or GIB debt fund.

The Commission proposes a broad range of types of products the GIB could offer in view of its activities, from grants and co-investments to insurance products and carbon price underwriting. Support should be focused on those areas with a maximum impact and short time to result. It does however underline that crowding out of the private sector should be prevented at all times and returns on public-provided funds should be reinvested.

Although still on the political agenda, to be discussed further after the spending review in the autumn, establishment of the GIB is not a certainty. Current discussions focus on funding of the GIB, primarily whether a sale of government assets will be part of this.

A Green Bank, as proposed in the UK, would be an important step towards centralizing the many dispersed government initiatives to boost SE funding – and would be favorable in many countries. Moreover, independence of public support from the political arena could reduce the policy risk and facilitate a more private sector-based approach.

Source: SEO Economic Research, based on Green Investment Bank Commission (2010), Hewett (2009), Cameron & Holmes (2009), Podesta & Kornbluh (2009), Holmes & Mabey (2009)

1.5 Developing Countries

1.5.1 Funding Requirements

The development of the non-industrialized economies will greatly affect energy use in the future. Wagner et al. (2009) conclude, "[t]he stark reality is that, even if emissions from industrialized countries and deforestation were reduced to zero by 2050, the climate goal cannot be met unless emerging economies also reduce their emissions". Kenney (2009, p. 2) point out that, if the economic growth of China, initially, and then India follows the historical trajectory of fossil fuel energy usage and resource consumption that Japan, Taiwan, and Korea followed, "the environmental impacts would be nothing short of monumental".

According to the IEA, the majority of energy infrastructure projects needed by 2030 will be in emerging markets like China and India (IEA, 2008). Table 9 summarizes the mitigation costs and financing needs developing countries face, according to different studies. Although the figures differ substantially, they do illustrate the magnitude of requirements.

Table 9 Estimated annual climate funding needed in developing countries (2005 US $billion)

Source of estimate		
Mitigation costs	*2010–20*	*2030*
McKinsey & Company		175
Pacific Northwest National Laboratory (PNNL)		139
Mitigation financing needs	*2010–20*	*2030*
International Institute for Applied Systems Analysis (IIASA)	63–165	264
International Energy Agency (IEA) Energy Technology Perspectives *	565	
McKinsey & Company	300	563
Potsdam Institute for Climate Impact Research (PIK)		384

Source: The World Bank (2010, p. 260); *IEA figures are annual averages through 2050

1.5.2 Risks and Barriers

Funding of SE investments in non-industrialized economies faces specific risks and barriers, requiring tailored mitigation instruments and mechanisms. Based on several studies (Liming, 2009; Ockwell, Watson, MacKerron, Pal, & Yamin, 2008; SEFI & Marsh, 2005; UNEP, 2009; UNEP & SEFI, 2008; UNEP et al., 2009), the following specific risks and barriers, and related solutions, are identified.

Political system and policy environment

Unstable and immature political systems pose additional risks. UNEP, SEFI, NEF et al. (2009) point to political risk insurance as a mitigation instrument (e.g., by the Multilateral Insurance Guarantee Agency). Aside from an uncertain policy regime in terms of regulations and support for the SE sector, legal and tax systems might provide insufficient comfort to conduct business. As in developed countries, long-term offtake contracts and a sound institutional environment are crucial in this regard.

Scale

Projects in developing countries are often even more small scale compared with those in industrialized countries, aggravating related risks. Developing countries face problems in managing the minimum required scale and the relatively high level of technology of RE projects. General training and education as well as specific technology transfer support are therefore an important part of measures to improve the success rate of investments.[78] In addition, economies of the least developed countries are small, and the wealth level is low. Foreign direct investments (FDI) and risk mitigation products will therefore not easily find their way to those countries in view of the low commercial attractiveness.[79] Public policy and intermediation by multilateral or bilateral agencies is therefore required (SEFI & Marsh, 2005).

Besides project and economy of scale issues, many developing countries have poorly developed financial markets and face comparative liquidity restrictions. Financial institutions have less experience with project finance structures and are relatively risk averse (UNEP & SEFI, 2008).

Economic and financial risk

Macroeconomic conditions are most often less stable. Elements like exchange rate, interest rate and (hyper)inflation risk – not assessed of specific importance for SE investments in industrialized countries – can result in considerable risk exposure in developing countries. Tools generally used in industrialized countries to mitigate these risks, like interest rate swaps, are often not available to the least developed countries (SEFI & Marsh, 2005). Development banks and ECAs are equipped to facilitate in this regard. In addition, counterparty risk, e.g., credit worthiness of final offtakers for generated power, might hamper financial attractiveness (UNEP et al., 2009).

78. For more information on technology transfer support, see for instance UNFCCC (2008) and Ockwell et al. (2008).

79. This is not so much a problem in growth economies like China and India.

Rural areas

Connecting rural areas to energy networks in developing countries will be a challenge in itself.[80] According to Liming (2009), costs will be higher than in urban areas (amongst many other factors, due to the need for accompanying infrastructure development). In general, the author assesses these investments as 'high risk and low profit'. On the bright side, sustainable energy is expected to be more cost effective than non-sustainable energy. The main reason is that stand-alone solutions are cheaper in these areas than connections to the central energy grid.

1.5.3 *How to Meet Funding Requirements of Developing Countries*

Required investments in developing countries are substantial. Delaying investments is not an option in view of the serious lock-in consequences. Though justifiable[81], counting on contributions by richer, developed countries will not cover the requirements either.[82] This leaves the private sector, which does not seem to favor taking on the additional funding requirements – expected returns simply do not meet risks on a sufficiently widespread basis.

The World Bank (2010) points to the Clean Development Mechanism (CDM), part of Carbon Trading, as the principal instrument for catalyzing mitigation in developing countries at this moment. They see a potential for improvements of CDM in terms of, e.g., efficiency, governance and operation, and enlarging the scope of benefits to low-income countries.[83] London School of Economics (2009) concludes, "carbon market finance may, in the longer term, generate sufficient additional investment to meet stringent emission targets".[84] (WEF, 2009b), on the other hand, is of the opinion that carbon markets and international offset schemes like CDM will not result in sufficient financial flows in the required time frame. Whether this holds true or not, additional instruments are needed to attract sufficient private funding at the least for the medium term.

---

80. And an important one: access would contribute to economic development and reduction of poverty.

81. Developing countries have contributed little, historically, to the underlying problem.

82. In Copenhagen it was agreed that developing countries would submit Nationally Appropriate Mitigation Actions (NAMAs) to the UNFCCC, which are "voluntary emission reduction measures undertaken by developing countries ... They are expected to be the main vehicle for mitigation action in developing countries under a future climate agreement" (Dalkmann et al., 2010). It is intended that these countries would get adequate support for implementing these plans, but it is a relatively new concept with success still to be proven. For sake of reference: in 2009, only some 25% of required funding was covered by public sector commitments from developed countries (UNEP, 2009). This figure is pre-Copenhagen but also pre-Greece's liquidity crisis. In general, most OECD countries face enormous public debt as it is, and increasing ODA does not seem a public policy priority.

83. For further information on CDM, see the chapter on Carbon trading.

84. Assumed investment requirements, however, are substantially lower than those in Table 9.

Public finance mechanisms are generally seen as a potential tool for closing the funding gap in developing countries. PFMs are financial commitments made by the public sector, which alter the risk-reward profile of private investments and thus catalyze investments.[85] Examples of these mechanisms include credit lines, guarantees, first loss equity positions and carbon finance facilities. In choosing the most appropriate government intervention, London School of Economics (2009) underlines the importance of appropriate risk allocation between the private and public sector. Public risk intervention should be limited to those risks "associated with market failures, policy credibility and equity consideration. Going beyond this would be inefficient … causing deadweight loss".

In the design of PFMs, both WEF (2009b) and UNEP (2009) point to the importance of institutional investors, by far the largest potential source of private funding. PFMs to stimulate SE funding in developing countries should therefore be designed to attract pension funds, insurance companies, etc. This implies the need for (sufficiently large and) low-risk funds focused on SE in developing countries.[86] At this moment, few large, diversified funds are available, and the involved risks and uncertainties remain considerable.

In specifying solutions to attract institutional investments with PFMs, WEF (2009b) focuses on the design of the funds. The report mentions two types of funds potentially catalyzing huge investment flows into developing country regions: challenge funds and regional cornerstone funds.[87] London School of Economics (2009) also mentions these funds as "proposals for a global architecture" to mobilize finance. In the *challenge fund*, fund management firms bid for access to regional packages of PFMs. The PFM packages, offered by multilateral development banks (MDBs), improve the risk-return profile, and the fund managers must explain in the bid how they will leverage these mechanisms. In *cornerstone funds*, regional MDBs would raise equity (the 'anchor equity') from major institutional investors and then invite fund management firms to bid on the distribution of part of the anchor equity. Based on their part of the anchor equity – and access to preferential risk mitigation instruments from the MDBs – the fund managers would attract additional (secondary) institutional investors. Since most of the funds would be invested in infrastructure-style investment characteristics, project portfolio funding could be further leveraged with debt. The regional cornerstone funds would thus invest in smaller funds that would invest in individual projects (i.e., a fund-of-funds). Further work is necessary as WEF (2009b) concludes by stating, "[t]he UN or negotiating parties are invited to ask a group of leading investors, financial experts and industry representatives to work with finance ministers and their officials to develop these ideas".

---

85. UNEP & SEFI (2008) calculate a multiplier of US$3 to US$15 per every US$1 of public investment.
86. Institutional investors typically invest in investment funds (WEF, 2009b).
87. The regions are ASEAN and Pacific, China, India, Latin America, Middle East/North Africa and Sub-Saharan Africa.

UNEP (2009) focuses on the design of the PFMs underlying the funds. They identify five key areas preventing institutional investors from engagement in low-carbon investment and propose PFMs for each of these areas. Figure 8 summarizes the result.

Figure 8 Five constraints on private sector engagement are matched with five operational PFM proposals

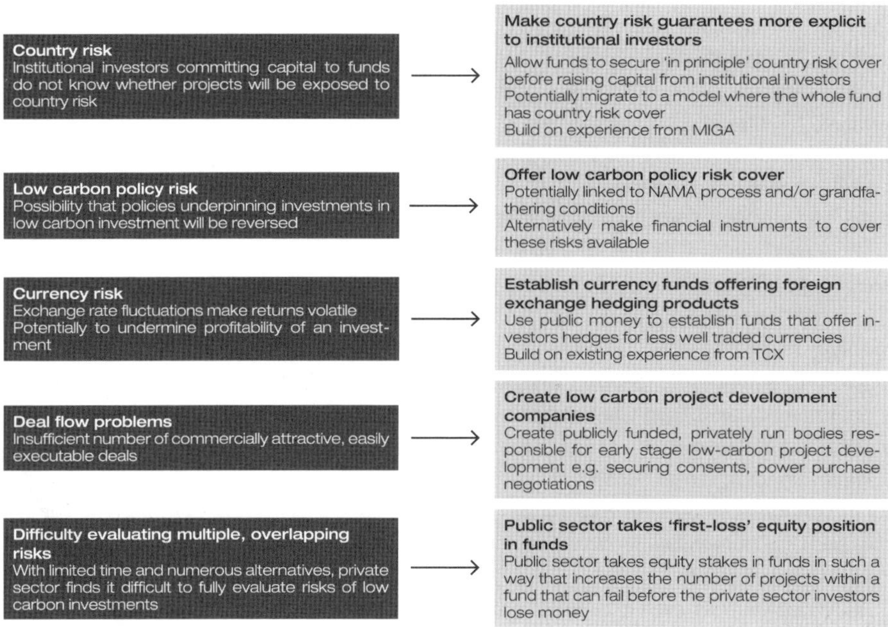

Source: UNEP (2009, p. 14)

According to London School of Economics (2009) the private sector favours concessional debt as a PFM. Concessional debt refers to lending at terms that are below market terms. Other instruments with a high leverage potential are risk mitigation and credit enhancement instruments, like full or partial guarantees and insurance, although these instruments are better suited for middle-income than for the least developed countries. Furthermore, the report sees an important role for multilateral development banks and recommends an enhanced mandate for MDBs to leverage private investments. Going forward, the report concludes "[the] private-public dialogue on innovative ways of using public funds to leverage private investment could become much stronger … so that private funds can flow at the necessary scale and speed". The discussion on innovative finance instruments is taken up again in chapter 4.

References

Auerswald, P. E., & Branscomb, L. M. (2003). Valleys of death and Darwinian seas: Financing the invention to innovation transition in the United States. *The Journal of Technology Transfer, 28*(3), 227-239.

Awerbuch, S. (2000). Investing in photovoltaics: risk, accounting and the value of new technology. *Energy Policy, 28*(14), 1023-1035.

Balachandra, P., Nathan, K., Salk, H., & Reddy, B. S. (2010). Commercialization of sustainable energy technologies. *Renewable Energy.*

Beard, T. R., Ford, G. S., Koutsky, T. M., & Spiwak, L. J. (2009). A Valley of Death in the innovation sequence: an economic investigation. *Research Evaluation, 18*(5), 343-356.

Biermans, M., Grand, H. l., Kerste, M., & Weda, J. (2009). *De kapitaalmarkt voor duurzame projecten: De regels van het spel zijn het zelfde maar het spel verloopt anders.* Amsterdam: SEO Economisch Onderzoek.

Brealey, R. A., & Myers, S. C. (2003). *Principles of corporate finance.* New York, NY: McGraw&Hill.

Bürer, M. J., & Wüstenhagen, R. (2009). Which renewable energy policy is a venture capitalist's best friend? Empirical evidence from a survey of international cleantech investors. *Energy Policy.*

Cameron, J., & Blood, D. (2009). *Catalyzing Capital Towards the Low-Carbon Economy.* Copenhagen: Copenhagen Climate Council.

Cameron, J., & Holmes, I. (2009). *Accelerating green infrastructure investment with green bonds.* London: Green Alliance.

City of London, The London Accord, & CEAG Ltd. (2009). *Delivering Copenhagen: The Role of the City's Financial Services Sector in Supporting Action on Climate Change.* London: CEAG Ltd.

CUPC. (2008). Retrieved 5-20-2010, 2010, from http://www.sourcewatch.org/index.php?title=Comparative_electrical_generation_costs

de Jager, D., Rathmann, M., Klessmann, C., Coenraads, R., Colamonico, C., & Buttazzoni, M. (2008). *Policy instrument design to reduce financing costs in renewable energy technology projects.* Utrecht: Ecofys.

Deutsche Bank. (2008). Electric Cars: Plugged In – Batteries must be included, *Global Autos Research Team.*

Dinica, V. (2006). Support systems for the diffusion of renewable energy technologies – an investor perspective. *Energy Policy, 34*(4), 461-480.

EC. (2008). *The support of electricity from renewable energy sources.* Brussels: The European Commission.

Edwards, R. (2009). *Carbon finance for developing country greenhouse gas emissions mitigation from 2010 – 2020 and the role of a Global Climate Change Fund.* London: Climate Change Capital.

Efiong, A. (2007). *Energy Efficiency: The potential for selected investment opportunities.* London: Merrill Lynch.

Eichholtz, P., Kok, N., & Quigley, J. M. (2009). Doing Well by Doing Good? Green Office Buildings. *American Economic Review, Forthcoming*

Eichholtz, P., Kok, N., & Quigley, J. M. (2010). *The Economics of Green Building.*

Enkvist, P.-A., Nauclér, T., & Rosander, J. (2007). *A cost curve for greenhouse gas reduction.* New York: McKinsey.

Farrell, D., & Remes, J. K. (2008). *How the world should invest in energy efficiency*. New York: McKinsey & Company.

Frondel, M., Ritter, N., & Schmidt, C. M. (2008). Germany's solar cell promotion: dark clouds on the horizon. *Energy Policy, 36*(11), 4198-4204.

Global Environment Facility. (2009). Innovative Renewable Energy Insurance Facility Introduced to Cover Risks in Developing Countries. Retrieved 7-5-2010, from http://www.thegef.org/gef/node/1603

Green Investment Bank Commission. (2010). *Unlocking Investment to Deliver Britain's Low Carbon Future*.

Grubb, M. (2004). Technology Innovation and Climate Change Policy: An overview of issues and options. *Keio economic studies, 41*(2), 103.

Helm, D. (2010). Government failure, rent-seeking, and capture: the design of climate change policy. *Oxford Review of Economic Policy, 26*(2), 182.

Hewett, C. (2009). Establishing a Green Investment Bank for the UK [Electronic Version].

Hoel, M. (2010). Is there a green paradox? University of Oslo, Department of Economics.

Holmes, I., & Mabey, N. (2009). *Accelerating Green Infrastructure Financing: Outline proposals for UK green bonds and infrastructure bank*. London: Climate Change Capital.

Houghton, T., & Cruden, A. (2009). An investment-led approach to analysing the hydrogen energy economy in the UK. *International Journal of Hydrogen Energy, 34*(10), 4454-4462.

IEA. (2008). *World Energy Outlook 2008*: International Energy Agency.

IEA. (2009). *World Energy Outlook 2009*: International Energy Agency.

IPCC. (2007). *Summary for policymakers*. Geneva: Intergovernmental Panel on Climate Change.

Jefferson, M. (2008). Accelerating the transition to sustainable energy systems. *Energy Policy, 36*(11), 4116-4125.

Junginger, M., Faaij, A., & Turkenburg, W. C. (2004). Cost reduction prospects for offshore wind farms. *Wind Engineering, 28*(1), 97-118.

Kann, S. (2009). Overcoming barriers to wind project finance in Australia. *Energy Policy, 37* (8), 3139-3148.

Kemfert, C. (2009). There is no green paradox. *Hürriyet Daily News and Economic Review*.

Kenney, M. (2009). Venture Capital Investment in the Greentech Industries: A Provocative Essay. *BRIE Working Paper 185*.

Kolk, A., & Pinkse, J. (2005). Business responses to climate change: identifying emergent strategies. *California Management Review, 47*(3), 6-20.

Kossoy, A., & Ambrosi, P. (2010). *State and trends of the carbon market 2010*. Washington, DC: The World Bank.

Krohn, S., Morthorst, P. E., & Awerbuch, S. (2009). The economics of wind energy. *preparado para a European Wind Energy Association*.

Lazard, L. (2008). *Levelized Cost of Energy Analysis – Version 2.0*.

Liming, H. (2009). Financing rural renewable energy: A comparison between China and India. *Renewable and Sustainable Energy Reviews, 13*(5), 1096-1103.

LSE. (2009). *Meeting the Climate Challenge: Using Public Funds to Leverage Private Investment in Developing Countries*. London: London School of Economics and Political Science.

McKinsey & Company. (2009). *Pathways to a Low-Carbon Economy: Version 2 of the Global Greenhouse Gas Abatement Cost Curve*.

Meijer, I. S. M., Hekkert, M. P., & Koppenjan, J. F. M. (2007). The influence of perceived uncertainty on entrepreneurial action in emerging renewable energy technology; biomass gasification projects in the Netherlands. *Energy Policy, 35*(11), 5836-5854.

Mills, E. (2003). Risk transfer via energy-savings insurance. *Energy Policy, 31*(3), 273-281.

Mills, E. (2009). *From risk to opportunity 2008: Insurer responses to climate change.* Boston MA: Ceres.

Mills, E., Kromer, S., Weiss, G., & Mathew, P. A. (2006). From volatility to value: analysing and managing financial and performance risk in energy savings projects. *Energy Policy, 34* (2), 188-199.

Mizuguchi, H., & Monoe, Y. (2009). *Green Industrial Revolution Gaining Momentum: Promising industries and players in next-gen eco, energy technologies.* Tokyo: Daiwa Institute of Research Ltd.

Müller, B. (2008). *International adaptation finance: The need for an innovative and strategic approach*: Oxford Institute for Energy Studies.

NEA, IEA, & OECD. (2005). *Projected Costs of Generating Electricity: 2005 Update.*

Neuhoff, K., Fankhauser, S., Guerin, E., Hourcade, J. C., Jackson, H., Rajan, R., et al. (2010). Structuring International Financial Support for Climate Change Mitigation in Developing Countries. *Discussion Papers of DIW Berlin.*

Nordhaus, W. D. (2007). To tax or not to tax: Alternative approaches to slowing global warming. *Review of Environmental Economics and Policy, 1*(1), 26.

Ockwell, D. G., Watson, J., MacKerron, G., Pal, P., & Yamin, F. (2008). Key policy considerations for facilitating low carbon technology transfer to developing countries. *Energy Policy, 36*(11), 4104-4115.

Owen, A. D. (2006). Renewable energy: Externality costs as market barriers. *Energy Policy, 34* (5), 632-642.

Paris Re. (2008). PARIS RE, Marsh and the UNEP/GEF develop innovative renewable energy insurance solutions.

Pindyck, R. S. (2007). Uncertainty in environmental economics. *Review of Environmental Economics and Policy, 1*(1), 45.

Pinkse, J. (2007). Carbon emissions trading: managing climate change through financial markets. *Aenorm, 56*, 17-20.

Plinke, E. (2008). *Energy Efficiency: Hidden Capital – How Investors Can Benefit From The Cheapest Source Of Energy* Basel: Bank Sarasin & Co. Ltd.

Podesta, J. D., & Kornbluh, K. (2009). *The Green Bank.*

Project Catalyst. (2009). *Enabling technologies for low carbon growth.* Brussels: ECF Energy Strategy Centre.

PwC. (2009). *Crisis or not, renewable energy is hot: To reap the rewards, governments and companies should act now.* Amsterdam: PricewaterhouseCoopers.

Ross, C., Mills, E., & Hecht, S. B. (2007). Limiting Liability in the Greenhouse: Insurance Risk-Management Strategies in the Context of Global Climate Change. *Stanford Journal of International Law, 43*, 251.

Roth, D. (2008). Driven: Shai Agassi's Audacious Plan to Put Electric Cars on the Road.

Schleich, J., & Gruber, E. (2008). Beyond case studies: Barriers to energy efficiency in commerce and the services sector. *Energy Economics, 30*(2), 449-464.

SEFI, & Marsh. (2005). *Scoping Study on Financial Risk Management Instruments for Renewable Energy Projects: United Nations Environment Programme.* Paris: SEFI/Marsh.

Shepherd, P. (2009). *Reshaping the capital markets for a sustainable recovery*. London: Green Alliance.

Sinn, H. W. (2008a). Das grüne Paradoxon. *Plädoyer für eine illusionsfreie Klimapolitik. Econ, Berlin.*

Sinn, H. W. (2008b). Public policies against global warming: a supply side approach. *International Tax and Public Finance, 15*(4), 360-394.

Sinn, H. W. (2009). *The Green Paradox*. Paper presented at the CESifo Forum 3/2009.

Sjöö, K. (2008). The Influence of Uncertainty on Venture Capital Investments in Renewable Energy Technology: an exploratory study.

Stack, J., Balbach, J., Epstein, B., & Hanggi, T. (2007). *Cleantech venture capital: How public policy has stimulated private investment.*

Stern, N., Peters, S., Bakhshi, V., Bowen, A., Cameron, C., Catovsky, S., et al. (2006). *Stern Review: The economics of climate change.*

SwissRe. (2009, November 3, 2009). *Climate Change Adaptation and the Role of Insurance Products*. Paper presented at the CC & Insurance Adaptation, Las Vega.

Tester, J. W. (2005). *Sustainable energy: Choosing among options*: The MIT Press.

The World Bank. (2010). *World Development Report 2010: Development and Climate Change*. Washington, DC: The International Bank for Reconstruction and Development / The World Bank.

Thompson, C. (2009). The Green Issue – Batteries Not Included. *The New York Times.*

Thompson, M., Elford, S., Glover, E., Prouty, E., & Quealy, J. (2007). *Sustainability: Investing in renewable energy*. London: Canaccord Adams.

UNEP. (2008, 13-14 October 2008). *Summary of Discussions*. Paper presented at the Roundtable on Financial Risk Management for Renewable Energy Projects in Emerging and Developing Countries, Paris.

UNEP. (2009). *Catalysing low-carbon growth in developing economies: Public Finance Mechanisms to scale up private sector investment in climate solutions*. Paris: UNEP.

UNEP, & GEF. (2008). Financial Risk Management Instruments for Renewable Energy projects, *Project Status Note – March 2008* (pp. 4).

UNEP, & MISI. (2009). *Why Clean Energy Public Investment Makes Economic Sense: The Evidence Base*. Basel: SEF Alliance.

UNEP, & SEFI. (2004). *Executive Briefing: Making it Happen: Renewable Energy Finance and the Role of Export Credit Agencies*. Paris: UNEP.

UNEP, & SEFI. (2008). *Public Finance Mechanisms to Mobilise Investment in Climate Change Mitigation*. Paris: United Nations Environment Programme.

UNEP, SEFI, NEF, & Chatman House. (2009). *Private Financing of Renewable Energy – A Guide for Policymakers*. Paris: UNEP.

UNEP, SEFI, & New Energy Finance. (2008). *Global Trends in Sustainable Energy Investment 2008: Analysis of Trends and Issues in the Financing of Renewable Energy and Energy Efficiency*. Paris: UNEP.

UNFCCC. (2007). *Investment and Financial flows to Address Climate Change*. Bonn.

UNFCCC. (2008). *Identifying, analysing and assessing existing and potential new financing resources and relevant vehicles to support the development, deployment, diffusion and transfer of environmentally sound technologies*. Bonn.

Van der Ploeg, R., & Withagen, C. (2010). Is There Really a Green Paradox?

Van Kooten, G. C., & Timilsina, G. R. (2009). *Wind Power Development: Economics and Policies*. Washington, DC: The World Bank.

Vattenfall, A. B. (2007). Global mapping of greenhouse gas abatement opportunities up to 2030. *Web: http://www. vattenfall. com/www/ccc/ccc/Gemeinsame_Inhalte/DOCUMENT/ 567263vattenfall/ P, 272860.*

Victor, D. (2009). *The Politics of Fossil-Fuel Subsidies.* Winnipeg/Geneva: The Global Subsidies Initiative.

Vine, E., Mills, E., & Chen, A. (2000). Energy-efficiency and renewable energy options for risk management and insurance loss reduction. *Energy, 25*(2), 131-147.

Vine, E. L. (1992). Persistence of Energy Savings: What do we know and how can it be ensured? *Energy, 17*(11), 1073-1084.

Wagner, G., Wang, J., Dudek, D., Haverkamp, J., Keohane, N., & Petsonk, A. (2009). *The CLEAR Path: Rewarding early actions by emerging economies to limit carbon.* Washington, DC: Environmental Defense Fund.

WEF. (2009a). *Green Investing: Towards a Clean Energy Infrastructure.* Cologny/Geneva: World Economic Forum.

WEF. (2009b). *Task force on low-carbon prosperity: Summary of Recommendations.* Cologny/ Geneva: World Economic Forum.

WEF. (2010). *Green Investing 2010: Policy Mechanisms to Bridge the Financial Gap.* Cologny/ Geneva: World Economic Forum.

WEF. (2011). *Green investing 2011 – A preview.*

Wustenhagen, R., & Teppo, T. (2004). *What makes a good industry for venture capitalists? Risk, return and time as factors determining the emergence of the European energy VC market.* St. Gallen: University of St. Gallen.

Wustenhagen, R., & Teppo, T. (2006). Do venture capitalists really invest in good industries? Risk-return perceptions and path dependence in the emerging European energy VC market. *International Journal of Technology Management, 34*(1), 63-87.

2. Carbon Trading

Chapter Overview

2.1 Introduction

In discussing the need for a transition from conventional to sustainable energy (SE) sources, Chapter 1 touched upon the vital importance of public policy geared towards overcoming investment barriers and stimulating SE investment in order to mitigate climate change. This chapter elaborates on one of the primary *market-based* policy instruments to reduce carbon emissions and stimulate investment in renewable energy technologies: carbon trading, also known as cap-and-trade systems. The following three sections provide an elaborate overview of the principles underlying carbon trading, from theoretical underpinnings to compliance and voluntary carbon markets, the regulatory environment, and market functioning. In the last section, the more descriptive first part is taken as a starting point to assess the success of carbon trading. This is measured in terms of effectiveness in reducing carbon emissions. Issues and improvements are discussed where effectiveness has not lived up to expectations.

2.2 Carbon Trading

2.2.1 *Theoretical Background*

The build-up of atmospheric greenhouse gases (GHGs) is expected to cause significant climate changes in the coming decades and beyond, such as an increasing global surface temperature, increasing precipitation and evaporation, and rising sea levels. Preventing climate change can be regarded as a *global public good*. Its impact is indivisible, and its influences are felt around the world rather than affecting one nation, town, or family. Global public goods are different from other economic activities, in the sense that only weak economic and political mechanisms exist for solving these issues efficiently and effectively. It is difficult to determine and reach agreement on efficient policies, because dealing with public goods involves estimating and balancing costs and benefits, neither of which is easy to measure, while both involve major distributional concerns (Kaul, Grunberg, & Stern, 1999; Nordhaus, 1999, 2006b, 2007).

Traditional fossil-fuel energy is relatively abundant and inexpensive. But while the private costs of fossil fuels (i.e., the costs to companies or individuals) are mostly relatively low, the total costs to society are not. The difference between private and societal costs is called an external cost, or *externality*. External costs are directly related to producing or delivering a good or service, but are not borne by its originator. GHG emissions are a classic example of externalities. There is a link between public goods and externalities. Some authors claim that public goods (notably those that have benefits that are non-rivalrous in consumption and are non-excludable, so-called *pure public goods*) can be thought of as special cases of externalities. In essence, both are different ways of talking about goods with non-private aspects (Cornes & Sandler, 1996; Miller, 2006).[1]

There are two principal market-based instruments to address climate change mitigation and the underlying issue of externalities: carbon taxes and carbon emissions trading, the latter also referred to as cap-and-trade or allowance trading. A *carbon tax* is a price instrument and is typically levied on the carbon content of fuel inputs, creating an incentive to either switch to lower-carbon inputs or to use inputs more efficiently.[2] Since governments have imperfect information about costs of fuel switching and energy efficiency improvement (i.e., mitigation costs), there is uncertainty how much abatement will occur for a given tax level. It is nearly impossible for governments to deduce a tax level that results in the mitigation efforts as intended by policymakers.[3] Nevertheless, carbon taxes continue to have a strong (theoretical)

---

1. In addition to externalities, subsidization also results in relatively low price for conventional fuels, as was discussed in chapter 1, *Financing the Transition to Sustainable Energy*. For more information on fossil-fuel subsidies, see Victor (2009).
2. Other price-based approaches include fees and subsidies.
3. If there were an emission cap under global agreement, governments could simply adjust tax rates iteratively to keep emissions within the cap.

appeal on economists worldwide, *inter alia* because of the potentially much greater price stability that this brings relative to an emissions trading system, its revenue-raising capabilities and simplicity, and its low administration and compliance costs (PwC, 2009). Drawbacks include the difficult political environment for taxation of emissions (national/international) and the fact that its impact on emission reduction targets is only indirect. Since this literature review concerns carbon trading, carbon taxes are not discussed further. This does not imply any inferiority (theoretical or otherwise) compared to carbon trading, however.[4]

Emissions trading (ET) is based on quantitative limits rather than being price-based. It regulates the corporate environmental impact by putting a quantity cap on emission output. Combined with the possibility to trade in the capped emission outputs, which become scarce due to the cap, this results in a price on units of emission and thus in pricing the negative externality. ET does not prescribe the means by which firms should comply with the quantity cap. As a result, emissions trading gives firms flexibility and the possibility to fit carbon management activities into their overall strategy. Carbon taxes and cap-and-trade schemes can and are used conjointly. The European Union opted for a trading scheme to address emissions from large sources (utilities, heat production, large energy-intensive industrial facilities), while several European countries introduced carbon taxes to target emissions from other sectors, notably residential and services, transport, waste management, and agriculture (Kolk & Pinkse, 2005; Nordhaus, 2007; Pinkse, 2007; The World Bank, 2010). These 'hybrid' systems provide evidence for the benefits of a combination of taxes and trading.

2.2.2 *Cap-and-Trade*

In a cap-and-trade scheme governments issue emission permits representing a legal right to emit pollutants, which are freely tradable between trading scheme participants. More specifically, a central authority sets a limit (or cap) on the permitted level of GHG emissions and allocates permits/allowances that bestow the right to emit GHG below the current or expected level of emissions. Allowances are either given to emitters for free or are auctioned to them – the latter creates a source of fiscal revenue. The capped level is aimed at creating an overall shortage of allowances. By granting an (increasingly) insufficient amount of emission allowances, emission rights have a (growing) value and, vice versa, emissions entail (growing) private costs. A price is put on external costs, thereby 'internalizing' the negative externality (Coase, 1960; Convery, 2009; Ellerman, 2005; Lai, 2008).[5]

An emitter faced with a shortage of allowances can chose between 3 options: cut its emissions (e.g., by lowering its production), invest in cleaner technology to reduce

4. For more information on carbon taxes, see for instance Nordhaus (2007).
5. Evidently, achieving this depends on whether caps result in sufficient scarcity. This is further discussed in section 2.5.

emissions per unit of output, or buy sufficient allowances to compensate its shortfall compared with its actual emissions level (City of London, The London Accord, & CEAG Ltd, 2009, p. 10). Firms and sectors will have different marginal compliance costs (i.e., the marginal costs of fuel switching or increasing energy efficiency), so there is potential for gains from trading permits. If a firm has high marginal costs of mitigation while another has much lower costs, the firm with the lower costs can sell a permit at a price above its marginal costs of mitigation, reduce its emissions accordingly, and make a profit. If the permit price is below the marginal mitigation costs of the buyer, the trade is profitable for both parties. In theory, carbon trading leads to a cost-effective reduction of emissions, as abatement will occur where marginal costs of mitigation are lowest (Böhringer & Rosendahl, 2009; Burniaux, Château, Dellink, Duval, & Jamet, 2009; Carbon Trust & Climate Strategies, 2009; Egenhofer, 2007; Flachsland, Marschinski, & Edenhofer, 2009; Heal, 2007; Leung, Yung, Ng, Leung, & Chan, 2009). Moreover, since cap-and-trade is based on quantitative limits, there is a high certainty that a country will stay within its cap, provided that enforcement is effective. It fixes the volume of emissions and then lets the market find the appropriate price level (The World Bank, 2010; WEF, 2009). This is not to say that emissions trading is not subject to theoretical criticism as well, including for instance the question of whether an efficient outcome is necessarily fair, equitable, or desirable (Hepburn, 2007; Woerdman, 2001).

2.2.3 *Emergence of Carbon Trading*

The conceptual underpinnings for carbon trading began with Pigou (1920) pointing out the social benefits of forcing companies to pay for the costs of their pollution by setting taxation equal to the value of the negative externality emanating from the pollution (Grubb, Laing, Counsell, & Willan, 2010).[6] Forty years later, Coase (1960) stated the basic idea underlying tradable permits, by noting the reciprocal nature of harmful effects and suggesting that property rights and allowing trade (i.e., market-based solutions) could regulate them effectively and efficiently (Ellerman, 2005; Hepburn, 2007). Other economists later applied his insight specifically to environmental problems (Crocker, 1968; Dales, 1968; Montgomery, 1972). Despite some early activities, tradable permits have only been implemented on a larger scale and deemed a real success since the mid 1990s, when a global agreement on carbon reduction targets was in the making (Ellerman, 2005).

The influence of regulation on carbon markets and carbon trading is substantial. The World Bank (Capoor & Ambrosi, 2008) concludes "[t]he carbon market has so far been essentially a compliance-driven market, where buyers largely engage in carbon transactions because of carbon constraints (current or anticipated) at international, national or sub-national levels". In 1997, the Kyoto Protocol to the United Nations Framework Convention on Climate Change (UNFCCC) provided for carbon trading

6. See Nordhaus (2006a; 2007) and Pezzey (2003) for further discussion on the concept of Pigovian Taxes.

through three "flexible mechanisms". The Kyoto Protocol made no provision for how emissions allowances should be traded or what form its market should take. Instead, the private sector was challenged to devise its own market solutions for emissions trading, from which a transparent carbon price would emerge to inform investment decisions. The first Kyoto commitment period runs from January 2008 to December 2012, and it has prompted the emergence of major international markets in carbon. The largest carbon trading market by far is the European Union Emissions Trading Scheme (EU ETS).[7]

7. The first forward carbon trades, however, occurred many years earlier, long before the Protocol came into force. For instance, in the 1970s the Environmental Protection Agency (EPA) in the US offered states the option to employ variants of tradable permits for the control of localized air pollutants. The first voluntary trades, by parties not subject to regulatory requirements, occurred in the late 1980s. Still, trading on a large scale only became reality due to the Kyoto Protocol. Nowadays, voluntary carbon trade is driven by two factors: corporate social responsibility (CSR) and the anticipation of legislation.

2.3 Carbon Markets and Regulatory Environment

2.3.1 *Compliance Markets*

Global Regulatory Background: Kyoto Protocol

At the heart of the regulation governing and impacting carbon emission trading is the Kyoto Protocol. Amongst many other sources, information on the background and regulatory content of the Protocol can be found in Part I of Carbon Trust (2009) and on the website of the UNFCCC.[8]

The Kyoto Protocol is complementary to the United Nations Framework Convention on Climate Change (UNFCCC), which entered into force in 1994 and enjoys near universal membership. The UNFCCC is aimed at tackling the challenge posed by climate change. Whereas the UNFCCC *encourages* stabilization of GHG emissions, the targets in the Kyoto Protocol are *binding*. More specifically, by signing the Kyoto Protocol in 1997, 37 industrialized countries and the European Community (the so-called *Annex B parties*) have committed to reducing their emissions[9] by an average of 5 percent against 1990 levels over the five-year period 2008-2012.[10]

Although the focus is on domestic action against climate change, the Kyoto Protocol also introduces three market-based mechanisms, thereby creating a 'carbon market' (UNCCF, 2010):

- Emissions Trading (ET);
- The Clean Development Mechanism (CDM);
- Joint Implementation (JI).[11]

The targets for the Annex B parties are expressed in allowed emissions under the Protocol and result in 'assigned amount units' (AAUs), thereby creating the necessary scarcity to enable carbon trading. Article 17 of the Protocol covers Emission Trading, allowing countries to sell excess emission units to countries that are over their targets.[12] Kyoto is thus a 'cap-and-trade system' that imposes national caps (limits) on the emissions of Annex B countries. The cap level, which indicates how many emissions the respective country can produce, is strongly related to the effectiveness of carbon trading, which is discussed in detail in section 2.5.

---

8. UNFCCC website: http://unfccc.int/2860.php (accessed on June 24, 2010).

9. 'Emissions' refer to six greenhouse gases: CO_2 (which is the most important GHG), methane, nitrous oxide, hydrofluorocarbons, perfluorocarbons and sulphur hexafluoride.

10. The Kyoto Protocol entered into force on 16 February 2005. The detailed rules for the implementation of the Protocol were adopted at COP 7 in Marrakesh in 2001, and are called the "Marrakesh Accords". The 38th country, USA, has not ratified the Kyoto Protocol (UNCCF, 2010).

11. Furthermore, credits can be earned for Land Use, Land-Use Change and Forestry (LULUCF) projects. These credits can be traded only at the country level. LULUCF is discussed in section 2.4.1.

12. Further defined in 'Modalities, rules and guidelines for emissions trading under Article 17 of the Kyoto Protocol', decision 11/CMP.1.

Under the Clean Development Mechanism (CDM), defined in Article 12, Annex B Parties can earn credits by implementing emission-reduction projects in developing countries. These credits can be counted towards meeting Kyoto targets. The Joint Implementation (JI) mechanism, defined in Article 6, is comparable to CDM but arranges the earning of emission units by one Annex B Party with projects in another Annex B Parties. In Kyoto terminology: with CDM parties can earn certified emission reduction (CER), with JI parties can earn emission reduction units (ERU). The trading mechanisms under the Kyoto Protocol are discussed further in section 2.4.

European Union Emissions Trading Scheme

EU Regulation

In 2002, the EU and all its member states ratified the Kyoto Protocol, thereby committing themselves to reducing GHG emissions by 8% in the period from 2008 to 2012. Based on a legally binding burden-sharing agreement (BSA), the 8%-target is shared between the Member States. The BSA sets individual emissions targets for each member state.[13]

An important instrument in achieving the EU emission reduction targets is the implementation of the EU Emissions Trading Scheme (EU ETS). Amongst many other sources, elaborate information on background, development towards and content of legislation underlying the EU ETS can be found in Convery & Redmond (2007), Egenhofer (2007), Ellerman & Buchner (2007) and EC.[14]

The legal foundation for the EU ETS is the Emissions Trading Directive, enacted in 2003, followed by the 'Linking Directive' which links Joint Implementation (JI) and Clean Development Mechanism (CDM) credits to the EU ETS.[15] The EU ETS was launched in 2005, covering a three-year trial trading period (2005–2007). This is not part of any obligation under the Kyoto Protocol but was designed to familiarize European firms with emissions trading. The second trading period covers the period 2008-2012, coinciding with the first commitment period under the Kyoto Protocol. From then on, consecutive five-year periods (starting from the 2013-2017 trading period) are intended the span the post-Kyoto commitment periods.

Both the Kyoto Protocol and the BSA allocate emission rights to nations, not to individual legal entities. Different from the Kyoto Protocol, under EU regulation each EU member state developed its own National Allocation Plan (NAP). The NAP allocates the country's total BSA target between the trading sectors (those that initially partici-

13. Council Decision 2002/358/EC of 25 April 2002. The Linking Directive makes emission credits from CDM and JI projects (CERs and ERUs, respectively) fungible with EUAs.

14. EU website: http://ec.europa.eu/environment/climat/emission/implementation_en.htm (accessed on June 24, 2010).

15. Directive 2003/87/EC of October 13, 2003, respectively Directive 2004/101/EC of November 13, 2004.

pate in the ETS) and the non-trading sectors. Moreover, it specifies how the permits, called European Union Allowances (EUAs), are distributed among the individual sources in the trading sector, thereby creating the potential supply and demand for allowances in the market. The NAPs are determined by discussion and negotiation between member states and the participating firms, and the NAPs are then submitted to the European Commission for approval.

During the first and second trading periods of the EU ETS, 95% and 90% of permits, respectively, have been assigned to companies based upon historical emissions and free of charge according to Article 10 of the Directive. This so-called *grandfathering* of emission rights has been subject to criticism. Permit prices are passed through to consumers – permits that were given away for free in the first place – resulting in (adverse) distribution effects (Woerdman, Arcuri, & Cló, 2008). For instance, electricity generators could earn windfall profits this way, by passing the market value of the allowances through to the final price. Moreover, allocation based upon historical emissions leads to perverse dynamic effects, where firms have an incentive to emit more now in order to receive a larger free allocation in the future. Grandfathering may also result in rent-seeking behavior by companies as they spend valuable resources in lobbying to obtain a higher allocation (Clò, 2010; Hepburn, 2007; Woerdman et al., 2008).

Critics therefore advocate auctioning permits instead of grandfathering, in order to solve the redistributive concerns. Indeed, auctioning of emission permits provides benefits over simply assigning them for free. First of all, auctions prompt the private sector to reveal their expected abatement costs, thereby dissolving information asymmetry between companies and governments. Second, auctioning promotes a greater managerial focus on ET, and thus on companies' abatement efforts. Finally, free allocation can be regarded as a regressive transfer of wealth from (relatively poor) citizens to (relatively wealthy) shareholders (Hepburn, 2007).[16] The new ETS Directive addresses the criticism on grandfathering through a bigger role for auctioning in Phase III.

EU ETS

The European Union Emissions Trading Scheme covers over 11,000 installations, including combustion plants, oil refineries, coke ovens, iron and steel plants, and factories making cement, glass, lime, brick, ceramics, pulp, and paper. Land and air transport are not included (see Box 1), and EU ETS only covers the most important greenhouse gas, CO_2. Former European trading schemes – the UK Emissions Trading Scheme (UK ETS) and schemes in Norway and Denmark – have all been subsumed within the EU Emissions Trading Scheme (Betsill & Hoffmann, 2009; City of London et al., 2009; Hepburn, 2007).

16. This does not mean grandfathering is less efficient than auctioning. For a discussion on the efficiency of both systems, see Woerdman et al. (2008). They conclude that the final verdict depends on the definition of efficiency – only if equality is taken into account is auctioning more efficient than grandfathering.

Box 1 Aviation and EU ETS[17]

In 2008, the Council of the EU and the European Parliament agreed the basis on which international aviation will be brought into EU ETS from 2012 (Phase 3).[18] This means airlines of all nationalities will need allowances to cover the emissions from their flights to, from or within the EU. The outcome, however, was contentious in light of rising oil prices and strong opposition by the International Civil Aviation Organization (ICAO), and led to strong rebukes from airlines and threats of legal action by some states (Rock, Baines, & LeBoeuf, 2008).[19]

After 2 'pre-trading' years in 2010 and 2011, trading will be possible in 2012 (first trading phase) and thereafter (second trading phase). The cap levels will be based on average 2004-2006 emission levels: in 2012, 97% of average 2004-2006 emission levels is allowed, from 2013 on the cap will be 95% of average 2004-2006 emission levels. Some 15% of allowances will be allocated via auction, 3% is specially reserved for new entrants and fast growers, the remainder are free allowances (Verschueren, 2009).

Transport (including international aviation) accounts for approximately 24% of total EU-27 GHG emissions (European Environment Agency, 2009), of which 3% stems from aviation (Anger, 2009). This percentage is expected to increase, due to rapid expansion and estimated future growth caused by globalization, economic growth, liberalization and business model innovation.

The first impact estimates show that the financial burden on the aviation industry will be rather modest in the first years after the introduction of the trading scheme, and therefore will induce only low competition distortions. It is also expected that emission reductions within air transportation will be comparably low unless the system design becomes more restrictive (Vespermann & Wald, 2010).

EU firms within the scope of the EU ETS now face a carbon-constrained reality in the form of legally binding emission targets.[20] It is regarded as the most important European climate policy instrument, since it covers almost half of the total European CO_2 emissions. As was mentioned in section 2.2, it is the largest carbon market in the world by a substantial margin, both by value and by volume, with annual trading quadrupling from US$24 billion in 2006 to US$101 billion in 2008, and still growing in 2009 (see Table 4). Combined with CDMs, it comprises over 90% of the world's

---

17. For more information on the implications of EU ETS for airlines, see: CE Delft (2007a; 2007b) and CE Delft & MVA (2007).

18. Directive 2008/101/EC (13 January 2009) and Directive 2003/87/EC (consolidated version).

19. See also http://ec.europa.eu/environment/climat/aviation/index_en.htm.

20. Firms whose emissions exceed the allowances they hold at the end of the accounting period must pay a fine (€40 for each extra metric ton of CO_2 emitted during the pilot period, and €100 during the commitment period). Those fined must also make up the deficit by buying the relevant volume of allowances (Convery and Redmond, 2007).

carbon markets. Through the implementation of the "Linking Directive", it has become the hub of the global carbon markets (Abadie & Chamorro, 2008; Ellerman, 2005; Hepburn, 2007).

Other Operational Compliance Markets[21]

New Zealand

On November 25, 2009, New Zealand's ETS expanded from forestry to become the first mandatory, economy-wide scheme outside Europe. This was decided by passing the Climate Change Response (Moderated Emissions Trading) Amendment of 2009 through Parliament. New Zealand is trying to align itself with Australia's proposed Australian Pollution Reduction Scheme (see below) in the hope of future linkage between the two markets.

New Zealand chose to implement this economy-wide scheme step by step, starting with a transition period in 2010-12. In the first period, there is a fixed price for government-issued NZ ETS allowances (called New Zealand Units, or NZUs) used for compliance purposes of NZ$25 (US$18 or €13). Importantly, however, during the transition period there is an unlimited supply of allowances, hence, there will be no cap on emissions.[22] This might pose a challenge in terms of commitment to its international emission reduction target. From the start, the scheme will regulate stationary energy, industrial process and liquid fossil fuels for transport. Thereafter sectors will be added in 2013 and 2015.

New South Wales Greenhouse Gas Abatement Scheme (NSW GGAS)

Until 2009, the Greenhouse Gas Abatement Scheme (NSW GGAS) in New South Wales, Australia, was the largest non-Kyoto trading scheme in terms of physical volume and financial value (Hepburn, 2007).[23] The scheme, which launched in 2003, is aimed at reducing GHG emissions associated with the production and use of electricity. In 2006, the NSW government decided to extend the GGAS to 2021 or until the establishment of a national ETS. The delay of the proposed Carbon Pollution Reduction Scheme (CPRS), potentially Australia's central instrument to manage GHG emissions, has created uncertainty about the scheme's future (certificates under the NSW GGAS would not be eligible under a federal scheme), and the number of new GGAS accreditations tapered off in 2009 as a result of the Australian senate's continued rejection of CPRS legislation (Hamilton, Sjardin, Peters-Stanley, & Marcello, 2010; Kossoy & Ambrosi, 2010). In 2008 there were still 18 million NSW greenhouse gas abatement credits (NGACs) transacted, representing €77 million in value (Tvinnereim, 2008).

---

21. The overviews of other operation and announced compliance markets are based on Kossoy & Ambrosi (2010) and WEF (2010).
22. No cap has yet been announced for 2013 and thereafter.
23. Since 2009, the RGGI is the largest non-Kyoto market (see Table 4).

Japan

Although there is not yet an active government-based ETS in Japan (proposed legislation is discussed below), there is a mandatory cap-and-trade scheme in the Tokyo metropolitan area, which targets 1,400 office and commercial buildings (including universities) and factories. The scheme covers 1% of Japan's emissions, but it regulates the energy use of services instead of the CO_2 emissions for industries.

North America

The most notable recent development in emissions trading in the US has been the Regional Greenhouse Gas Initiative (RGGI), a cap-and-trade scheme covering ten Northeast and Mid-Atlantic states, which began its first three-year compliance period at the start of 2009. The initiative caps emissions from the power sector. Emission rights are auctioned and can thereafter be traded between electric power generators. This scheme is significant for the fact that it was established in a country that has not yet signed up to any international emission reduction targets, and for generating proceeds of over US$430 million in its quarterly emission auctions. These proceeds have been distributed back to the states to invest in energy efficiency and renewable energy (WEF, 2010).

Alberta (Canada) initiated a compliance market in 2007. The Climate Change Emissions Management Act was amended to require companies with an emission intensity of more than 100kt CO_2e per year to reduce their emissions by 12% from their baseline (an average of 2003-2005 emissions). Reduction deficits can be met through trade, payments into the Climate Change and Emissions Management Fund at a set price or by buying Emission offsets (Goddart, Haugen-Kozyra, & Ridge, 2008).

Announced Compliance Markets

Table 1 gives an overview of cap-and-trade schemes that were in their deliberation or design phase as of April 2009 and that will be mandatory, once operational.

Table 1 Future cap-and-trade policies that are mandatory (partly) (as of April 2009)

Deliberation Phase	Design Phase
Canada	Australia
Florida	California
Japan	Korea*
NAFTA-CEC*	Copenhagen Accord
PEMEX*	Western Climate Initiative
US Congress	

Source: SEO Economic Research, adapted from Betsill & Hoffmann (2009)
* = Mandatory or voluntary status still unsure

US: Waxman-Markey and Kerry-Boxer

In 2009, progress seemed to be made towards the long-awaited US Federal cap-and-trade scheme as the *Waxman-Markey American Clean Energy and Security Act* passed the House of Representatives. This act pledges to cut US emissions by 17% by 2020 and 83% by 2050 (compared to 2005 levels) and includes a cap-and-trade provision. According to this act, the majority of the cap-and-trade permits (85%) will be given away for free to the most heavily emitting industries, grandfathering their emission rights. As of now it is uncertain whether the act in its current form will pass the US Senate.[24]

Meanwhile, the *Kerry-Boxer Climate Bill* has been working its way through committee stages. It is similar to the Waxman-Markey Act in many ways, but would set a slightly more stringent target (a 20% reduction from 2005 levels by 2020), places greater emphasis on the use of domestic rather than international offsets, and gives the US President more control over what types of offsets would be eligible under the scheme (WEF, 2010). Mid-2010, after months of heavy debate between Democrats and Republicans, the plans for an energy bill including cap-and-trade were abandoned as the leader of the senate majority presented a more restricted energy bill.[25]

At the state level, California is set to introduce a cap-and-trade scheme in 2012 as a way of meeting the requirements for emissions reductions under its global warming legislation, AB32.[26]

Japan

On March 12, 2010, the government of Japan proposed the *Basic Act on Global Warming Countermeasures*. Thus far, the climate policy of Japan has excluded market-based approaches and price instruments. With the 'Basic Act' a mandatory ETS is established, a carbon tax is implemented, and a feed-in tariff for all renewable energy sources is included. Furthermore, the Act aims to achieve a 10% share of total primary energy supply from renewable sources by 2020, and is in line with Japan's mid-term and long-term GHG emissions reduction goals. There is growing opposition to the proposed bill from leading business organizations that have concerns about the costs to the economy. The ETS will be active in one year, but observers believe that, due to the opposition, this will take longer. This is not the case for the carbon tax and feed-in tariff.

---

24. See also http://thinkcarbon.wordpress.com/2009/07/11/comparison-of-waxman-markey-eu-ets-and-cprs-emissions-trading-schemes/ for a snapshot comparison of the proposed Waxman-Markey Cap-and-Trade Scheme, the EU Emissions Trading Scheme and the Carbon Pollution Reduction Scheme in Australia (website accessed on July 9, 2010).

25. See http://www.csmonitor.com/USA/Politics/2010/0727/Stripped-down-energy-bill-leaves-out-cap-and-trade.

26. AB32 is the California Global Warming Solutions Act of 2006. It requires California's state-wide GHG emissions to be reduced to the 1990 level by 2020. Based on the current understanding, this is a reduction of about 25%.

Australia

Unlike in New Zealand, the Australian economy-wide trading scheme, the Australian Pollution Reduction Scheme (CPRS), did not make it through the Senate (twice). Therefore, the Prime Minister announced that further plans on this subject would be postponed and re-examined by the end of 2012. The CPRS would have covered approximately 75% of Australia's emissions. This would have been in line with its mid-term commitment of reducing GHG emissions by at least 5% below 2000 levels by 2020.

Future Developments

UNFCCC: Beyond Kyoto

Emission reduction targets in the Kyoto Protocol, at the heart of catalyzing carbon trading, go only as far as 2012. It was hoped and believed that the 15th Conference of the Parties to the UNFCCC in Copenhagen in December 2009 would address this issue. Copenhagen, however, did not deliver in this regard: no agreement was reached on post-2012 emission reduction targets, nor on a new deadline for a post-2012 agreement. Negotiations were deferred to the next conference (COP 16 in Mexico), "with significant issues between the major players still to be resolved" (WEF, 2010).

This does not mean nothing good came out of Copenhagen. According to the World Bank, "probably the most significant aspect of the Accord is that it enshrines the continuation of the Kyoto Protocol" (WEF, 2010). Table 2 summarizes the main results of the conference.[27]

Table 2 Main elements of Copenhagen Accord

Item	Content
Shared vision	Recognize need to keep rise in global temperatures to less than 2°C based on scientific evidence
Mitigation	Developed nations to set national emission reduction targets for 2020 by end of Jan 2010 Signatories to Kyoto Protocol to cut emissions further. Developing nations to submit emissions mitigation plans by end of Jan 2010
Technology	Technology mechanisms for technology development and transfer to be established
Funding	Copenhagen Green Climate Fund (CGCF) to be set up. Majority of funding for adaptation measures, deforestation relief, clean-tech development to be channelled through CGCF. Developed nations to provide $30bn in additional funding in 2010-12, $100bn in annual funding to be mobilized by 2020 predicated on implementation and transparency of mitigation actions by developing nations
Verification	Assessment of progress in implementing accord to be completed by 2015. Strengthening of long-term targets to be considered.

Source: Mizuguchi (2010)

27. For further information on the outcome of the Conference, see UNFCCC (2010).

Box 2 Bali/COP13: Bali Action Plan

'Copenhagen' was preceded by the Bali conference in December 2007. It consisted of 2 ad hoc working groups: one on Long-term Cooperative Action under the Convention (AWG LCA), and the other on further commitments for Annex I Parties under the Kyoto Protocol (AWG KP). The conference resulted in a definition of the negotiation process for post-2012 commitments, the Bali Action Plan (part of the Bali Road Map), which should have been completed in Copenhagen in 2009. The main subjects of negotiation were technology transfer, the fight against deforestation, market mechanisms, and the scope and content of Article 9 of the Kyoto Protocol, which stipulates the first review of the Protocol.[28] Also, the Adaption Fund was launched, which is geared towards innovative financing leverages. This funding mechanism has its own independent source of finance. Its main income source is the 2% levy on Clean Development Mechanisms (discussed in detail in section 2.4.1) that could raise between $300 million and $600 million over the medium term, depending on the carbon price (The World Bank, 2010).

To differentiate between developing and developed countries, the Conference stated different targets for each. Developing countries did not receive quantified emission targets but should take mitigation actions that are "measurable and reportable". Developed countries committed to the Kyoto Protocol were to agree on new quantified emission limitation and reduction commitment (Pew Center on Global Climate Change, 2007).

EU ETS Phase 3

The strong link between Kyoto and EU ETS could cast identical uncertainty on the post-2012 period for the EU carbon market. Recent EU policy indicates otherwise. In April 2009, the Council of the European Union adopted a climate-energy legislative package.[29] The main goal of this act is to achieve a one-fifth part of energy from renewable sources in the final consumption of energy and a 10% share of energy from renewable sources in each member state's transport energy consumption by 2020. Each member state gets a mandatory national target for this commitment in order to provide certainty for investors and to give an incentive for technological development in the renewable energy sector.

---

28. UNFCCC website: http://unfccc.int/meetings/cop_13/items/4049.php and http://unfcccbali.org/unfccc/ (accessed on July 7, 2010).

29. European Commission, *Directive 2009/29/EC of the European Parliament and of the Council of 23 April 2009 amending Directive 2003/87/EC so as to improve and extend the greenhouse gas emission allowance trading system of the Community* (Brussels, April 23, 2009). This Directive was amended and adopted by the European Parliament (EP) and the Council of the European Union in April 2009 (Parker, 2010).

To achieve this main goal, the EU designed several new rules for a better implementation. In summary:

- The EU decided that heavy industry will contribute more to the overall target of GHG emission reduction;
- GHG emissions permits will increasingly be auctioned instead of given away for free (see below);
- Up to 300 million emissions allowances are set aside to finance clean technologies;
- There are new rules for cleaner cars, new quality standards for fuel and biofuels, and a carbon capture framework.[30]

The shift from giving away allowances for free – grandfathering – to auctioning follows from criticism of grandfathering, as explained previously. Auctioning, however, entails higher private costs for the regulated sectors. This generally causes companies (or sectors) to resist the auctioning of permits and lobby for the allocation of free permits. In Europe, industrial lobbies pointed to the risk of 'carbon leakage' by claiming that the unilateral and stricter European climate policy imposes higher costs on European companies, worsening their market position against international competitors and forcing them to either shut down plants or move their production activity to non-EU countries. Substantial asymmetric costs on the European economic agents could be detrimental for both the European economic growth and ineffective for the environment. Emissions would decrease in Europe, but proportionally increase in the rest of the world (Clò, 2010; The World Bank, 2010). To limit the risk of carbon leakage, the new ETS Directive differentiates between energy sectors (full auctioning from 2013 onwards), energy-intensive sectors not exposed to carbon leakage (80% grandfathering in 2013, gradually declining to 30% in 2020 and full auctioning in 2027) and energy-intensive sectors exposed to carbon leakage (pure grandfathering).[31] Grandfathering in Phase III will not be based on historic emissions, as in Phase I and Phase II, but on a performance benchmark. This implies than only the most efficient plants will really receive permits for free (Clò, 2010).

Furthermore, the European Union has formally, but conditionally, increased its emission target for 2020. For the period beyond 2012, the EU will commit to reach a 30%, instead of 20%, reduction by 2020 compared with 1990 levels if a "satisfactory international agreement" is reached, i.e., if other developed countries make comparable commitments for emission reduction, and if developing countries make their contribution "dependent on their responsibilities and respective capabilities".[32] This decision was taken at the end of January 2010, after the Copenhagen meeting.

---

30. *Council adopts climate-energy legislative package*, Council of the European Union, Brussels, 6 April 2009.
31. This solution is not without its flaws, see section 2.5.4.
32. http://unfccc.int/files/meetings/application/pdf/europeanunioncphaccord_app1.pdf (accessed on July 17, 2010) and *Questions and Answers on the Commission's proposal to revise the EU Emissions Trading System* (EU MEMO/08/35).

The World Economic Forum (2009, p. 37) claims that regardless of whether a new international agreement on emission reduction is reached (i.e., a post-Kyoto treaty), "the future of the EU ETS is secure [since the] EU has shown a strong commitment to climate goals in general ... and to the EU ETS in particular". This suggests that EU ETS will persevere, even in the absence of a new legally binding international agreement. Only a more stringent European emission reduction target is dependent on a new international agreement.[33] The latest development, the adoption of a cap for 2013 on July 9, 2010, confirms the EU ETS's fortitude.[34] However, detailed deliberation on the relationship between legally binding international agreement and the future of the EU's emission reduction efforts is virtually non-existent in the current debate.

2.3.2 *Voluntary Markets*

Background

The voluntary market represents purchases of carbon credits by organizations or individuals who are not legally obliged to make any emission reductions, or who wish to make emission reductions claims over and above that legally required, and therefore are under no legal constraints governing the kind of emission offsets that they purchase. Although the concept of voluntary offsets predates regulation-based ET, it was stimulated when the Kyoto mechanisms came into force in 2005 and the concept of carbon trading became more of a reality.

Hamilton et al. (2009) divide voluntary markets in the legally binding Chicago Climate Exchange (CCX) and the broader, non-binding Over-The-Counter (OTC) offset markets. The CCX is a cap-and-trade system, further detailed below, while OTC offset markets are not.[35] Most credits purchased in the OTC market originate from emission reduction projects and are thus offsets. Credits are called Verified (or Voluntary) Emission Reductions (VERs). OTC trading can also refer to voluntarily buying credits from compliance markets, such as CDMs.[36]

On the supply side, voluntary markets reach projects and locations outside the scope of the regulated market mechanisms, as well as projects with high transaction costs or other barriers (e.g., land use). Hence, voluntary markets increase project supply and project diversity.

---

33. See the answer to question 6 in *Questions and Answers on the Decision on effort sharing* (EU MEMO/08/797).

34. *Commission decision of 9 July 2010 on the Community-wide quantity of allowances to be issued under the EU Emission Trading Scheme for 2013*, C(2010) 4658 final, European Commission, Brussels. Aviation is not included in this decision. The cap to be allocated to aircraft operators will be determined by a separate decision of the Commission.

35. OTC markets include several Government Voluntary Offset Programs, which are discussed below.

36. For all clarity: some voluntary markets are OTC markets, but not all OTC markets are voluntary markets.

Buyers in voluntary markets are generally driven by 'pure voluntary' or 'pre-compliance' motives. The former is focused on offsetting their own emissions and strongly relates to "public relations and ethics" (Hamilton et al., 2009). This market is developing as consumers come to understand climate change and want to take personal action. Projects typically demonstrate community benefits or strong sustainability components. A large number of these projects is within close range of the trading place, which makes it easier for traders to identify the source of their credits – e.g., a lot of credits traded on the CCX in Chicago concern North American projects. Well-known examples include projects to offset emissions from air travel, and carbon labelling of consumer products. The latter, pre-compliance, refers to the purchase of rights that are expected to become part of future regulatory systems. Companies that expect to face a shortage of rights in the future hope to buy emission rights at a low price now, while other companies hope to sell the purchased rights at a higher price in the future. Pre-compliance driven trade is particularly dominant in countries where legislation is imminent, such as the US and Australia (countries in a so-called *regulatory vacuum*), and buyers are seeking pre-compliance and early action offsets (Capoor & Ambrosi, 2008; Hepburn, 2007).

The volume and value of credits traded on voluntary markets are much smaller than the compliance markets of the Kyoto Protocol (see Table 4 at the end of this section), and the credit price is much lower. Since there is no regulatory framework, voluntary markets grow organically. They are still regarded as being in their early days of evolution, as was underlined by rapid growth in 2006, 2007 and 2008. In 2009, however, the voluntary carbon market saw a sharp decline in trading volume (see 2009 data in Table 4) as companies and individuals cut back on discretionary spending in view of the financial crisis. In the second half of 2009 the market did recover slightly, thanks to the *American Clean Energy and Security Act* passing the House of Representatives in the US (as discussed above), though by far not enough to balance the discretionary cut-backs. It has led companies to start securing credits in the voluntary market which they eventually hope to use to meet their compliance needs (Carbon Trust & Climate Strategies, 2009; WEF, 2010).

The quality of offset credits has been an important concern, hampering the development of voluntary OTC markets. Signalling market maturation, recent years have seen the emergence of third-party verification and voluntary standards. This has improved the quality assurance. Most popular standards in the voluntary OTC market were Voluntary Carbon Standards (48% of VERs in 2008), Gold Standard (12%), Climate Action Reserve (10%) and American Carbon Registry (9%).[37] Third-party verification generally follows the development of standards.

37. For a full overview and description of standards, see Hamilton et al. (2009).

Figure 1 Voluntary Market Supply Chain

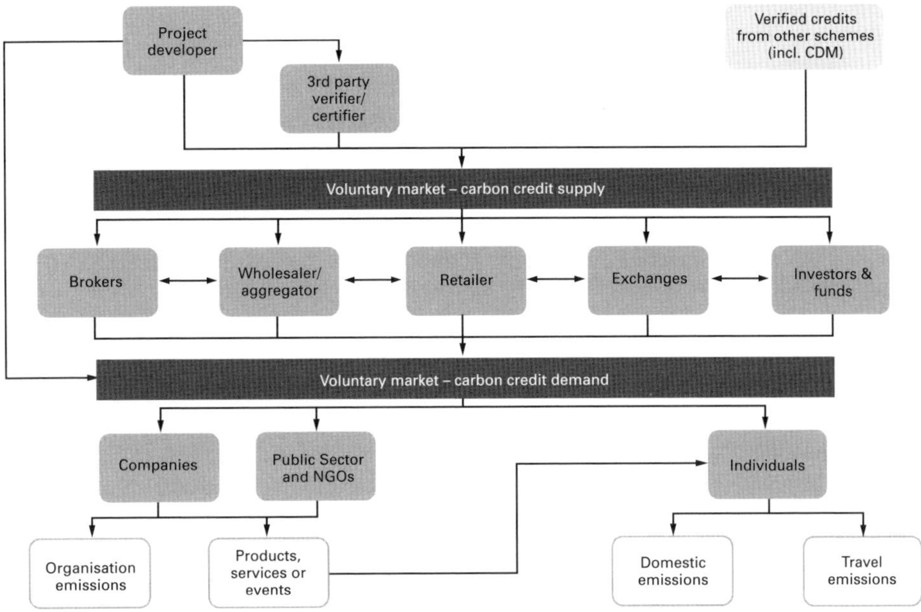

Source: Carbon Trust & Climate Strategies (2009, p. 66)

Operational Voluntary Markets

North America: Chicago Climate Exchange (CCX) and Climate Action Reserve

The Chicago Climate Exchange (CCX), a voluntary scheme launched in 2003, is currently North America's only cap-and-trade system for all six greenhouse gases with projects and global affiliates worldwide. CCX Members allegedly represent 17% of the Dow Industrials, 22% of the largest coal-burning electric utilities and 11% of the Fortune 100. Two US states (Illinois and New Mexico) and several cities and counties are also active on the CCX. The CCX is the only voluntary but legally binding cap-and-trade system. That is, although a voluntary scheme, companies that decide to participate (members) make a legally binding commitment to reduce GHG emissions. Trade is between the members.

An example of a voluntary OTC scheme in North America is the Climate Action Reserve. This is an offsets program which establishes regulatory-quality standards for the development, quantification and verification of GHG emission reduction projects and issues carbon offset credits known as Climate Reserve Tonnes (CRT) generated from these projects. Account holders can trade CRTs, but it also possible for individuals or organizations to offset their emissions for activities like travel and business operations by purchasing small quantities of CRTs. In 2009, trade in CRTs almost tripled in value because it was considered likely these rights would become eligible under a federal (compliance) scheme.[38]

Japan

Japan has a voluntary Experimental Integrated ETS (as from October 2008), which includes several existing initiatives such as the Keidanren Voluntary Action Plan, for a domestic offsets scheme, and the Japan-Voluntary Emissions Trading Scheme (J-VETS), which targets smaller emitters. It covers about 70% of CO_2 emissions from industrial sectors. Transaction activity is reported to be extremely limited so far (Kossoy & Ambrosi, 2010).

Upcoming Markets[39]

China has three voluntary environmental exchanges that do not involve the central government:

- The China Beijing Environmental Exchange (CBEEX) provides a market platform, amongst others for trading emission rights from CO_2, and facilitates CDM transactions;
- The Tianjin Climate Exchange (TCX) is an integrated exchange for the trading of environmental financial instruments;
- The Shanghai Environment Energy Exchange (SEEE) provides a platform for trading all kinds of rights focusing on the environment and energy. It is exploring a new market mechanism aligned with the requirements of the CDM. The aim of the exchange is to reduce transaction costs and bring more transparency to CER pricing.

In **Mexico**, 21% of national emissions is currently covered by the voluntary program for GHG accounting and reporting. The aim is to expand this to 80%. The program establishes baselines and develops standards, and the expectation is that sectoral crediting complements CDM as the source of carbon market finance for Mexico.

The **Republic of Korea** has the Korean Certified Emission Reduction (KCER) Program, a government-operated GHG reduction program. The KCERs are issued by the government for five-year crediting periods and benchmarked using CDM, ISO standards and IPCC guidelines. The KCERs are either purchased by the government, sold into the voluntary market or banked in preparation for emissions trading. A trading scheme is under development through the Basic Act for Low Carbon Green Growth and will be completed by the fall of 2010.

38. This scheme is just one example. As explained above, more standards and 3rd party registrations exist.

39. The overview in this section is based on Kossoy & Ambrosi (2010).

Future Developments

Announced Voluntary Markets

Brazil is exploring the possibility of introducing a domestic cap-and-trade scheme, primarily covering the energy, transport, industrial and agribusiness sectors. This country has a voluntary target of emission reduction (38.9% by 2020), and the scheme would help realize this target (Kossoy & Ambrosi, 2010).

In **India** there are two schemes active under the National Action Plan on Climate Change. With the use of market-based instruments, the aim is to increase energy efficiency and the use of renewable energy. The first scheme is the Perform Achieve and Trade (PAT) mechanism for trading energy efficiency certificates, which is expected to become operational in 2011, with an initial commitment period of three years. The second scheme, the Renewable Energy Certificate (REC) mechanism, is intended to support an increase in installed renewable capacity from 15-65 GW in five years and is expected to become operational in 2011. RECs will only be issued to renewable energy generators, but will be freely tradable. RECs will be traded through regulator-approved power exchanges, within a price band (Kossoy & Ambrosi, 2010).

Market Development

Especially the emergence of commonly accepted standards points to the maturation of voluntary carbon markets. This feeds purchasers' trust in transactions and should increase their popularity. The current number of standards, totalling 17 in 2009, is seen as rather high, however, and some consolidation is expected. Pre-compliance motives are expected to become more important as it becomes clearer which offset credits will qualify for future compliance markets, as was seen with CRTs in the US. At the same time, uncertainty of future legislation as well as the length and impact of the economic downturn could hinder voluntary market growth. These uncertainties make it hard to predict future voluntary market growth, but estimates have projected annual volumes of between 200 and 550 $MtCO_2e$ by 2012 (Carbon Trust & Climate Strategies, 2009).

There is an overlap between voluntary and compliance markets, as companies and individuals outside the regulatory regime partly fulfil their need for credits from the compliance markets (CERs) or credits from CDM projects in the process of validation or registration. Some analysts predict that CERs could grow to form half of all voluntary trades (Carbon Trust & Climate Strategies, 2009).

2.3.3 *Summary*

An overview of operational cap-and-trade policies around the globe is presented in Table 3 (a snapshot dating from April 2009).

Table 3 Operational cap-and-trade policies as of April 2009 (excluding inactive policies)

Operational Phase	Initiated	Regulatory Status	Allocation*	Compliance
Chicago Climate Exchange (US)	2000	Voluntary (not binding)	Free	Purchase of CFIs[40]
EU Emissions Trading Scheme	1999	Mandatory	Free	Penalty
Japan (Experimental Integrated ETS)	2002	Voluntary	Free	Return government subsidy
New Zealand	2007	Mandatory	Free	Penalty
New South Wales GGAS	1998	Mandatory	Free?	Penalty (A$12/excess ton)
Regional Greenhouse Gas Initiative (US)	2003	Mandatory	Auctioning	N/A
Switzerland	2000	Voluntary (but binding)	Free	Carbon tax

Source: SEO Economic Research, adapted from Betsill & Hoffmann (2009)
* = Allocation during current compliance period

Currently, the most liquid emissions trading markets are EU-ETS, global Kyoto compliance markets and the US's Regional Greenhouse Gas Initiative (Table 4). Voluntary markets are significantly smaller than regulated markets, in terms of traded volume and value, but are growing rapidly. In addition, several voluntary markets have been announced in developing countries.

40. The tradable instrument on CCX is called the Carbon Financial Instrument (CFI) contract, which represents 100 metric tons of Exchange Allowances or Exchange Offsets.

Table 4 Carbon market at a glance, volumes and values[41]

	Volume ($mtCO_2e$)				Value (MUS$)			
	2006	2007	2008	2009	2006	2007	2008	2009
Allowances Markets								
EU ETS	1,104	2,060	3,093	6,326	24,436	49,065	100,526	118,474
New South Wales	20	25	31	34	225	224	183	117
Chicago Climate Exchange	10	23	69	41	38	72	309	50
RGGI	na	na	62	805	na	na	198	2,179
AAUs	na	na	23	155	na	na	276	2,003
Subtotal	1,134	2,108	3,278	7,362	24,699	49,361	101,492	122,822
Spot & Secondary Kyoto offsets								
Subtotal	25	240	1,072	1,055	445	5,451	26,277	17,543
Project-based Transactions								
Primary CDM	537	552	404	211	5,804	7,433	6,511	2,678
JI	16	41	25	26	141	499	367	354
Voluntary market	33	43	57	46	146	263	419	338
Subtotal	586	636	486	283	6,091	8,195	7,297	3,370
Total	1,745	2,984	4,836	8,700	31,235	63,007	135,066	143,735

Source: The World Bank (Capoor & Ambrosi, 2008, 2009; Kossoy & Ambrosi, 2010)

41. See Hamilton, Sjardin, Peters-Stanley, & Marcello (2010) for a comparable overview.

2.4 Market Functioning

2.4.1 *Market Characteristics*

Introduction

What changes hands in Emissions Trading (ET) is the right to emit a certain volume of CO_2 (or an equivalent amount of another greenhouse gas). The intention is to put a price on emissions that have until now been cost-free, and to allow trade in permits, so that those who can most easily reduce emissions have the greatest incentive to do so. Cap-and-trade fixes the volume of emissions and then lets the market find the appropriate price level.[42]

Mechanisms[43]

The Kyoto Protocol makes provision for four instruments that provide flexibility to its signatories in implementing their reduction goals: Emissions Trading (ET), Joint Implementation (JI), Clean Development Mechanism (CDM) and Land Use, Land-Use Change and Forestry (LULUCF). The underlying philosophy of flexible mechanisms is that the Annex B countries can make some of the reductions to which they have committed themselves outside of their own country (Abadie & Chamorro, 2008).[44] Within the EU ETS, mechanisms either resemble or are linked to the Kyoto mechanism.

Emissions Trading

Emission reduction targets for Annex B Parties are expressed as levels of allowed emissions, or Assigned Amount Units (AAUs) for the 2008-2012 commitment period. Emissions Trading (ET), set out in Article 17 of the Kyoto Protocol, allows countries that have AAUs to spare – i.e., emissions permitted but not used – to trade their excess capacity with countries that are over their targets (UNFCCC, 2010). Within EU ETS, trading is arranged rather the same way, with emission rights called European Union Allowances (EUAs).

---

42. The difference between carbon markets and markets for standard commodities (like oils, coals and gas) is that the former is structurally less liquid and deep than the oil market (Reinaud, 2007). Temporary mismatches between supply and demand therefore give rise to wide fluctuations in price. This is one of the reasons why price volatility in carbon markets may well be above standard levels in financial markets (Abadie & Chamorro, 2008). Carbon prices and price volatility are further discussed in section 2.4.2.

43. For an elaborate discussion of the Kyoto mechanisms, see for instance Carbon Trust et al. (2009).

44. For more information on flexible mechanisms: Carbon Trust & Climate Strategies (2009) provide an excellent and elaborate introduction to and assessment of all three Kyoto mechanisms, updated in a review article by one of the authors of the report (Grubb et al., 2010).

Related to Kyoto's AAU trade are Green Investment Schemes (GIS). In these schemes, the seller agrees with the buyer to use the proceeds of the sale of AAUs for climate change mitigation programmes.[45]

Clean Development Mechanisms

Clean Development Mechanism (CDMs) are projects that reduce emissions in developing and newly industrializing countries (Article 12 of the Kyoto Protocol). By investing in these projects, countries or companies acquire Certified Emission Reductions (CERs), which can be used to meet their own commitments without having to reduce emissions themselves. Over 200 types of CDM projects are eligible under the Kyoto Protocol, including renewable energy, energy efficiency, forestry, and industrial gas capture.

According to the Kyoto Protocol, developing countries have no quantified emission targets for the first Kyoto period (2008-2012) – see Box 3 for an elaboration on the pros and cons of emissions trading in developing countries. Instead, the CDMs of the Kyoto Protocol are intended to induce technological change in developing countries. The purpose is twofold: it is a means of reducing compliance costs for industrialized countries, and it is a means of assisting developing countries in achieving sustainable development. In developing countries a lot of additional investment is needed to "green" the annual investment in power sectors, in order to keep up with economic and population growth.[46] Unless investments are specifically directed towards low-carbon technology (at a larger scale than is currently being achieved), they will go towards a carbon-intensive development path. Carbon finance mechanisms such as CDM potentially play an important role in redirecting these investments (Hagem, 2009; J. I. Lewis, 2010).[47]

Box 3 Developing countries: CDM or Emissions Trading?

Submitting developing countries to cap-and-trade schemes could eliminate level-playing field concerns. EU countries, for example, are only willing to accept a higher reduction target (30% instead of 20% compared to 1990 levels) if developing countries "contribute adequately according to their responsibilities and respective capabilities".[48] Also, it could prevent detrimental re-location of production sites. Regulatory inequalities regarding GHG emissions can cause companies to move their production sites to countries where environmental requirements are the least strict. The *Pollution Haven Hypothesis* (PHH) predicts that poor countries with lax environmental regulations can become pollution havens as

45. Green Investment Schemes have developed due to the virtually non-existent trade of AAUs between countries because of current excess supply. This is further discussed in section 2.5.2.
46. Much of this investment will need to take place in China.
47. In recent years there has been criticism of CDMs, which is further discussed in section 2.5.3.
48. UNFCCC website: http://unfccc.int/home/items/5264.php (accessed on July 6, 2010).

polluting industries migrate to these countries from rich countries with stringent pollution standards (Cave & Blomquist, 2008; Silva & Zhu, 2009).

There are, however, important downsides to submitting developing countries to emissions trading. The World Bank (2010) points out that the cost of administering climate policy and the institutional and human capital required are substantial. Setting up a market for auctioning and trading permits can be highly complex. A regulator is required to monitor the exercise of market power by participants and to monitor and enforce rules at the level of individual emitters.

Figure 2 Accumulation of CERs by project type

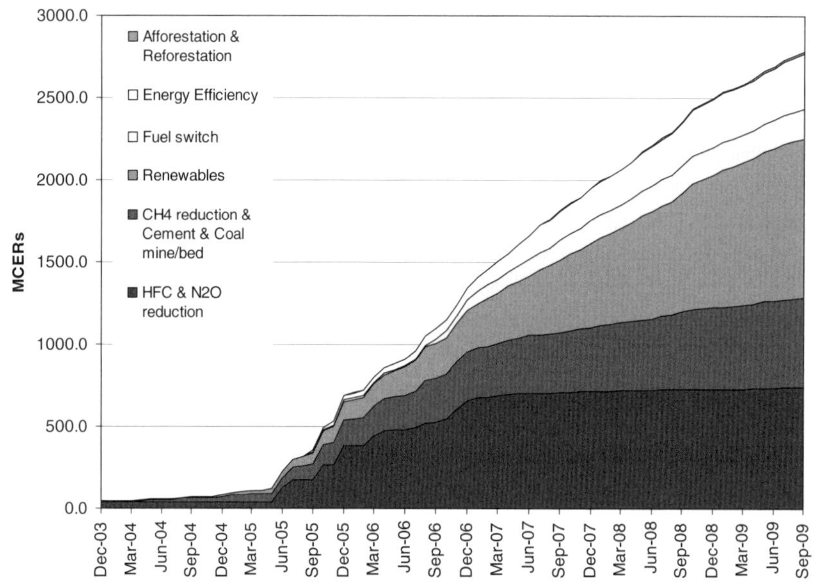

Source: Grubb et al. (2010, p. 4)

In 2008 and 2009, 37% of CERs were based on renewable energy or energy efficiency (Figure 2). This proportion is expected to grow to nearly 60% by 2012, as the potential for industrial gas projects has largely been exhausted.[49] By the end of 2012, New Energy Finance estimates that the CDM will have caused around US$15 billion to flow from developed to developing countries for investment in low-carbon projects (WEF, 2010).

49. This point is also made by Grubb et al. (2010). For a more detailed analysis, see Michaelowa et al. (2008).

Figure 3 Accumulation of CERs by host country

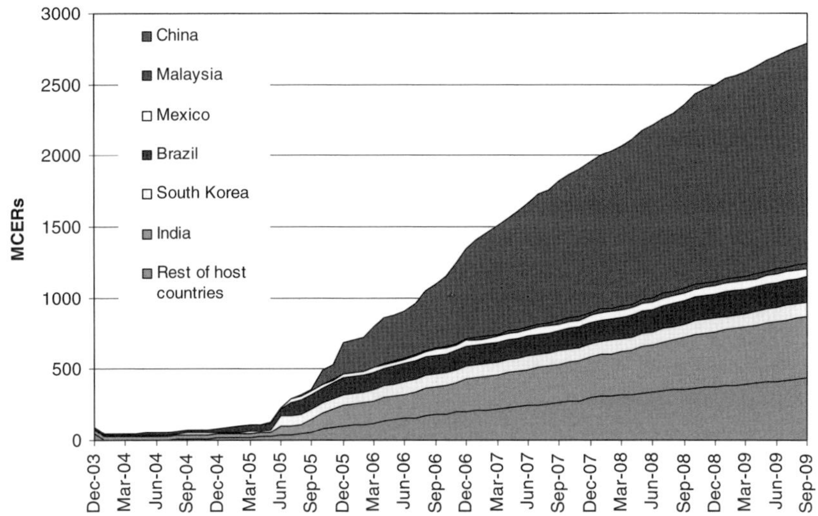

Source: Grubb et al. (2010, p. 6)

Rights under the CDM are also eligible within the EU ETS. CERs accounted for 17% by value of carbon trading under the EU-ETS in 2009 (WEF, 2010).

Joint Implementation

Joint Implementation (JI) are projects carried out jointly by industrial countries. It refers to the opportunity for countries or companies to implement climate protection projects in other countries that have signed the Kyoto Protocol. After successful completion of a JI, a country or company is awarded Emission Reduction Units (ERUs) that can be offset against their initial commitments (Article 6.1 of the Kyoto Protocol). While Clean Development Mechanisms are targeted at developing countries, JI mechanisms are targeted at industrial countries. In practice, these are mostly "economies in transition", i.e., former Soviet Bloc countries. As is the case with awarding credits for CDM projects, ERUs are only awarded if a JI project is considered supplemental (as opposed to substitutive) to domestic actions (Hepburn, 2007; WEF, 2010). In Europe, potential overlap between savings from JI projects and EU ETS is tackled by 'double counting' rules: ERUs from projects at facilities under the EU ETS scope are prohibited, and emissions savings from power stations under EU ETS as a result of JI energy efficiency projects are discounted before awarding ERUs (Grubb et al., 2010).

Russia accounts for almost two-thirds of the projected savings to 2012 from JI projects, the remainder is divided roughly equally between Ukraine and the EU's new member states (Figure 4). Since Russian projects are dominated by coal mine methane projects and N_2O reductions, so are the total expected ERUs by 2012 – i.e., ERUs that could be generated by the end of 2012 from all of the projects currently in the JI pipeline, across all stages from beginning of public comments to those already registered (Figure 5).

Figure 4 Accumulation of ERUs by host country

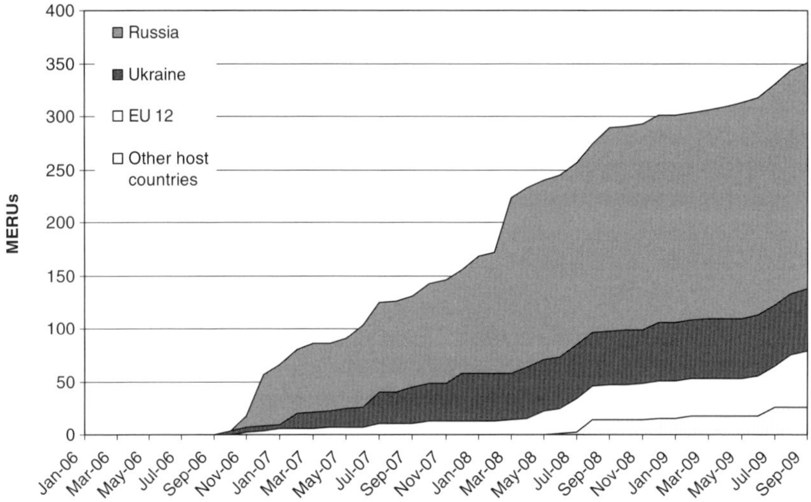

Source: Grubb et al. (2010, p. 8)

Figure 5 Accumulation of ERUs by project type

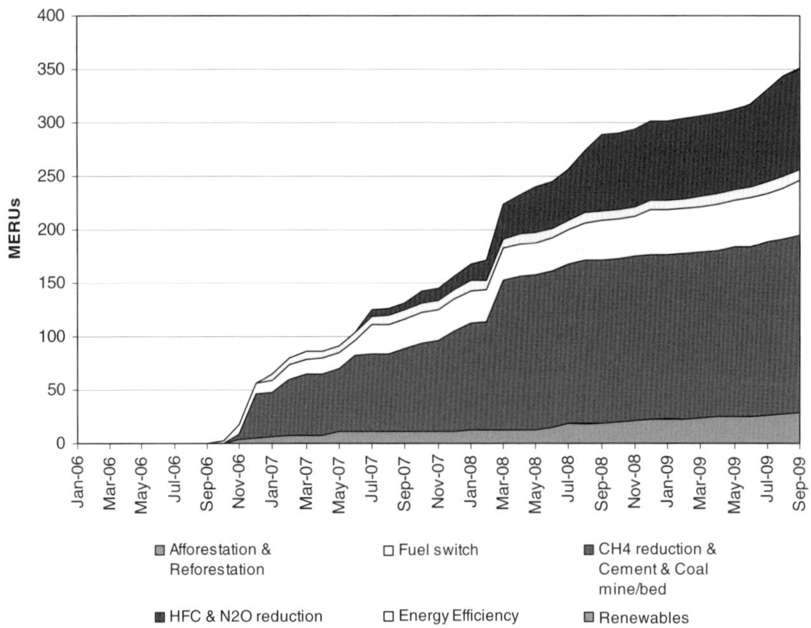

Source: Grubb et al. (2010, p. 7)

Initially, JI projects were intended to involve minimal international oversight, as projects would originate in countries that had complied with the complete array of Kyoto Protocol provisions for annual reporting and review of national emission inventories. As transition economies were worried that they could not meet these requirements, a second 'track' of JI was established through the Marrakech Accords, which resembles CDM procedures (Table 5), with projects being directly endorsed through a multilateral Joint Implementation Supervisory Committee (JISC), supported by the UNFCCC. Under *Track 1* procedures, which parties can use if they meet all eligibility conditions, ERUs can be issued upon its own verification of emission reductions; *Track 2* projects require determination acceptance by the JISC before the host party can issue and transfer ERUs (Grubb et al., 2010; Korppoo & Gassanzade, 2008).

Table 5 Joint Implementation: Track 1 versus Track 2 requirements by stages

Type of Eligibility	Key Requirements (Eligibility for previous levels is required at each level)	Stage at which eligibility is checked	When eligibility is established
Kyoto eligibility	Party to Kyoto Protocol, target under Annex B	Publication of the Project Design Document (PDD)	Submission of the PDD to the UNFCCC Secretariat
Eligibility to participate in the mechanisms	Designated Focal Point and JI procedures	Final determination by the JISC	Project's submission to the JISC
Eligibility for Track 2	Assigned Amount, registry	ERUs transfer out of the national registry	Every year starting from 2008
Eligibility for Track 1	Inventory system, annual inventories, incl. most recent	ERUs transfer out of or to (procurement) the national registry	Every year starting from 2008

Source: Korppoo & Gassan-zade (2008, p. 6)

Land Use, Land-Use Change and Forestry

Land use, land-use change and forestry (LULUCF) activities are set out in Article 3 of the Kyoto Protocol. It allows Annex B parties to take into account GHG emissions associated with afforestation, reforestation and deforestation since 1990 in assessing compliance with their Kyoto targets. Additional allowances (called Removal Units, RMUs) can be issued for each tonne of CO_2 sequestered by LULUCF. RMUs have limitations because they cannot be banked for use to offset emissions after 2012, and because EU ETS does not allow sequestration as an eligible activity, nor does it allow the use of RMUs for compliance with its scheme (City of London et al., 2009).

LULUCF project activities that are not eligible under CDM, except afforestation and reforestation, are permitted under the Joint Implementation mechanism. JI allows any other LULUCF projects, such as promoting improved forest management, increased fire and pest controls, and preservation of old growth forests. There are however some institutional problems with crediting LULUCF projects under JI. Only RMUs (not AAUs) can be converted into ERUs for JI, and therefore if a country has not met its Kyoto reporting obligations or if its accounting does not generate RMUs, the country cannot host JI LULUCF projects (Korppoo & Gassan-zade, 2008).

Summary

Figure 6 and Table 6 provide an overview of Kyoto mechanisms:

Figure 6 Characteristics of the Global Carbon Mechanisms

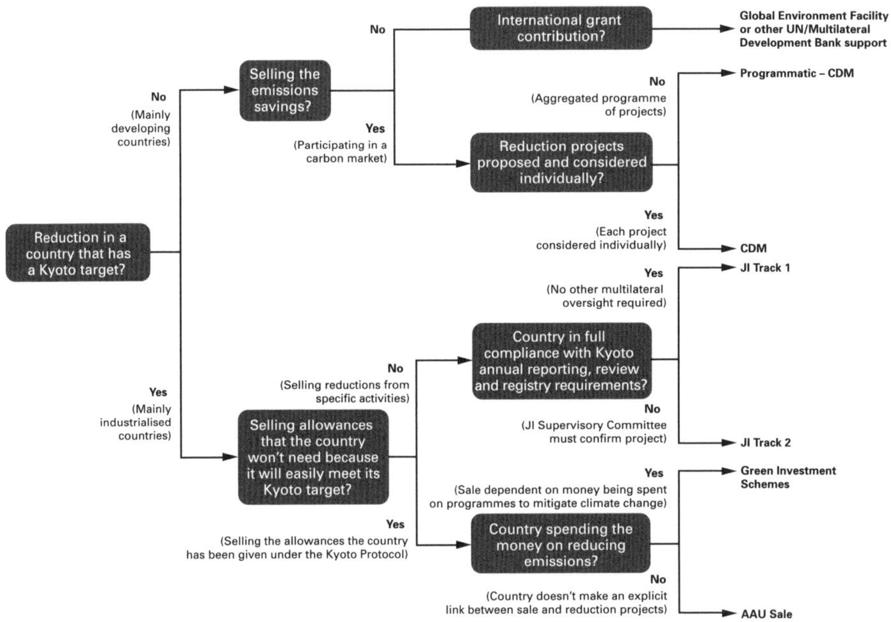

Source: Carbon Trust & Climate Strategies (2009)

2.4.2 *Carbon Price*

Carbon prices are determined in a system of interlinked, policy-led financial markets, similar to currency markets. A single global price for carbon[50] is not (yet) in sight because there is no global carbon market and thus no political consensus or supporting infrastructure. Still, market-linking through project-based and other mechanisms encourages arbitrage, and this should reveal a global carbon price range, one that could drive significant behavioral change (Houser, 2009; WEF, 2009).[51]

---

50. As is advocated by Stern (2006, p. 468).
51. For instance, European companies obtaining emission rights via the Clean Development Mechanism (CDMs), which is part of the Kyoto mechanisms, can also use these rights to fulfil their obligations under the EU ETS. In this way, Kyoto and EU ETS are linked.

Table 6 Summary of mechanisms for Annex I countries under the Kyoto Protocol

	Joint Implementation (JI) 'Track 2'	JI 'Track 1'	Green Investment Schemes (GIS)	Industry-level cap-and-trade (EU ETS)
Supervision of transactions	Multilateral supervision	Bilateral supervision subject to national compliance with full-scope Kyoto Protocol MRV procedures		
Reduction unit	Emission Reduction Unit (ERU)	ERU	Assigned Amount Unit (AAU)	EUA backed by AAU
Governing body and procedure	JI Supervisory Committee, 'final determination'	Host country	Host country	EU
Units issued by Crediting period	Host country Kyoto first period: from 1st Jan 2008, currently to end 2012.	Host country as JI track 2	Kyoto Protocol Variable	EU Kyoto Protocol first period with banking forward allowed
Eligibility of land-related activities	Afforestation and reforestation plus other uses as selected under KP Article 3.4	Afforestation and reforestation plus other uses as selected under KP Article 3.4		CO_2 only from qualifying sources which excludes for example land use
Third-party verification	'Determination' of Project Design Document by 'Accredited Independent Entity'	Kyoto Protocol provisions for national emissions, bilateral agreement for projects plus ITL procedures		KP + EU + ITL procedures
Methodologies	Projects can use: - Approved CDM methodologies - Elements of CDM methodologies - New methodologies	Bilateral	Bilateral	n/a
Additionality	Projects can use: - additionality tool from CDM; - other cenario or comparability approaches	Host country determination	Not explicitly required	Not explicitly required

Source: Grubb et al. (2010); Adapted by SEO Economic Research

The primary drivers of prices are – at least in the long term – the number of credits created, the expected demand from industry, and the ease of closing any shortfall between supply and demand, using technology and investments available during the relevant commitment period (WEF, 2009).

Determination of Prices

Emission Caps and Allowance Allocation

Policy drivers, such as cap levels and the availability of offsets, are essential in the supply of and demand for allowances and therefore have major consequences for allowance prices. In January 2008, the EC proposed putting 1974 million tons of EUAs on the market in 2013, and reducing this to 1720 million EUAs in 2020 (Figure 7). Emissions by participants of the ETS are thereby expected to be reduced by 21%, compared to the 2005 allowance level. Increasing scarcity of EUAs should increase allowance prices accordingly (Abadie & Chamorro, 2008; Edwards, 2009).

Figure 7 Allocation and emission in the EU ETS

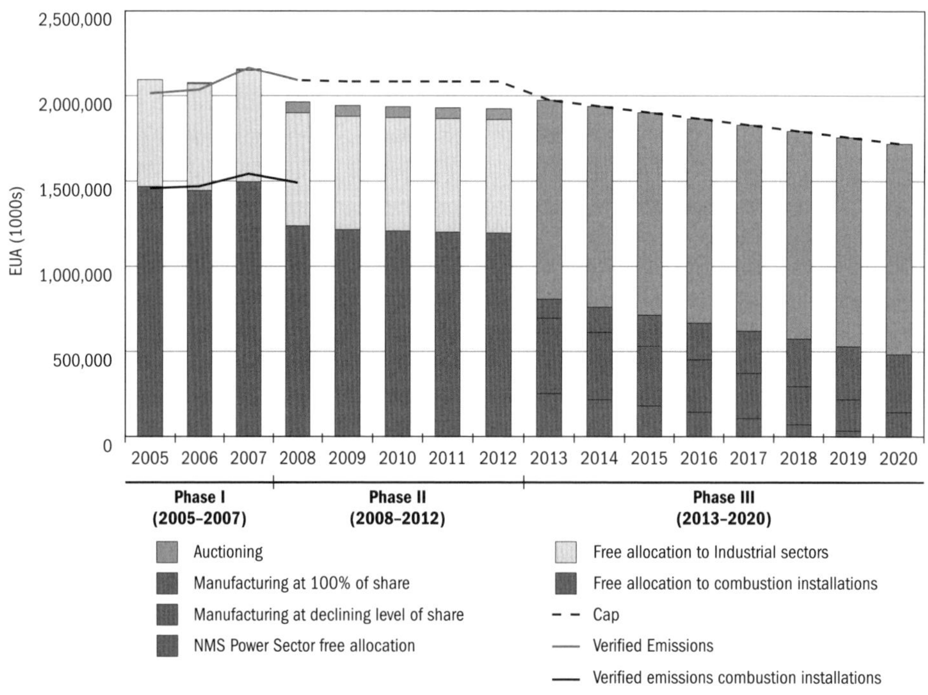

Source: Grubb, Brewer, Sato, Helmayr, & Fazekas (2009, p. 25)

Economic and Production Growth

Economic prosperity and levels of industrial production, notably in countries that participate in an emissions trading scheme, have a major impact on demand and supply of emission allowances (Alberola, Chevallier, & Chèze, 2009; Edwards, 2009; The World Bank, 2010). That is, companies in (industrial) sectors in which production grows faster (slower) than anticipated in their baseline projections – projections on which caps are based and on which the companies consequently base their allocation needs and permit stock – exhibit a 'short' ('long') compliance position. They have less (more) allowances than verified emissions and thus become allowance buyers (sellers) or, provided that there is allowance surplus elsewhere within the company, pool their company allowances. These companies have a positive (negative) impact on allowance prices.

Prices of Energy Commodities

In some industries, particularly power generation, the price of natural gas relative to the price of coal affects operating choices and therefore the demand for emission allowances. For example, a high gas price vis-à-vis coal prices stimulates the use of coal which, with coal emitting twice the CO_2 content of natural gas, leads to more demand for emission allowances (Edwards, 2009; Reinaud, 2007). The other way around, emissions trading also has an effect on energy prices. For instance, if utilities pass through some or all of the compliance costs related to emissions trading. This has led to windfall profits, which are discussed in section 2.5.

Policy Uncertainty

While climate change is inherently a long-term, uncertainty-ridden challenge, political systems are skewed towards addressing more immediate concerns and are therefore ill-prepared to consider and adopt long-term action against long-term risks (Blyth & Yang, 2006).[52] This is most importantly reflected in the short commitment periods, in both Kyoto and EU ETS. Because allocations and targets can change in future commitment periods, investors will only have short foresights into the trading scheme while committing themselves to investments that span 20 to 30 years (Reinaud, 2007). Irreversible investment decisions will be based on pre-implementation expectations of climate change policy, so investors bear the risk that the actual marginal cost of abatement may differ from those expectations. As a result, policy uncertainty may lead to a delay in investment, thereby impacting the prices of CO_2 allowances. A delay of 'green investments' would lower the supply of emission rights, a delay of 'dirty investments' would lower the demand of emission rights. Measuring the exact impact is challenging. IEA (2007) have attempted to model policy risk as an element of price uncertainty. They have used one-off price jumps as a proxy for the influence of policy change on prices and find this is a dominant factor in price uncertainty.

52. More generally, being regulation-based, the development of carbon trading cannot be seen separately from the political arena. In other words, development may be influenced by elements influencing public policy in general, like the short-term political agenda and the lobby industry. An example of the former is the vast amount of 'green deals' promised by many governments during the financial crisis. Examples of the latter include the aviation industry trying to keep it from being subject to an emission cap, and energy-related industries trying to prevent emission rights from being auctioned instead of grandfathered.

Macroeconomic Risk Factors

Carbon allowances form a specific market among energy commodities. Carbon futures – which have been traded since 2005 on EU ETS – are only remotely connected to macroeconomic risk factors. As was mentioned above, prices on the carbon market are essentially a function of allowance supply (fixed by a regulator) and power demand arising from electric operators. The transmission of macroeconomic shocks to the carbon market through volatility spillovers between energy markets appears a promising area for future research (Chevallier, 2009). The impact of the recent financial crisis could be an interesting starting point. In this regard, Chevallier (2009, p. 614) states, "The sensitivity of carbon futures to macroeconomic influences is carefully identified following a sub-sample decomposition before and after August 2007, which attempts to take into account the potential impact of the 'credit crunch' crisis. Collectively, these results challenge the market observers' viewpoint that carbon futures prices are immediately correlated with changes in the macroeconomic environment".

Other Factors

Other CO_2 price drivers include other policies (including non-carbon trading) aimed at climate change (e.g., support for renewable electricity production), the external supply of project-based mechanisms (e.g., an abundance of CERs and ERUs dampens CO_2 prices), weather (e.g., a dry year in countries producing hydro power, such as Norway and Sweden, leads to more demand for fossil fuels in those countries and the countries that import hydro power from them), and hedging strategies of power producers engaged in forward transactions (Edwards, 2009; Reinaud, 2007).

Price Uncertainty and Volatility

For carbon trading to affect long-term infrastructure investment decisions, a stable price signal is essential. Carbon prices, however, are inherently volatile since the traded commodity is artificially 'created' from a whole set of dissimilar practices; practices ranging from energy efficiency improvements in industrial processes to capturing coal mine methane and generating hydro-electric power. Putting a price on carbon is therefore highly arbitrary. Some strategies currently practised to track or estimate future carbon prices are looking at energy prices (i.e., the difference between coal and gas prices) or speculating about future political decisions (Gilbertson & Reyes, 2009).

Since the supply of allowances is fixed, cap-and-trade makes the market intrinsically more volatile and may lead to uncertainty about price shifts in the business cycle or in the relative prices of low-carbon and high-carbon (fossil) fuels directly affecting permit prices. For instance, costs for new low-carbon technologies may decrease through economies of scale as they achieve greater market penetration, but then again they may rise if greater penetration leads to greater scarcity in the underlying resource, or if supply chain constraints are hit. These factors feed through to uncertainty in carbon prices, and the resulting price volatility makes it difficult to plan abatement strategies and reduces the incentive to spend R&D on new abatement technologies. Two ways to reduce price volatility are the provision to take abundant emission rights from one compliance period to the next (banking or carry-over) – which is allowed in EU ETS (Betsill & Hoffmann, 2009) – and by allowing borrowing (Blyth, 2010; Edwards, 2009; The World Bank, 2010).

2.4.3 *A New Financial Market*

Starting Point: Trading Emission Units

Four types of emission units can be traded and sold under the Kyoto Protocol's emissions trading schemes.[53] They are each equal to one tonne of CO_2 and correspond to the previously discussed flexible mechanisms (UNFCCC; Allianz Glossary of Emissions Trading; Hepburn, 2007):

- Assigned Amount Units (AAUs): emission units that represent the targets accepted by Annex B countries (countries with commitments under the Kyoto Protocol) for limiting or reducing GHG emissions. Article 17 of the Protocol allows countries to sell their spare emission units;
- Certified Emission Reductions (CERs): certificates issued by bodies of the UNFCCC for successful completion of Clean Development Mechanism (CDM) projects (project-based exchanges between industrialized countries and developing countries);
- Emission Reduction Units (ERUs): emission certificates issued for the successful completion of Joint Implementation (JI) projects (project-based exchanges between industrialized countries). Emission credits are accompanied by a corresponding transfer of emission caps;[54]
- Removal Units (RMUs): credits arising from emission reductions created by countries by means of projects that reduce emissions, on the basis of land use, land-use change and forestry (LULUCF) activities. These project-based emission credits are only traded at the country level and can be used towards fulfilling national obligations as of 2008.

Financial Products and Intermediation

The Kyoto Protocol challenged the private sector to devise its own market solutions for trading emissions allowances, which should ultimately lead to a transparent carbon price that is intended to inform (energy) investment decisions. The financial services industry subsequently developed a range of contractual and financial instruments that allow companies to buy and sell allowances (to comply with legislation),

---

53. As explained, EU ETS provides for trading in EUAs in a similar manner as well as for a link with Kyoto mechanisms CDM and JI.

54. The formal crediting period for JI is aligned with the first commitment period of the Kyoto Protocol (Grubb et al., 2010).

to manage their emissions price risk, and to underwrite the economics of carbon-reducing investments (City of London et al., 2009).

By putting a price on carbon, emissions trading creates a whole new financial market, a market strongly linked to other commodity markets such as oil, coal and gas. As a result, managing climate change has also become the domain of managers with expertise in financial and commodity markets (Pinkse, 2007). These financial intermediaries include brokers, traders, exchanges and platforms, the private sector financial companies (e.g., banks, asset managers, insurance companies) and large compliance buyers (see Figure 8).

Figure 8 Players and Institutions in the Carbon Market

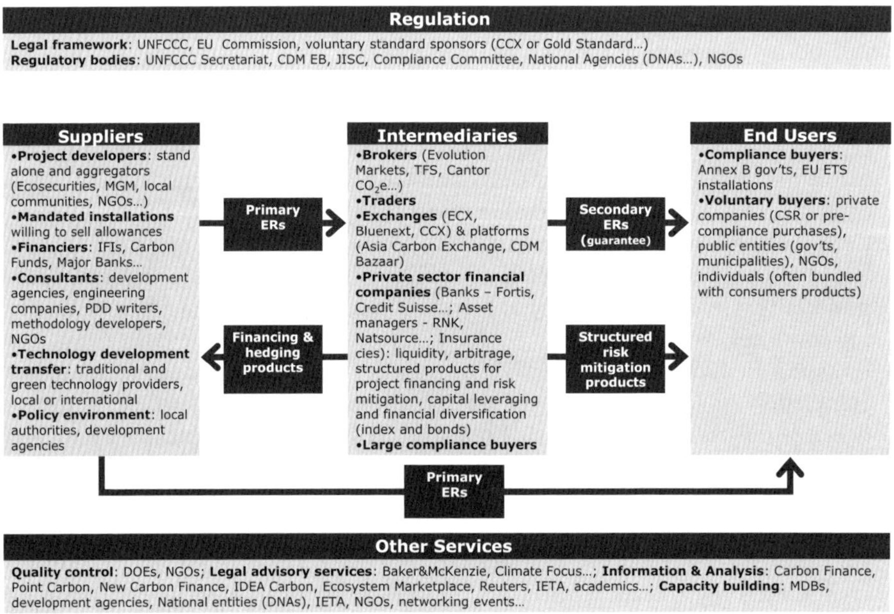

Source: Capoor & Ambrosi (2008)

Over the past few years, the financial industry has created several financial products related to carbon trading, such as (Capoor & Ambrosi, 2008; City of London et al., 2009):

- Monetization of future carbon receivables: loans provided by financial institutions against future carbon credit proceeds in forward purchase contracts;
- Carbon delivery guarantees: credit enhancement and guarantees for the delivery obligation of primary market projects to secondary market buyers;

- Derivatives: e.g., swaps between CERs and EUAs and between CERs and ERUs, carbon spread options based on the differential price between CERs and EUAs, call options on future carbon credits[55];
- Insurance/guarantees: e.g., protection from pricing fluctuation, delivery risks and projects or credit eligibility under the regulatory schemes;
- Miscellaneous: e.g., green credit cards, carbon-neutral products.[56]

In Europe, the imminence of EU ETS spurred the opening of a futures market in allowances in 2004. When EU ETS commenced in 2005, 7 brokers were operating in the market. In 2006 they had been joined by 5 exchanges. The European Climate Exchange (ECX), which manages the European Climate Exchange Financial Instruments (ECX CFI), is the largest futures market in terms of volume of operations and liquidity. Others include Nord Pool, Bluenext and the European Energy Exchange (EEX) and share the remainder of the market (Abadie & Chamorro, 2008; Capoor & Ambrosi, 2008; Daskalakis, Psychoyios, & Markellos, 2009).[57]

Figure 9 Monthly EUA trading

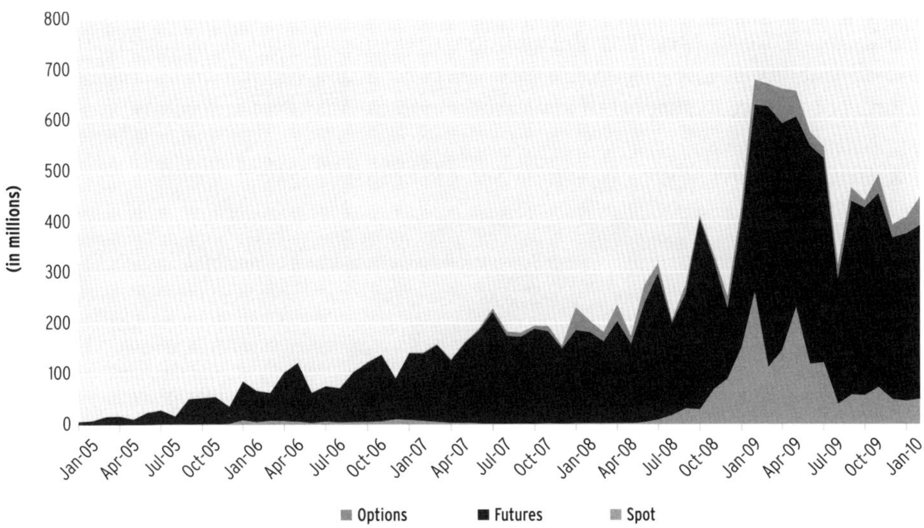

Source: Kossoy & Ambrosi (2010, p. 8)

In the years following 2004, futures were dominant in EUA transactions (see Figure 9). In 2009, spot contracts became more substantial, amounting to more than 22% of

55. Derivatives are traded either between two or more parties in over-the-counter markets (where trading is non-public and largely outside government regulation) or on exchanges (where trading is public, multilateral and closely regulated by governments and the exchanges themselves).

56. The financial sector is also constantly working on financial innovations in the field of carbon trading. For example, City of Londen et al. (2009) have proposed the issuance of carbon-linked bonds. These are government-issued bonds where the base interest rate is fixed, but actual interest payments vary depending on whether or not the issuer keeps an environmental promise.

57. For up-to-date figures, see for instance www.ecx.eu.

EUA transactions (Kossoy & Ambrosi, 2010).[58] The reason for this was that companies were cashing in on allowances in view of the tight credit environment and – with a slowly recovering economy – spot volumes have stabilized in 2010, accounting for 10-15% of EUA volume.[59]

Kossoy et al. (2010) estimated the value of the EU ETS option market at US$10.6 billion in 2009. EUAs accounted for the major part of this – 83% compared to 17% in CERs. The carbon options market has matured and is behaving more and more like other option markets, with financial and technical trades outweighing asset-backed trades (i.e., trades for compliance purposes).

Carbon Finance

Carbon Finance (CF) refers to resources provided to activities generating (or expected to generate) GHG emission reductions through the transaction of the related emission reduction rights. It is the generic name for the revenue streams generated by projects from the sale of their GHG emission reductions or from trading in carbon permits (Bosi, Cantor, & Spors, 2010; Kossoy & Ambrosi, 2010, p. 71). The orange blocks in Figure 10 exemplify the additional revenues from CF, which enhance the overall viability of low-carbon projects. CF plays a catalytic role in leveraging other sources of finance in support of low-carbon investments (debt and equity).

Figure 10 Additional project revenue streams provided by carbon finance

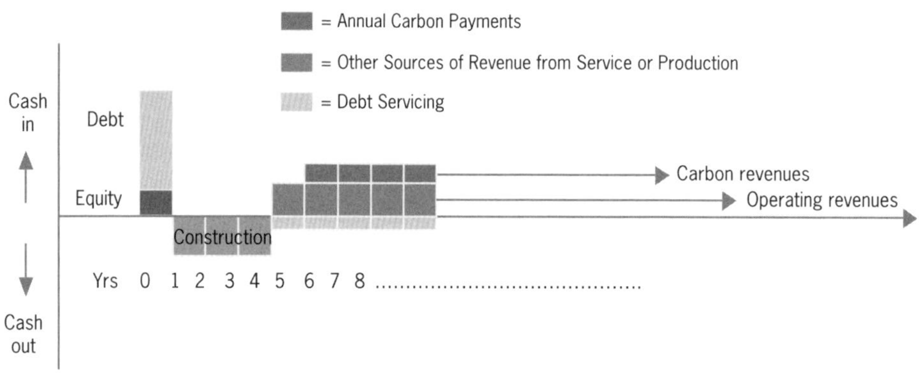

Source: Bosi et al. (2010, p. 11)

Carbon finance is accessible through regulated mechanisms – project-based compliance markets such as CDMs and JI under the Kyoto Protocol – and through voluntary markets. Carbon finance, particularly under CDM, enables projects in developing countries to access additional sources of financing, provided they can

58. In terms of volume (billions tCO_2e). EUA transactions totaled US$118.5 billion in 2009.

59. For an elaborate overview of EU ETS spot, futures and option carbon markets and more information on the effect of the economic downturn on the European emission market, see Kossoy et al. (2010).

demonstrate that the project is generating additional emission reductions – i.e., additional to those in the baseline or 'business-as-usual' (BAU) scenario (Ranade & Bhada, 2010).[60] The difference in (marginal) abatement costs between OECD and developing counties (short-run marginal abatement costs per ton CO_2 are at least 5 times lower in developing countries) implies that the international trade in emission reduction credits is mutually beneficial (The World Bank, 2006).

The global market for GHG reductions through project-based transactions has doubled in value between 2006 and 2007, reaching US$13.6 billion in 2007, of which US$5.5 billion were traded on the secondary CDM market (Girishankar, 2009). Figure 11 underlines the growing value of CDM and JI transactions until 2007, then the market declined significantly in 2009, largely due to the global economic downturn, the emergence of competing carbon assets (AAUs) and the approaching end of the first Kyoto Protocol commitment period in 2012, which closes the window for new projects that otherwise would have entered the CDM/JI pipeline (Bosi et al., 2010).

*Figure 11 Value of CDM & JI transactions (per year)**

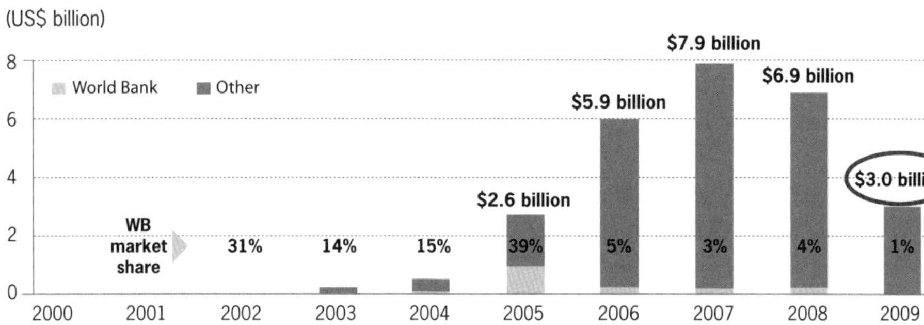

Source: Bosi et al. (2010, p. 13)

The World Bank, in conjunction with public and private sector partners in the Prototype Carbon Fund (PCF), established the first global carbon fund in 2000. This is a compliance fund: the return for fund participants is their pro rata share of emission reductions generated by the fund portfolio and is thus not a financial return. Currently, there are 11 World Bank funds and facilities, including the administration of country carbon funds for Italy (ICF), Denmark (CCF), Spain (SCF) and the Netherlands (NCDMF and NECF). In terms of number of projects, the WB has one of the largest portfolios, with at present 211 active projects worldwide (Bosi et al., 2010).

The World Bank Carbon Finance Unit (CFU) does not lend or grant resources to projects, but rather contracts to purchase project-based emission reductions in developing countries (CERs) and economies in transition (ERUs), paying for emission reductions annually or periodically once they have been verified by a third-party

60. The challenge of additionality is discussed further in section 2.5.3.

auditor, using resources provided by governments and private participants in industrialized countries (Girishankar, 2009).

Investments in sustainable energy in developing countries are skewed towards the wealthiest nations within developing regions,[61] which mirrors the presence of significant investment barriers in the poorest countries in these regions, e.g., lack of sources for funding (Girishankar, 2009; Kossoy & Ambrosi, 2010).

The World Bank identifies 5 actions that can make Carbon Finance fit better into public and private sector investment decision-making (Kossoy & Ambrosi, 2010):

- Scale up: expand the demand side of the market (implementing more stringent emission reduction targets) and build a credible supply to scale;
- Long-term predictability (lengthier contracts and long-term pricing signals);
- Comprehensive insurance/guarantee products (e.g., underwrite political risks and contract-frustration risk at the country and sector levels);
- Frontload future demand (e.g., the issuance of bonds and monetization of future receivables);[62]
- Combine (blend) limited financial resources.

61. E.g. in 2008 88% of investment in South America went to Brazil, while China and India jointly accounted for 80% of investment in Asia/Oceania (Kossoy & Ambrosi, 2010, p. 42). Only 2% of current and proximal global CDM/JI projects are located in Africa (Bosi et al., 2010).

62. Payment for carbon credits generally occurs on delivery (i.e. once the project is operational, "pay-upon-performance"), as opposed to frontloading (advance payments). Monetization of Emission Reduction Purchase Agreements (ERPAs) is rare due to high inherent project risk, CF regulatory risk and market uncertainties (Kossoy & Ambrosi, 2010).

2.5 Assessing Carbon Trading

2.5.1 *Introduction*

It seems logical, 13 years after establishing the Kyoto Protocol and 5 years after the start of EU ETS, to evaluate carbon trade. Has it so far lived up to the high hopes and optimism surrounding its international implementation with Kyoto and – if not – how can it be improved? The latter has been touched upon by many authors, discussing a multitude of options which could contribute to a better functioning of specific carbon markets or carbon trading in general. More often than not, however, the question of *how* to assess the functioning of trading and markets has not been addressed.

There are exceptions. For instance, Hepburn (2007, p. 383) clearly defines the assessment process stating, "[a]ssessment of the performance of current carbon trading arrangements requires two preliminary stages, namely the specification of a plausible counterfactual and the specification of criteria of assessment". Counterfactuals can range from 'no current nor future action' to 'full implementation of carbon reduction policies', implying a world of differences in the outcome of assessments. As assessment criteria Hepburn (2007) mentions "effectiveness (in delivering emission reductions), efficiency (at least cost) and equity (with acceptable distributional consequences)".

Although not always explicit, in most cases analysis seems focused on effectiveness, which requires a definition of the underlying goal(s). Examples include:

- Hepburn (2007) sees emission reductions as the primary task of carbon trading arrangements, which should be achieved efficiently while respecting distributional consequences.
- Focusing on EU ETS regulation, Deutsche Bank (M. C. Lewis & Curien, 2009, p. 16) also sees this as one of the aims but adds "incentivizing CCS technology for power generation such that it becomes commercially viable by 2020, and providing proof that a market can achieve this in a cost-efficient, transparent and predictable manner".
- According to the Environmental Audit Committee (2010, p. 9) the EU ETS has twin objectives, namely "limiting emissions and encouraging investment in low-carbon technology".
- The World Economic Forum (WEF, 2009, p. 35) sees as the intention of carbon markets to "put a price on emissions that have until now been cost-free, and second to allow trade in permits, so that those who can most easily reduce emissions have the greatest incentives to do so". In its 2010 Green Investing report the pricing goal is further detailed as providing "a price signal which shifts investment decisions towards low-carbon technologies" (WEF, 2010, p. 47).

Keeping in mind that most authors (more or less explicitly) see reducing carbon emissions as the primary goal, this section first provides an overview of the literature on the accomplishments of Kyoto and EU ETS in terms of emission reduction. It subsequently investigates relating issues and potential improvements to these systems.[63] Thereafter, the more indirect channel towards emission reduction is discussed: how do carbon markets/prices influence decisions on emission reduction investments?

2.5.2 *Kyoto Mechanisms: Emissions Trading*

Accomplishments

Under the Kyoto Protocol governments can trade emission rights (AAUs, see Section 2.4). Trade in AAUs has been minimal, however, accounting for less than 1% of total $MtCO_2e$ volume traded on allowance markets in 2009 (Kossoy & Ambrosi, 2010). This mechanism has obviously failed to contribute to climate change according to its original design.

Issues and Potential Improvements

The primary reason for the low level of trade is the high targets set under Kyoto, inciting concerns about the environmental legitimacy of trading in AAUs. Although not intended to be lax, especially targets for former Soviet Union and Eastern European countries failed to impose real constraints because the baseline projections overestimated economic developments in the 1990s.[64] Emissions of these countries remained well below Kyoto targets, "for reasons that have little to do with their climate change policies" (Grubb et al., 2010), as is illustrated in Figure 12. Because this surplus has not resulted from efforts to transition to a low-carbon economy, it is widely referred to as *hot air*.

Trading in AAUs would therefore in many cases give countries with a shortage of emission rights the opportunity to fulfill their targets by buying AAUs without requiring additional emission reduction effort by the country selling the rights. Some countries, including Austria, Germany, and The Netherlands, have stated that they will not buy hot air unless payments are "greened" by being directed to producing other environmental benefits (Hepburn, 2007).[65]

By linking the proceeds of selling (hot air) AAUs to projects that would reduce emissions – so-called Green Investment Schemes (GIS) – transition countries have found

63. For sake of reference: an idea of the magnitude of the environmental challenge can be derived from the IEA World Energy Outlook scenarios (IEA, 2008). Starting from a baseline in 2005 of 27,000 mega tonnes (Mt) of CO_2 emissions, its reference scenario (i.e. status quo) results in emissions of 40,000 Mt in 2030. The 450ppm (i.e. the required CO_2 concentration level) results in emissions of 25,700 Mt in 2030.

64. These countries faced a recession following the collapse of the Soviet Union.

65. That trading has been low can be seen as a system design failure, but on the other hand also as a success in culture shift: market parties have not fully exploited the hot air potential at the cost of climate change.

a way to monetize their excess AAUs favoring emission reduction.[66] Although challenges remain, mainly in credibly linking proceeds to sound emission reduction, this is a promising development. The first trade of allowances to fund GIS only materialized in 2008 due to required legislation, thus it is too early to evaluate the practical experience (Carbon Trust & Climate Strategies, 2009).

Figure 12 Kyoto targets set too high

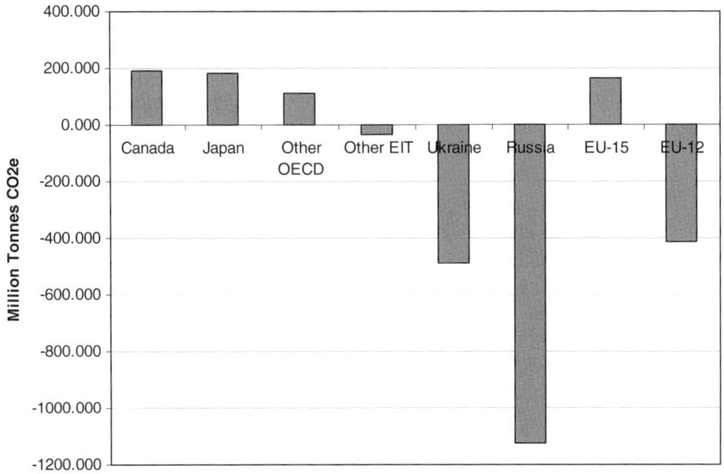

Source: Grubb et al. (2010); 2007 emissions relative to Kyoto targets; based on UNFCCC data as at 10-2009

2.5.3 *Kyoto Mechanisms: CDM and JI*

Accomplishments

The Clean Development Mechanism (CDM) and Joint Implementation (JI) are project-based mechanisms under the Kyoto Protocol. Whereas CDM has been a greater success in terms of emission savings than expected (Grubb et al., 2010), JI saw a slow start with projected emission savings in 2012 only amounting to 10% that of CDM based on projects submitted per September 2008 (Carbon Trust & Climate Strategies, 2009). The first reason for this is that the formal crediting period of JI was aligned with the first commitment period of Kyoto, which started later than expected in 2008.[67] In anticipation of this, the first JI projects were initiated late in 2006. Administrative processes were an issue as well. Track 2 JI projects (see Section 2.3) must pass a verification procedure. Independent Entities (IEs), responsible for verifying projects, could not cope with the large demand for project determination. In addition,

66. GIS is distinctively different from CDM and JI, since the former involves up-front finance (as opposed to finance against future emission credits of CDM and JI projects) and it is led by governments as part of national strategies complying with Kyoto obligations (Grubb et al., 2010; Hepburn, 2007).

67. Compared to CDM starting in 2000.

Central European countries entering the EU joined the EU ETS in which they could trade emission reductions more effectively and obtain higher prices than under JI (Korppoo & Gassan-zade, 2008). According to New Energy Finance, the trade volume of JI will remain low until 2012 (NEF, 2009).

As said, CDM has proven to be a success. It is the dominant mechanism within Kyoto. One of CDM's main objectives is to involve developing countries in climate change, which is essential for total emission reductions.[68] The mechanism has lived up to this primary task, having played "an important role in driving private-sector interest in projects to reduce emissions [in developing countries]" (Hepburn, 2007, p. 385). In terms of financial flows, UNFCCC estimates the value of CDM credits amounting to US$4.5-8.5 billion per year, with an expected private capital leverage multiple of ten (UNFCCC, 2008).[69] More conservatively, WEF (2010) states that CDM will have stimulated roughly US$15bn in low-carbon investment flows from developed to developing countries by the end of 2012.[70] Underlining the measurement difficulties, Grubb et al. (2010) conclude, "the Mechanisms clearly represent a substantial share – perhaps a quarter to a half – of the total mitigation technology investment in developing countries".

The starting period of the mechanism saw a focus of investments on hydrofluorocarbons (HFC-23, industrial gases used in refrigerators). These gases have a high (adverse) climate change potential compared to CO_2 but require only modest investments (Pinkse, 2007; WEF, 2009). Although attracting criticism (see below), this is also used to indicate the efficiency of CDM – stimulating emission reductions at low cost (Hepburn, 2007).

Carbon Trust & Climate Strategies (2009) assess the performance of CDM projects in terms of actual versus expected CERs produced and find that 'project type' is the dominant driver in determining whether projects live up to expectations.[71] Other factors include project size (smaller projects have higher yield) and host country (in terms of e.g., investment stability).[72]

Issues and Potential Improvements

Required Funding

It is important to see the above accomplishments, positive as they are, in perspective. According to McKinsey, total mitigation funding needs by developing countries

68. See for instance IEA (2007) and Wagner et al. (2009).
69. JI credits are included in this figure.
70. This immediately points to the measurement challenge. Background of the difference between the two estimates is not clear.
71. E.g. in terms of technology used, N_2O projects have the highest yield.
72. For a more detailed analysis of CDM project performance, see for instance New Carbon Finance (2008), 'False expectation: why CDM projects underperform'.

amount to US$300 billion (in 2005$) per year (McKinsey & Company, 2009). Evidently, there is still a long way to go, and carbon trading cannot be expected to fulfill total investment needs – it should go hand-in-hand with other public and private funding solutions. Lewis (2010) concludes that "the scale of CDM mitigation currently occurring in developing countries is insufficient", partly based on previous findings (Hultman, 2009; Schneider, 2007; Teng, Chen, & He, 2008; Wara, 2009). However, from a political point of view as well as from an effectiveness standpoint, it seems impossible to expect that developed countries will buy the CERs representing the total required investments in the developing countries. This was underlined after the G8 in 2008, where it was stated that all of the major economies, including China, should take additional action to reduce emissions (G8, 2008).[73]

Additionality

One of the most hotly debated issues of the CDM mechanism from the start is project additionality (Grubb et al., 2010; J. I. Lewis, 2010; NEF, 2009).[74] Because host countries of CDM projects are not restricted by emission caps, the CDM mechanism effectively creates new emission credits. In other words, "[i]f carbon finance is being used to promote renewable energy projects that are not necessarily replacing fossil fuel energy projects, then they may not be contributing to a deviation from business as usual greenhouse gas emission, and may in fact be contributing to global emissions by allowing developed countries to emit more as they offset their reduction targets with these projects" (J. I. Lewis, 2010, p. 8).

It is therefore essential that reductions are explicitly assessed as 'additional' to those that would occur without the project. The CDM Executive Board governs assessment of additionality. This has proven to be a challenging task, prone to a lack of certainty due to its subjective nature and focus on judgment.[75]

A major concern regards the incentives for sellers and buyers alike to inflate baseline emissions to maximize emission reduction of the CDM. To this end, 'bad policies' – policies driving up baseline emissions – that are implemented after adoption of the Kyoto Protocol are not taken into account when assessing additionality (the 'E+' rule). On the other hand, policies directed at low-carbon technologies are also not taken into account so as not to diminish incentives to implement 'good policies' (the 'E-' rule). Performance of additionality assessment shows mixed results and is ex-

73. One of the options to address this problem is introducing an emission cap on (some) developing countries. For an analysis of the difference in impact on incentives to invest between the two mechanisms – CDM versus a cap for developing countries – see for instance Hagem (2009).

74. A condition for the approval of a CDM project is that the reduction achieved by the project shall be additional to any that would occur without project activity (UNFCCC, 1998, article 12). The problem with this criterion is that it must be based on a counterfactual baseline for emissions (Hagem, 2009).

75. Notwithstanding the design of various methodologies to assess additionality.

pected to become more challenging as time goes by (Grubb et al., 2010).[76] In terms of future development or improvement, the authors conclude "[a]n honest political debate is required based on recognition that project-by-project additionality is an imperfect art with an unavoidable trade-off between administrative costs and the level of assurance".[77]

Although different in nature, JI faces similar challenges. Especially in terms of the relatively young GIS practice, more attention is required to establish norms of good conduct – like the E+ and E- rules for CMD – including international oversight.

Coverage

The majority of supply of CDM credits is concentrated in relatively few countries China has a 59% share (WEF, 2010). Especially the small role of African countries and the least developed countries has attracted criticism. In this regard, the mechanism does not address emission reduction in the poorest countries. In addition, the focus has been on only a few sectors (energy supply, industry and waste), while other sectors like energy efficiency in buildings or forestry have been largely left untouched. This limits the mechanism to exploit its full potential – covering only some 50% of total mitigation potential (Grubb et al., 2010). The background for this can differ per type of project. For instance, McKinsey's abatement cost curve shows that most energy efficiency projects have a *negative net cost*, implying they should be financially attractive.[78] Apparently, other barriers prevent these projects from being funded and thus the CDM mechanism from being effective.[79] These barriers should be addressed before the abatement potential can be exploited. On the other hand, the abatement cost curve also shows projects with a *positive net cost*, implying a requirement for additional policy support for them to become financially interesting.

As stated above, the initial focus was on non-CO_2 gases. This meant that investments were flowing to a small number of industry sectors, not addressing the lock-in risk of investments in high-carbon assets by the energy sector. As such, the design of the mechanism does not provide clear signals regarding the key technologies of central importance (Hepburn, 2007). Notwithstanding this, the share of credits referring to renewable energy (RE) and energy efficiency (EE) projects has been increasing. With the potential for industrial gas projects becoming exhausted, RE and EE are expected to amount to 60% by 2012 (WEF, 2010). This focus on high-yielding projects has

76. The main reason for this is that the number of projects initiated before the start of CDM is decreasing. For more information on the assessment of CDM additionality, see for instance: Michaelowa et al. (2008).

77. According to Bosi et al. (2010), the problem could be mitigated by exogenous criteria, standards and benchmarks.

78. McKinsey (2009) defines a global abatement cost curve, categorizing abatement opportunities in terms of costs and abatement potential. Costs are taken net of potential energy savings and are referred to as 'net costs'.

79. For more information on barriers to SE investments, see the previous chapter *Financing the Transition to Sustainable Energy*.

spurred criticism on the excessive profits made in the system. It is, however, not surprising that a new market provides excessive opportunities at the start (inframarginal rents), which is not 'wrong' in terms of market economics principles (Grubb et al., 2010).

Economic Efficiency

The transaction costs of CDMs are high. For a large part this is caused by the necessity to prove additionality on a project-by-project basis – possibly a logical requirement but certainly not an easy one to live up to. The bureaucracy is extensive (Lewis, 2010), while the approval process is long and laborious (Grubb et al., 2010). Early experience showed transaction costs amounting to several hundred thousand Euros per project (Fichtner, Graehl, & Rentz, 2003; Michaelowa, Stronzik, Eckermann, & Hunt, 2003). Simplified rules for smaller projects – by now presenting almost half of the projects – have decreased costs.[80]

Concerns continue with regard to timely verification and validation of projects in the system, as well as the issuance of credits for an increasing number of projects. Both indicate the need for additional capacity in the Executive Board.

2.5.4 *EU ETS*

Accomplishments

The Environmental Audit Committee indicates "[t]he effectiveness of the EU ETS will be determined primarily by its success in reducing emissions" (Environmental Audit Committee, 2010, p. 9). Although Phase I (2005-2007) showed an increase in emissions, caused by an over-allocation of permits, it is generally not seen as a failure but as a success – mainly in terms of the implementation of the system as such (Environmental Audit Committee, 2010; Hepburn, 2007). The EU ETS Phase I laid the groundwork, correctly measuring and recording emissions (NEF, 2009).

But maybe the main achievement of the system has been that it resulted in an explicit carbon price (Hepburn, 2007). The question of whether this has prompted abatement efforts is more difficult to answer.[81] In general, EAC (2010) points to the difficulties to assess the effectiveness of the EU ETS. Reasons include that it is "impossible" to separate effects from the impact of economic factors and policy instruments, and that emissions at or below the cap do not necessarily imply success because of potential over-allocation of emission rights.

80. For a more detailed review of how to streamline the CDM processes, see for instance Purdy (2009).

81. Hepburn (2007) provides some evidence to support a positive answer, based on surveys and other "tentative" results.

Issues and Potential Improvements

Cap Level

Cap levels during the ETS pilot trading period (2005-2007) were too high (Clò, 2009; Environmental Audit Committee, 2010; M. C. Lewis & Curien, 2009; Pearson & Worthington, 2009). This results in an abundance of allowances (or a lack of permit scarcity) and therefore a falling CO_2 price and insignificant incentives to reduce emissions. During the pilot phase of the EU ETS, the emission reduction burden imposed on *ETS sectors* was thus too weak. Indirectly, the amount of emissions that the *non-trading sectors* should have abated to grant compliance with the Kyoto target was excessive when compared with their abatement potential and marginal abatement costs (Clò, 2009, 2010; Kettner, Koeppl, Schleicher, & Thenius, 2007; Neuhoff, Keats, & Sato, 2006).[82]

Phase II is again expected to show over-allocation (Carbon Trust & Climate Strategies, 2009; Environmental Audit Committee, 2010; M. C. Lewis & Curien, 2010; Pearson & Worthington, 2009). The recession is an important reason for this, lowering emissions without underlying efforts towards a low-carbon economy. In addition, though reduced compared to Phase I, caps were unevenly distributed, with stringent caps imposed on the power sector while providing the industrial sector with allowances based on business-as-usual projections.[83] Shortfall in the power sector can therefore be purchased from the industrial sector without much additional reduction effort. Finally, the New Entrants Reserve (NER)[84] is collecting permits due to the recession instead of disbursing them to new entrants. These permits are expected to be given away by most countries, effectively weakening the emission caps because no emission reduction is attached to these permits (Pearson & Worthington, 2009). In its update on emission shortfall/surplus of January 2010, Deutsche Bank (M. C. Lewis & Curien, 2010) shows that it is whether or not NERs are released during Phase II that will determine the difference between a surplus or (a small) short position. In order to address the surplus in Phase II, Sandbag (Pearson & Worthington, 2009) advises cancelling excess NERs – a commitment already made by France and Ireland – and to provide incentives to companies to cancel permits 'voluntarily' (e.g., by means of tax measures). Others advocate tightening post-2020 caps, which are not set in stone yet, providing signals to affect the current price level (for instance Tilford (2009)).[85]

---

82. Emission reductions in line with commitments under the Kyoto Protocol are divided over sectors which are part of EU ETS (the trading sectors) and those that are not. The latter category should be stimulated to reduce emissions in other ways, e.g., through public policy instruments.

83. Industry was thus provided with 'hot air' emission permits.

84. The EU ETS allows member states to set aside a national pool of spare allowances for new or expanding industrial installations. Unused allocations from installations that are closed down are also added to this pool of allowances.

85. This only works if the market is efficient and reacts now to future (expected) developments, which is subject to discussion. See below under 'Price signals'.

Given these former inefficiencies and in light of the European unilateral commitment to a stricter emission reduction target, the new ETS Directive 2009/29/EC imposes a progressively stricter cap for the third post-Kyoto trading period (2013-2020), making the ETS regulation costlier each year (Clò, 2010). Deutsche Bank (M. C. Lewis & Curien, 2010) indeed estimates a short position during Phase III.

Options to further support more efficient cap levels include buying emission units for retirement by leading industrialized countries (although politically difficult in this time of recession in view of the costs involved), early commitment to increase post-2012 emission cutbacks in advance of global agreement, and protection against import from, e.g., CERs although this would isolate Europe from global mechanisms and distort the international price (Carbon Trust & Climate Strategies, 2009).

Allocation of Permits

Determination of National Allocation Plans (NAPs) is not without its pitfalls, as it involves asymmetric information and lobbying. Governments are relying on companies to reveal their abatement cost curve in order to determine an appropriate NAP. Companies have an incentive to exaggerate their cost estimates, however, in order to obtain a more generous allowance and a looser emission cap (Abadie & Chamorro, 2008; Hepburn, 2007).

In Phase I and Phase II, emission rights have largely been given away for free.[86] This so-called grandfathering of emission rights has been subject to criticism. In the new ETS Directive this has been addressed by creating a bigger role for auctioning. To avoid 'carbon leakage' – substantial asymmetric costs on the European companies, forcing them to either shut down plants or move their production activity to non-EU countries – the directive defines a hybrid system of grandfathering and auctioning:

- Energy sectors: full auctioning from 2013 onwards;
- Energy-intensive sectors not exposed to carbon leakage: 80% grandfathering in 2013, gradually declining to 30% in 2020 and full auctioning in 2027;
- Energy-intensive sectors exposed to carbon leakage: pure grandfathering (see also Section 2.3.1).

Clò (2010) analyses this aspect of the new directive and concludes that (i) grandfathering does not necessarily reduce the risk of carbon leakage because Phase III includes – unilaterally – a more stringent cap on European industry; (ii) the criteria to determine whether sectors are exposed to leakage risk are highly arbitrary and inefficient; and (iii) despite its declared intentions, grandfathering remains dominant under the new directive for the ETS manufacturing sectors. The first conclusion should be seen in light of the general pros and cons of grandfathering versus auction-

86. Under the ETS, utilities have received at least 95% of the allocated permits for 2005-2007 free of charge. For 2008-2012, this percentage drops to 90%.

ing, as discussed in section 2.3. As to the third conclusion, with auctioning as default for the energy sector which covers 65% of emissions within ETS, auctioning will still become the dominant overall mechanism in assigning EUAs in Phase III (Kossoy & Ambrosi, 2010). The importance of this point also depends on further work in terms of the second conclusion: the high percentage of grandfathering in the manufacturing industries is the result of an arbitrary method; if sound economic reasoning would result in an equally high share of the manufacturing industry being exposed to carbon leakage, grandfathering as a dominating mechanism might be justifiable for these sectors.

Price Signals

Coming to an explicit carbon price has been an essential part of EU ETS – pricing carbon emissions means pricing externalities and providing incentives for low-carbon investments. Emission prices (and revenues from potential emission sales) are included in investment decisions. Evidently, incentives diminish with a decreasing price level as well as with volatility of prices, making it more difficult to predict future price levels. Figure 13 shows the development of the carbon price within the EU ETS.

Figure 13 EU ETS emissions allowance prices: April 2005 – December 2009

Source: Environmental Audit Committee (2010, p. 21)

The figure shows how the carbon price has developed towards zero during Phase I due to caps being too low. A good start in Phase II was again followed by a sharp decline in price level during the second half of 2008 and 2009. This does not necessarily mean the market is not functioning well. On the contrary, a declining price due to the recession is a sign of natural adaptation to changed circumstances, and thus shows market flexibility. This is not the whole story, however. Because of the full bankability of Phase II allowances in Phase III, in an efficient market compliance parties with short positions (over the entire period of Phase II and III) would buy now in view of the low prices.[87] In other words, in a rational market "the mechanism mandating the bankability of EUAs should ensure that today's price trades at the level required to clear the market in Phase 3 adjusted for the time value of money" (M. C. Lewis & Curien, 2009, p. 27).[88] According to the authors, there are two reasons why this is not happening:

1. *Supply of EUAs is fixed until 2020*
   Uncertain demand – how prolonged will the recession be? – leads to volatile demand. In efficient markets the supply would adapt to the changing demand. This is not possible in the EU ETS, preventing the market from being cleared. Deutsche Bank (M. C. Lewis & Curien, 2009) proposes introducing targets subject to periodic review or even introducing some sort of central bank for allowances.[89] Although this seems to add to market uncertainty, Deutsche Bank advocates that it forces market participants to take into account what authorities want to achieve in the long term.
2. *Free allocation of allowances*
   Because all installations start off with a long position, they behave differently than when they had to buy permits as they went along. Grandfathering thus leads to market distortions, reducing market efficiency. For instance, because many installations have been given more allowances than needed, they have an incentive to sell permits in times of need for cash while facing a reluctant credit environment – even if they might need these permits in the future.

The low carbon price has led many to advocate implementing reserve price auctions – in addition to lower caps – or at least investigating this option further (Carbon Trust & Climate Strategies, 2009; Environmental Audit Committee, 2010; Grubb et al., 2009; M. C. Lewis & Curien, 2009; Pearson & Worthington, 2009; Tilford, 2009).[90] The general idea is to set a minimum price level for the EAUs to be auctioned in Phase III. If the price falls below this level, permits are not sold, effectively resulting in a withdrawal of permits from the market.[91] Deutsche Bank (M. C. Lewis

87. Important in this regard is that 2008-2020 is expected to show a net short position on average, even after correcting for the use of CERs and ERUs and the net demand of the aviation sector (M. C. Lewis & Curien, 2010).

88. For further theoretical background on this, see the Deutsche Bank reports 'Banking on Higher Prices' and 'It takes CO_2 to Contango'.

89. This requires a change of the Directive.

90. Interestingly, in reaction to recent solutions proposed in this direction in the UK, anonymous employees of the European Commission stated that intervention is not expected. The reasons lie in EC policy not to react to short-term developments as investments are based on long-term expectations. In short, prices should reflect the long-term supply and demand (press release, http://www.businessweek.com/news/2010-02-08/u-k-lawmakers-call-for-stricter-co2-caps-market-intervention.html). Evidently, this contrasts with the analysis by Deutsche Bank – discussed above – on market inefficiencies.

91. Exact design varies between authors. For additional background information, see for instance: Hepburn et al. (2006) and Grubb et al. (2006).

& Curien, 2009) concludes that the Directive does not prohibit setting reserve prices, although a final conclusion taking the "spirit of the text" into consideration is open to debate.[92]

Long-term Incentives

The phases within EU ETS design, as is the case in Kyoto, are relatively short. Investments in energy-generating assets, however, are based on expectation over decades. Regulation uncertainty on future phases can result in suboptimal investment decisions (Hepburn, 2007).[93] By lengthening the trading allowance periods, more certainty would be created for the companies involved. In addition, there is less chance of betting on Emission Trading failure – e.g., by building fossil-fueled power plants – and less opportunity for companies to influence policy design by lobbying for a generous allocation (Pinkse, 2007).

Policy Overcrowding

Policy measures to decrease CO_2 emission aimed at the sectors under the EU ETS reduce the effectiveness of emission trading. Generally, emission reduction projections in view of setting emission caps do not take emission reduction policies into account (Carbon Trust & Climate Strategies, 2009). That means that when emissions are reduced due to policy measures, it will be easier for companies to fulfil their emission obligations without having to buy rights or invest in emission reduction. For instance, subsidizing a certain renewable energy technology is intended to decrease emissions in that sector. If the emission cap is not reduced, meeting obligations is partly funded by society, and companies do not face incentives to decrease emissions further. New climate policies within the boundary of the cap-and-trade scheme aiming to reduce emissions should therefore be combined with an equal reduction in emission caps to ensure that emission reduction actually takes place (Blyth, 2010).[94]

---

92. More practically, a problem might arise due to allowances not going to the market, preventing full bankability.

93. Future policy decisions will impact the price of allowances and thus business cases surrounding energy investments. Regulatory risk will be included in business case metrics, which is economically logical from the perspective of the investor but might lead to sub-optimality in terms of climate change. The longer policy is 'fixed', the lower the regulatory risk.

94. In reality, policy measures as such do not decrease emissions. In many cases, governments provide financial incentives to decrease emissions. This still requires companies to take action. The point here is that these policy initiatives should be aligned with cap-and-trade regulation so as not to undermine the incentives that are at the heart of carbon trading.

2.5.5 *Impact on Emission Reduction Investment Decisions*

Impact on Cash Flows and Risk

Emissions trading impacts cash flows in a given period through four mechanisms (Abadie & Chamorro, 2008; Laurikka & Koljonen, 2006):

1. Existing cost categories: fuel costs;
2. New costs: the value of surrendered allowances;
3. Energy outputs: the price of power and heat; and
4. Additional revenues: free allowances.

The most direct channel is via allowance prices (for more information on the determination of emission price and its volatility, see Section 2.4).Because carbon prices influence cash flows, the uncertainty surrounding these prices poses a risk to be taken into account in assessing the cost of capital[95] (Abadie & Chamorro, 2008). In addition to the direct effect of volatile emission prices on revenues of selling and costs of buying these rights, the way in which CO_2 and fuel price variations feed through to electricity price variations is an important determinant of the overall investment risk. In their thorough report on climate policy uncertainty and investment risk, IEA (2007)[96] have modelled two elements of price uncertainty:

- Policy risk: reflected by a one-off price jump;
- Market price volatility: reflected by an annual price fluctuation.

The authors have thus separated the total effect of changes in prices into a policy and a volatility effect. In general, they find that policy uncertainty is the dominant factor in the risk premium.

Policy Uncertainty

Public policy impacts the pricing of carbon emissions. The international carbon cap-and-trade market is a direct consequence of regulation, reflected in international law (Kyoto Protocol) with some of the practical requirements – like NAP levels – determined at the country level. At a supranational level governments have imposed emission caps, thereby determining the total supply. In addition, market mechanisms have been created to facilitate a match of supply and demand. City of London et al. (2009, p. 5) conclude "[t]o ensure that scarce investment resources are deployed on the climate change mitigation effort, institutions and businesses need firm regulatory ground on which to base their investment decisions. However, recently businesses

95. Or: discount rate. Note that also in developing countries, which are not restricted by emission caps, projects will have to take these cash flows and risk impacts into account.

96. The report looks at how investments by the power sector in coal, gas, oil, nuclear and CCS technologies is affected by climate change policy uncertainty. Their conclusions are based on a quantitative analysis and provide a conceptual framework to assess the scale of effects of policy uncertainty.

have been receiving mixed messages from politicians around the world". As an important recent example, the outcome of Copenhagen resulted in "a significant step backwards" for the prospects of international carbon markets (Blyth, 2010). Also, the recent developments in the US imply serious uncertainty for the future of CO_2 pricing.

Climate policy risk will not impact all investment business cases in the same way. IEA (2007) indicates:

- Policy risk will be greater for investment decisions made close to a potential policy change. This is relevant for the timing of policy setting: a regulation should be announced well ahead of implementation. A practical example is the post-2012 regime which is drawing closer without clarity about its design;
- Policy risk is more pronounced if climate policy is a dominant economic driver. For instance, Carbon Capture and Storage (CCS) exists because of climate policy and will thus be relatively sensitive to regulatory risk;
- Price-regulated sectors will be dependent on the regulator for the degree to which price increases can be passed on to consumers, which could increase the impact of policy risk;
- Risk premiums depend on the technology being considered, the market context and the exact climate change policy mechanism under consideration.

With specific regard to CDM projects, J.I. Lewis (2010) points to the uncertainty of project approval. The incoming cash flows by selling the emission rights are therefore an uncertain parameter. The author concludes that "while the CDM could certainly help tip a project that is on the borderline of being profitable towards profitability, this is unlikely to be a sufficient factor for determining whether to invest in the first place".

Low-carbon investment business cases require an assessment of expectations over the long term (see previous section). In terms of regulatory risk, this implies that public policy should provide clarity on the future direction and design and the assurance this will be adhered to. Hepburn (2007) points to short commitment periods in both the Kyoto protocol and EU ETS, preventing investors from properly assessing the return on low-carbon assets. IEA (2007) indicate that the period of 5 to 15 years into the future is generally the most important period to recoup investments. Policy should therefore be fixed for a period of approximately 10 years ahead. Their results suggest that "climate policy risk may be brought down to modest levels compared to other risks if policy is set over a sufficiently long timescale into the future".[97] A second prerequisite is signaling creditability that 'fixed' really means fixed. In other words, promising that policy will not change is as valuable as the degree to which policymakers have not broken their promises in the past.

97. Climate policy which is set over a sufficiently long time results in fuel price risk being the dominant variable, with policy risk only contributing relatively little.

In conclusion, companies will have to incorporate regulatory risk surrounding carbon markets in business cases for low-carbon investments. In practice, this is generally reflected in the cost of capital. Based on their findings, IEA (2007) do not see policy risk as a serious threat to capacity levels in the long run but do indicate that it weakens investment incentives for low-carbon technologies.[98]

Long-Term Investment Decisions

Carbon pricing/emissions trading tends to under-deliver on investment in long-term solutions. There are three main reasons for this. First, markets may under-deliver on investment in R&D if companies are unable to retain the eventual commercial – emission reduction – benefits of such expenditure.[99] Second, there is a moral hazard problem in long-term investment incentives stemming from regulatory uncertainty: future governments may not feel bound by the commitments of their predecessors to provide continued levels of pay-off that are sufficiently high to recoup the companies' initial investments. Third, emissions trading enables opportunistic behaviour of carbon traders. Emission credits that can be purchased on the market sometimes represent reductions achieved through reductions from projects that merely utilize existing technologies or over-allocation of allowances, thereby not realizing one of the key arguments of an emissions trading scheme: to spur innovation and motivate firms to invest in more sustainable production technologies that lower GHG emissions (Pinkse, 2007). Finally, some authors argue that carbon market risks tend to accumulate in a non-linear way: the variance in possible prices increases at an accelerating rate over time. This means that the long-term risk profile (more than 25 years ahead) is disproportionately higher than the medium-term risk profile, and that companies tend to discount any price signals (e.g., policy announcements and targets) at a higher rate if they refer to longer timescales. This phenomenon is amplified by risk aversion on the part of companies. If companies apply a discount rate that increases over time, there is a growing divergence with the socially optimal discount rate for environment-related projects, which most economists argue should *decrease* over time (Blyth, 2010; Gagelmann & Frondel, 2005; Menanteau, Finon, & Lamy, 2003; Pinkse, 2007).

Project Selection and Threshold Prices

Companies under a cap-and-trade scheme have the choice between investing in emission reduction projects in order to stay within their emission cap or even obtain

98. Finally, it is valid to question whether companies are able to cope with policy risks or whether governments should underwrite them. For additional information on policy instruments and regulatory risk, see the previous chapter *Financing the Transition to Sustainable Energy*.

99. This type of market failure – positive externalities – creates a rationale for additional grants for the development of new technologies.

excess emission rights they can sell on the one hand and purchasing emission rights for emission above their cap level on the other.[100]

Generally, the carbon market price is assessed too low [for instance: WEF (2009); City of London et al. (2009)]. With the recent developments in carbon prices, there does not seem to be much debate about this conclusion. Various authors provide more perspective for this discussion by analyzing the threshold carbon price necessary to make investments in specific low-carbon technologies financially attractive – mostly with a focus on carbon capture storage [see for instance Abadie & Chamorro (2008) quoting a selection of previous results (Blyth et al., 2007; Martinsen, Linssen, Markewitz, & Vögele, 2007; Newell, Jaffe, & Stavins, 2006; Sekar, Parsons, Herzog, & Jacoby, 2007)]. The choice between investing in projects to reduce emissions or purchasing emission allowances (or a combination of the two) implies the need for project selection methodologies. Project selection will normally be based on standard finance theory (net present value) or cost/benefit analysis. Risks will be reflected in the discount rate, with the choice for the cost of capital potentially having a significant impact on the outcome of the business case. If managers face options to change course during a project or are able to postpone investments[101], real option analysis might be used to facilitate risk-neutral valuation based on the risk-free rate.[102] In determining threshold prices, many times 'trigger' prices are determined above which it is optimal to invest in emission-reducing projects *immediately*, i.e., when the value of the option to invest is highest. Real option analysis can be used for this kind of exercise. This also has the benefit that the riskless rate of return can be used instead of having to value project risk, both on the revenue and on the expenditure side.

Evidently, calculation of threshold prices and the outcome of project selection depend on the choice between these methodologies – as well as the choice for a discount rate when discounting cash flows.[103] As yet, there does not seem to be a clear consensus on methodology nor on final threshold prices.[104]

---

100. Choices can be made based on various selection methodologies, including net present value, cost/benefit analysis (CBA) and real option theory. See for instance Copeland et al. (2000).

101. Called 'managerial flexibility'.

102. For more information on real option analysis, see for instance Copeland & Keenan (1998).

103. In addition, the choice for the econometric calculation methods (models) applied are also of importance.

104. A quick check results in threshold prices calculated for CCS varying between 12 and 55 €/ton CO_2.

References

Abadie, L. M., & Chamorro, J. M. (2008). European CO2 prices and carbon capture investments. *Energy Economics, 30*(6), 2992-3015.

Alberola, E., Chevallier, J., & Chèze, B. (2009). Emissions compliances and carbon prices under the EU ETS: A country specific analysis of industrial sectors. *Journal of Policy Modeling, 31*(3), 446-462.

Anger, A. (2009). Including aviation in the European emissions trading scheme: Impacts on the industry, CO2 emissions and macroeconomic activity in the EU. *Journal of Air Transport Management, 16*, 100-105.

Betsill, M. M., & Hoffmann, M. J. (2009). *Constructing "Cap and Trade": The Evolution of Emissions Trading Systems for Greenhouse Gases.* Paper presented at the Open Meeting of the Human Dimensions of Global Environmental Change Research Community, Bonn, Germany.

Blyth, W. (2010). *Climate Policy after Copenhagen: Managing Carbon Price Risk in an Uncertain World.* London: Chatham House.

Blyth, W., Bradley, R., Bunn, D., Clarke, C., Wilson, T., & Yang, M. (2007). Investment risks under uncertain climate change policy. *Energy policy, 35*(11), 5766-5773.

Blyth, W., & Yang, M. (2006). *Impact of Climate Change Policy Uncertainty in Power Investment.* Paris: IEA/OECD.

Böhringer, C., & Rosendahl, K. E. (2009). Strategic partitioning of emission allowances under the EU Emission Trading Scheme. *Resource and Energy Economics, 31*(3), 182-197.

Bosi, M., Cantor, S., & Spors, F. (2010). *10 Years of Experience in Carbon Finance: Insights from working with Kyoto mechanisms.* Washington, DC: The World Bank.

Burniaux, J. M., Château, J., Dellink, R., Duval, R., & Jamet, S. (2009). *The economics of climate change mitigation: how to build the necessary global action in a cost-effective manner.*

Capoor, K., & Ambrosi, P. (2008). *State and trends of the carbon market 2008.* Washington, DC: The World Bank.

Capoor, K., & Ambrosi, P. (2009). *State and trends of the carbon market 2009.* Washington, DC: The World Bank.

Carbon Trust, & Climate Strategies. (2009). *Global Carbon Mechanisms: Emerging lessons and implications.* London: Carbon Trust.

Cave, L. A., & Blomquist, G. C. (2008). Environmental policy in the European Union: Fostering the development of pollution havens? *Ecological Economics, 65*(2), 253-261.

CE Delft. (2007a). *Allocation of allowances for aviation in the EU ETS: The impact on the profitability of the aviation sector under high levels of auctioning.* Delft: CE Delft.

CE Delft. (2007b). *Competitiveness issues for Dutch aviation from EU ETS.* Delft: CE Delft.

CE Delft, & MVA. (2007). *Implications of EU emission Trading Scheme for Competition Between EU and Non-EU Airlines.* Delft: CE Delft.

Chevallier, J. (2009). Carbon futures and macroeconomic risk factors: A view from the EU ETS. *Energy Economics, 31*(4), 614-625.

City of London, The London Accord, & CEAG Ltd. (2009). *Delivering Copenhagen: The Role of the City's Financial Services Sector in Supporting Action on Climate Change.* London: CEAG Ltd.

Clò, S. (2009). The effectiveness of the EU Emissions Trading Scheme. *Climate Policy, 9*(3), 227-241.

Clò, S. (2010). Grandfathering, auctioning and Carbon Leakage: Assessing the inconsistencies of the new ETS Directive. *Energy Policy, 38*(5), 2420-2430.

Coase, R. H. (1960). The Problem of Social Cost. *Journal of Law and Economics, 3*, 1-44.

Convery, F. J. (2009). Origins and Development of the EU ETS. *Environmental and Resource Economics, 43*(3), 391-412.

Convery, F. J., & Redmond, L. (2007). Market and Price Developments in the European Union Emissions Trading Scheme. *Review of Environmental Economics and Policy, 1*(1), 88-111.

Copeland, T., Koller, T., Murrin, J., & McKinsey, I. (2000). *Valuation: measuring and managing the value of companies*. New York: John Wiley & Sons.

Copeland, T. E., & Keenan, P. T. (1998). How much is flexibility worth? *The McKinsey Quarterly*(2).

Cornes, R., & Sandler, T. (1996). *The theory of externalities, public goods, and club goods*: Cambridge Univ Pr.

Crocker, T. D. (1968). *The Structuring of Atmospheric Pollution Control Systems*. New York: Norton.

Dales, J. H. (1968). *Pollution, Property and prices*. Toronto: University Press.

Daskalakis, G., Psychoyios, D., & Markellos, R. N. (2009). Modeling CO2 emission allowance prices and derivatives: Evidence from the European trading scheme. *Journal of Banking & Finance, 33*(7), 1230-1241.

Edwards, R. (2009). *Carbon finance for developing country greenhouse gas emissions mitigation from 2010 – 2020 and the role of a Global Climate Change Fund*. London: Climate Change Capital.

Egenhofer, C. (2007). The Making of the EU Emissions Trading Scheme: Status, Prospects and Implications for Business. *European Management Journal, 25*(6), 453-463.

Ellerman, A. D. (2005). A note on tradeable permits. *Environmental and Resource Economics, 31*(2), 123-131.

Ellerman, A. D., & Buchner, B. K. (2007). The European union emissions trading scheme: Origins, allocation, and early results. *Review of Environmental Economics and Policy, 1*(1), 66.

Environmental Audit Committee. (2010). *The role of carbon markets in preventing dangerous climate change*. London: The Stationery Office Limited.

Fichtner, W., Graehl, S., & Rentz, O. (2003). The impact of private investors transaction costs on the cost effectiveness of project-based Kyoto mechanisms. *Climate Policy, 3*(3), 249-259.

Flachsland, C., Marschinski, R., & Edenhofer, O. (2009). Global trading versus linking: Architectures for international emissions trading. *Energy Policy, 37*(5), 1637-1647.

G8. (2008). *G8 Statement on Climate Change and Environment.*

Gagelmann, F., & Frondel, M. (2005). The impact of emission trading on innovation-science fiction or reality? *European Environment, 15*(4), 203-211.

Gilbertson, T., & Reyes, O. (2009). Carbon Trading: How it works and why it fails. *Dag Hammarskjöld Foundation Occasional Paper Series*(7).

Girishankar, N. (2009). *Innovating development finance-from financing sources to financial solutions*. Washington, DC: The World Bank.

Goddart, T., Haugen-Kozyra, K., & Ridge, A. (2008). *Alberta: North America's First Compliance Offset Carbon*. Edmonton: Alberta Agriculture and Rural Development.

Grubb, M., Brewer, L., Sato, M., Helmayr, R., & Fazekas, D. (2009). *Climate Policy and industrial competitiveness: Ten insights from Europe on the EU Emissions Trading System.*

Grubb, M., Laing, T., Counsell, T., & Willan, C. (2010). Global carbon mechanisms: lessons and implications. *Climatic Change*, 1-35.

Grubb, M., & Neuhoff, K. (2006). *Allocation and competitiveness in the EU emissions trading scheme: policy overview*. Cambridge, UK: Faculty of Economics, University of Cambridge, UK.

Hagem, C. (2009). The clean development mechanism versus international permit trading: the effect on technological change. *Resource and Energy Economics, 31*(1), 1-12.

Hamilton, K., Sjardin, M., Peters-Stanley, M., & Marcello, T. (2010). *Building Bridges: State of the Voluntary Carbon Markets 2010*. New York/Washington: Bloomberg New Energy Finance/Ecosystem Marketplace.

Hamilton, K., Sjardin, M., Shapiro, A., & Marcello, T. (2009). *Fortifying the Foundation: State of the Voluntary Carbon Markets 2009*. Washington, DC & New York, NY: Ecosystem Marketplace & New Carbon Finance.

Heal, G. (2007). A celebration of environmental and resource economics. *Environmental Economics and Policy, 1*(1), 7-25.

Hepburn, C. (2007). Carbon trading: a review of the Kyoto mechanisms. *Annual Review of Environment and Resources, 32*, 395-393.

Hepburn, C., Grubb, M., Neuhoff, K., Matthes, F., & Tse, M. (2006). Auctioning of EU ETS phase II allowances: how and why. *Climate Policy, 6*(1), 137-160.

Houser, T. (2009). Ensuring US Competitiveness and International Participation.

Hultman, N. E. (2009). How can the Clean Development Mechanism better contribute to sustainable development. *AMBIO: A Journal of the Human Environment, 38*(2), 120-122.

IEA. (2007). *World Energy Outlook 2007*: International Energy Agency.

IEA. (2008). *World Energy Outlook 2008*: International Energy Agency.

Kaul, I., Grunberg, I., & Stern, M. A. (1999). *Global public goods: International cooperation in the 21st century*. New York: United Nations Development Programme.

Kettner, C., Koeppl, A., Schleicher, S., & Thenius, G. (2007). Stringency and distribution in the EU Emissions Trading Scheme–the 2005 Evidence. *Nota di Lavora, 22*, 2007.

Kolk, A., & Pinkse, J. (2005). Business responses to climate change: identifying emergent strategies. *California Management Review, 47*(3), 6-20.

Korppoo, A., & Gassan-zade, O. (2008). *Joint Implementation: Looking Back and Forward*. Cambridge: Climate Strategies.

Kossoy, A., & Ambrosi, P. (2010). *State and trends of the carbon market 2010*. Washington, DC: The World Bank.

Lai, Y. B. (2008). Auctions or grandfathering: the political economy of tradable emission permits. *Public Choice, 136*(1), 181-200.

Laurikka, H., & Koljonen, T. (2006). Emissions trading and investment decisions in the power sector–a case study in Finland. *Energy Policy, 34*(9), 1063-1074.

Leung, D. Y. C., Yung, D., Ng, A.;, Leung, M. K. H., & Chan, A. (2009). An overview of emissions trading and its prospects in Hong Kong. *Environmental Science & Policy, 12*(1), 92-101.

Lewis, J. I. (2010). The evolving role of carbon finance in promoting renewable energy development in China. *Energy Policy, 38*(6), 2875-2886.

Lewis, M. C., & Curien, I. (2009). *The ETS Review: Unfinished Business*. London: Deutsche Bank AG.

Lewis, M. C., & Curien, I. (2010). *The Crying of Lot 2013: Phase-3 Auctions and the EUA Price Outlook*. London: Deutsche Bank AG.

Martinsen, D., Linssen, J., Markewitz, P., & Vögele, S. (2007). CCS: A future CO2mitigation option for Germany? A bottom-up approach. *Energy policy, 35*(4), 2110-2120.

McKinsey & Company. (2009). *Pathways to a Low-Carbon Economy: Version 2 of the Global Greenhouse Gas Abatement Cost Curve.*

Menanteau, P., Finon, D., & Lamy, M.-L. (2003). Prices versus quantities: choosing policies for promoting the development of renewable energy. *Energy Policy, 31*(8), 799-812.

Michaelowa, A., & Castro, P. (2008). *Empirical Analysis of Performance of CDM Projects.* London, UK: Climate Strategies.

Michaelowa, A., Stronzik, M., Eckermann, F., & Hunt, A. (2003). Transaction costs of the Kyoto Mechanisms. *Climate policy, 3*(3), 261-278.

Miller, N. H. (2006). *Notes on Microeconomic Theory.*

Mizuguchi, H. (2010). *Likely Green Investment Trends in 2010.* Tokyo: Daiwa Institute of Research Ltd.

Montgomery, W. D. (1972). Markets in licenses and efficient pollution control programs. *Journal of Economic Theory, 5*(3), 395-418.

NEF. (2009). *Global Carbon Quarterly Q3 2009.* London: Bloomberg New Energy Finance.

Neuhoff, K., Keats, K., & Sato, M. (2006). Allocation, incentives and distortions: the impact of EU ETS emissions allowance allocations to the electricity sector.

Newell, R. G., Jaffe, A. B., & Stavins, R. N. (2006). The effects of economic and policy incentives on carbon mitigation technologies. *Energy Economics, 28*(5-6), 563-578.

Nordhaus, W. D. (1999). *Global public goods and the problem of global warming.* Toulouse: The Institut d'Economie Industrielle (IDEI).

Nordhaus, W. D. (2006a). After Kyoto: Alternative mechanisms to control global warming. *The American Economic Review, 96*(2), 31-34.

Nordhaus, W. D. (2006b). *Paul Samuelson and global public goods: A commemorative essay for Paul Samuelson.*

Nordhaus, W. D. (2007). To tax or not to tax: Alternative approaches to slowing global warming. *Review of Environmental Economics and Policy, 1*(1), 26.

Parker, L. (2010). *Climate Change and the EU Emissions Trading Scheme (ETS): Looking to 2020.* Washington, DC: Congressional Research Service.

Pearson, A., & Worthington, B. (2009). *ETS S.O.S.: Why the flagship 'EU Emissions Trading Policy' needs rescuing.* London: Sandbag.

Pew Center on Global Climate Change. (2007). Thirteenth Session of the Conference of the Parties to the UN Framework Convention on Climate Change and Third Session of the Meeting of the Parties to the Kyoto Protocol.

Pezzey, J. C. V. (2003). Emission Taxes and Tradeable Permits A Comparison of Views on Long-Run Efficiency. *Environmental and Resource Economics, 26*(2), 329-342.

Pigou, A. C. (1920). *The economics of welfare.* London: Macmillan.

Pinkse, J. (2007). Carbon emissions trading: managing climate change through financial markets. *Aenorm, 56*, 17-20.

Purdy, R. (2009). Governance Reform of the Clean Development Mechanism after Poznan. *CCLR The Carbon & Climate Law Review, 3*(1), 5-15.

PwC. (2009). *Carbon Taxes vs Carbon Trading: Pros, cons and the case for a hybrid approach.* London: PricewaterhouseCoopers LLP.

Ranade, M., & Bhada, P. (2010). *A City-Wide Approach to Carbon Finance.* Washington, DC: The World Bank.

Reinaud, J. (2007). *CO2 allowance & electricity price interaction: Impact on industry's electricity purchasing strategies in Europe*: OECD/International Energy Agency.

Rock, N., Baines, T., & LeBoeuf, D. (2008). Aviation and the EU Emissions Trading Scheme: Turbulence Ahead? In K. Carnahan (Ed.), *Geenhouse Gas Market Report 2008: Piecing Together a Comprehensive International Agreement for a Truly Global Carbon Market*. Geneva: International Emissions Trading Association, IETA.

Schneider, L. (2007). *Is the CDM fulfilling its environmental and sustainable development objectives? An evaluation of the CDM and options for improvement.*: Report prepared for WWF by Öko-Institut EV Berlin.

Sekar, R. C., Parsons, J. E., Herzog, H. J., & Jacoby, H. D. (2007). Future carbon regulations and current investments in alternative coal-fired power plant technologies. *Energy Policy, 35*(2), 1064-1074.

Silva, E. C. D., & Zhu, X. (2009). Emissions trading of global and local pollutants, pollution havens and free riding. *Journal of Environmental Economics and Management, 58*(2), 169-182.

Stern, N., Peters, S., Bakhshi, V., Bowen, A., Cameron, C., Catovsky, S., et al. (2006). *Stern Review: The economics of climate change.*

Teng, F., Chen, W., & He, J. (2008). *Possible Development of a Technology Clean Development Mechanism in a Post-2012 Regime*: Harvard Project on International Climate Agreements
Belfer Center for Science and International Affairs
Harvard Kennedy School.

The World Bank. (2006). *The Role of the World Bank in Carbon Finance: An Approach for Further Engagement*. Washington, DC: The World Bank.

The World Bank. (2010). *World Development Report 2010: Development and Climate Change*. Washington, DC: The International Bank for Reconstruction and Development / The World Bank.

Tilford, S. (2009). Carbon price collapse threatens the EU's climate agenda [Electronic Version]. *CER Bulletin*. Retrieved July 2010 from http://www.cer.org.uk/articles/65_tilford.html.

Tvinnereim, E. (2008). The First Six Months of 2008. In K. Carnahan (Ed.), *Geenhouse Gas Market Report 2008: Piecing Together a Comprehensive International Agreement for a Truly Global Carbon Market*. Geneva: International Emissions Trading Association, IETA.

UNCCF. (2010). Retrieved June 24, 2010, from http://unfccc.int/2860.php

UNFCCC. (2008). *Identifying, analysing and assessing existing and potential new financing resources and relevant vehicles to support the development, deployment, diffusion and transfer of environmentally sound technologies*. Bonn.

UNFCCC. (2010). Retrieved June 24, 2010, from http://unfccc.int/2860.php

Verschueren, K. (2009, November 12). *European Emission Trading system for Aviation*. Paper presented at the Airneth Seminar, The Hague.

Vespermann, J., & Wald, A. (2010). Much Ado about Nothing?-An analysis of economic impacts and ecologic effects of the EU-emission trading scheme in the aviation industry. *Transportation Research Part A: Policy and Practice*.

Victor, D. (2009). *The Politics of Fossil-Fuel Subsidies*. Winnipeg/Geneva: The Global Subsidies Initiative.

Wagner, G., Wang, J., Dudek, D., Haverkamp, J., Keohane, N., & Petsonk, A. (2009). *The CLEAR Path: Rewarding early actions by emerging economies to limit carbon*. Washington, DC: Environmental Defense Fund.

Wara, M. (2009). The Clean Development Mechanism's early performance. In S. Schneider, A. Rosencrantz & M. Manstrandrea (Eds.), *Climate Change Science and Policy*. Washington: Island Press.

WEF. (2009). *Green Investing: Towards a Clean Energy Infrastructure*. Cologny/Geneva: World Economic Forum.

WEF. (2010). *Green Investing 2010: Policy Mechanisms to Bridge the Financial Gap*. Cologny/Geneva: World Economic Forum.

Woerdman, E. (2001). Emissions trading and transaction costs: analyzing the flaws in the discussion. *Ecological Economics, 38*(2), 293-304.

Woerdman, E., Arcuri, A., & Cló, S. (2008). Emissions Trading and the Polluter-Pays Principle: Do Polluters Pay under Grandfathering? *Review of Law & Economics, 4*(2), 565-590.

Appendix A Glossary

Accredited Independent Entity (AIE): Accredited independent entities (AIEs) are independent auditors that assess whether a potential project meets all the eligibility requirements of the JI (determination) and whether the project has achieved greenhouse gas emission reductions (verification).

Additionality: A project activity is additional if anthropogenic GHG emissions are lower than those that would have occurred in the absence of the project activity.

Afforestation: The process of establishing and growing forests on bare or cultivated land, which has not been forested in recent history.

Annex I (Parties): Annex I Parties include the industrialized countries that were members of the OECD (Organisation for Economic Co-operation and Development) in 1992, plus countries with economies in transition (the EIT Parties), including the Russian Federation, the Baltic States, and several Central and Eastern European States.

Annex B (Parties): The 39 industrialized countries (including the European Economic Community) listed in Annex B to the Kyoto Protocol have committed to country-specific targets that collectively reduce their GHG emissions by at least 5.2% below 1990 levels on average over 2008–12.

Assigned Amount Unit (AAU): Annex I Parties are issued AAUs up to the level of their assigned amount, corresponding to the quantity of greenhouse gases they can release in accordance with the Kyoto Protocol (Art. 3), during the first commitment period of that protocol (2008–12). One AAU represents the right to emit one metric ton of carbon dioxide equivalent.

Backwardation: A downward sloping forward curve (i.e., the price of the future is less than the spot price of the underlying commodity). Antonym: contango.

Banking or carry over: Compliance units under the various schemes to manage GHG emissions in existence may or may not be carried over from one commitment period to the next. Banking may encourage early action by mandated entities depending on their current situation and their anticipations of future carbon constraints. In addition banking brings market continuity. Banking between Phase I and Phase II of the EU ETS is not allowed but is allowed between Phase II and further phases. Some restrictions on the amount of units that can be carried over may apply: for instance, EUAs may be banked with no restriction while the amount of CERs that can be carried over by a Kyoto Party is limited to 2.5% of the assigned amount of each Party.

Baseline: The emission of greenhouse gases that would occur without the policy intervention or project activity under consideration.

Biomass Fuel: Combustible fuel composed of a biological material, for example, wood or wood by-products, rice husks, or cow dung.

California Global Warming Solution Act AB32 (AB32): The passage of Assembly Bill 32 (California Global Warming Solution Act AB32) in August 2006 sets economy-wide GHG emissions targets as follows: Bring down emissions to 1990 levels by 2020 (considered to be at least a 25% reduction below business-as-usual) and to 80% of 1990 levels by 2050. Covering about 85% of GHG emissions, a cap-and-trade scheme (still being designed) would be a major instrument, along with renewable energy standards, energy efficiency standards for buildings and appliances as well as vehicle emissions standards.

Cap and trade: Cap-and-trade schemes set a desired maximum ceiling for emissions (or cap) and let the market determine the price for keeping emissions within that cap. To comply with their emission targets at least cost, regulated entities can either opt for internal abatement measures or acquire allowances or emission reductions in the carbon market, depending on the relative costs of these options.

Carbon Asset: The potential of greenhouse gas emission reductions that a project is able to generate and sell.

Carbon Finance: Resources provided to activities generating (or expected to generate) greenhouse gas (or carbon) emission reductions through the transaction of such emission reductions.

Carbon Dioxide Equivalent (CO2e): The universal unit of measurement used to indicate the global warming potential of each of the six greenhouse gases regulated under the Kyoto Protocol. Carbon dioxide—a naturally occurring gas that is a byproduct of burning fossil fuels and biomass, land-use changes, and other industrial processes—is the reference gas against which the other greenhouse gases are measured, using their global warming potential.

Certified Emission Reductions (CERs): A unit of greenhouse gas emission reductions issued pursuant to the Clean Development Mechanism of the Kyoto Protocol, and measured in metric tons of carbon dioxide equivalent. One CER represents a reduction in greenhouse gas emissions of one metric ton of carbon dioxide equivalent.

Chicago Climate Exchange (CCX): Members to the Chicago Climate Exchange make a voluntary but legally binding commitment to reduce GHG emissions. By the end of Phase I (December, 2006), all members will have reduced direct emissions 4% below a baseline period of 1998-2001. Phase II, which extends the CCX reduction program through 2010, will require all members to ultimately reduce GHG emissions 6% below baseline. Among the members are companies from North America as well as municipalities or US states or universities. As new regional initiatives began to take shape in the US, membership of the CCX grew from 127 members in January 2006 to

237 members by the end of the year, while new participants expressed their interest in familiarizing themselves with emissions trading.

Clean Development Mechanism (CDM): The mechanism provided by Article 12 of the Kyoto Protocol, designed to assist developing countries in achieving sustainable development by allowing entities from Annex I Parties to participate in low-carbon projects and obtain CERs in return.

Climate Action Reserve (CAR): The Climate Action Reserve is a US-based offsets program that establishes regulatory-quality standards for the development, quantification, and verification of greenhouse gas (GHG) emissions reduction projects in North America; issues carbon offset credits known as Climate Reserve Tonnes (CRT) generated from such projects; and tracks the transaction of credits over time in a transparent, publicly accessible system.

Community Independent Transaction Log (CITL): The Community Independent Transaction Log (CITL) conducts "supplementary checks" to those by the ITL for transactions involving registries of at least one EU member state, such as the issuance, transfer, cancellation, retirement, and banking of EUAs.

Conference of Parties (COP): The supreme body of the Convention. It currently meets once a year to review the Convention's progress. The word "conference" is not used here in the sense of "meeting" but rather of "association", which explains the seemingly redundant expression "fourth session of the Conference of the Parties."

Conference of the Parties serving as the Meeting of the Parties (CMP): The Convention's supreme body is the COP, which serves as the meeting of the Parties to the Kyoto Protocol. The sessions of the COP and the CMP are held during the same period to reduce costs and improve coordination between the Convention and the Protocol.

Contango: A term used in the futures market to describe an upward sloping forward curve (i.e., futures prices are above spot prices). Antonym: backwardation.

Crediting period: The crediting period is the duration of time during which a registered, determined or approved project can generate emission reductions. For CDM projects, the crediting period can be either seven years (renewable twice) or ten years (non-renewable).

Designated Focal Point (DFP): Parties participating in the Joint Implementation (JI) mechanism are required to nominate a Designated Focal Point (DFP) for approving projects.

Designated National Authority (DNA): An office, ministry, or other official entity appointed by a Party to the Kyoto Protocol to review and give national approval to projects proposed under the Clean Development Mechanism.

Designated Operational Entities (DOEs): Designated operational entities are independent auditors that assess whether a potential project meets all the eligibility requirements of the CDM (validation) and whether the project has achieved greenhouse gas emission reductions (verification and certification).

Determination: Determination is the process of evaluation by an independent entity accredited by the host country (JI Track 1) or by the Joint Implementation Supervisory Committee (JI Track 2) of whether a project and the ensuing reductions of anthropogenic emissions by sources or enhancements of anthropogenic removals by sinks meet all applicable requirements of Article 6 of the Kyoto Protocol and the JI guidelines.

Eligibility Requirements: There are six Eligibility Requirements for Participating in Emissions Trading (Art. 17) for Annex I Parties. Those are: (i) being a Party to the Kyoto Protocol, (ii) having calculated and recorded one's Assigned Amount, (iii) having in place a national system for inventory, (iv) having in place a national registry, (v) having submitted an annual inventory, and (vi) submittingsupplementary information on assigned amount. An Annex I party will automatically become eligible after 16 months have elapsed since the submission of its report on calculation of its assigned amount. Then, this Party and any entity that has opened an account in the registry can participate in Emissions Trading. However, a Party could lose its eligibility if the Enforcement Branch of the Compliance Committee has determined the Party is non-compliant with the eligibility requirements.

Emission Reductions (ERs): The measurable reduction of release of greenhouse gases into the atmosphere from a specified activity, over a specified period of time.

Emission Reductions Purchase Agreement (ERPA): Agreement which governs the transaction of emission reductions.

Emission Reduction Units (ERUs): A unit of emission reductions issued pursuant to Joint Implementation. One EUA represents the right to emit one metric ton of carbon dioxide equivalent.

Emissions Trading Scheme (ETS): see cap and trade.

EU-10: Bulgaria, Czech Republic, Estonia, Hungary, Latvia, Lithuania, Poland, Romania, Slovakia, and Slovenia.

EU-15: Austria, Belgium, Denmark, Finland, France, Germany, Greece, Ireland, Italy, Luxembourg, the Netherlands, Portugal, Spain, Sweden, United Kingdom.

European Union Allowances (EUAs): the allowances in use under the EU ETS. An EUA unit is equal to one metric ton of carbon dioxide equivalent.

European Union Emission Trading Scheme (EU ETS): The EU ETS was launched on January 1, 2005 as a cornerstone of EU climate policy towards its Kyoto commitment and beyond. Through the EU ETS, member states allocate part of the efforts towards their Kyoto targets to private sector emission sources (mostly utilities). Over 2008–12, emissions from mandated installations (about 40% of EU emissions) are capped at 6% below 2005 levels on average. Participants can internally reduce emissions, purchase EUAs or acquire CERs and ERUs (within a 13.4% average limit of their allocation over 2008–12). The EU ETS will continue beyond 2012, with further cuts in emissions (by 21% below 2005 levels in 2020 or more, depending on progress in reaching an ambitious international agreement on climate change).

First Commitment Period: The five-year period, from 2008 to 2012, during which industrialized country have committed to collectively reduce their greenhouse gas (or "carbon") emissions by an average of 5.2% compared with 1990 emissions under the Kyoto Protocol.

Green Investment Scheme (GIS): A GIS is a voluntary mechanism through which proceeds from AAU transactions will contribute to contractually agreed environment- and climate- friendly projects and programs both by 2012 and beyond.

Greenhouse gases (GHGs): Both natural and anthropogenic, greenhouse gases trap heat in the Earth's atmosphere, causing the greenhouse effect. Water vapour (H_2O), carbon dioxide (CO_2), nitrous oxide (N_2O), methane (CH_4), and ozone (O_3) are the primary greenhouse gases. The emission of greenhouse gases through human activities (such as fossil fuel combustion or deforestation) and their accumulation in the atmosphere are responsible for an additional forced contribution to climate change. The Kyoto Protocol regulates six GHGs: carbon dioxide (CO_2), methane (CH_4), and nitrous oxide (N_2o), as well as hydrofluorocarbons (HFCs), perfluorocarbons (PFCs), and sulfur hexafluoride (SF_6).

Global Warming Potential (GWP): An index representing the combined effect of the differing times greenhouse gases remain in the atmosphere and their relative effectiveness in absorbing outgoing infrared radiation.

Internal rate of return: The annual return that would make the present value of future cash flows from an investment (including its residual market value) equal the current market price of the investment. In other words, the discount rate at which an investment has zero net present value.

International Transaction Log (ITL): the ITL links together the national registries and the CDM registry and is in charge of verifying the validity of transactions (issuance, transfer and acquisition between registries, cancellation, expiration and replacement, retirement, and carry-over). It is the central piece of the emissions trading under the Kyoto Protocol.

Japan-Voluntary Emissions Trading Scheme (JVETS): Under the J-VETS, companies receive subsidies to implement mitigation activities in line with voluntary commitments and can resort to emissions trading (incl. offsets) to meet their commitments with more flexibility. Though growing, its impact remains limited: over the first three years of the scheme, participants (288 companies) have reduced their emissions by about one million tCO2e. The J-VETS has contributed to the development of MRV system, third-party verification system, and the registry system. The J-VETS has been incorporated to the Experimental Integrated ETS as one of the participating options.

Joint Implementation (JI): Mechanism provided by Article 6 of the Kyoto Protocol, whereby entities from Annex I Parties may participate in low-carbon projects hosted in Annex I countries and obtain Emission Reduction Units in return.

Kyoto Mechanisms (KMs): the three flexibility mechanisms that may be used by Annex I Parties to the Kyoto Protocol to fulfill their commitments. Those are the Joint Implementation (JI, Art. 6), Clean Development Mechanism (CDM, Art. 12) and International Emissions Trading (Art. 17).

Kyoto Protocol: Adopted at the Third Conference of the Parties to the United Nations Convention on Climate Change held in Kyoto, Japan, in December 1997, the Kyoto Protocol commits industrialized country signatories to collectively reduce their greenhouse gas emissions by at least 5.2% below 1990 levels on average over 2008–12 while developing countries can take no-regret actions and participate voluntarily in emission reductions and removal activities through the CDM. The Kyoto Protocol entered into force in February 2005.

Monitoring Plan: A set of requirements for monitoring and verification of emission reductions achieved by a project.

National Allocation Plans (NAPs): The documents, established by each member state and reviewed by the European Commission, that specify the list of installations under the EU ETS and their absolute emissions caps, the amount of CERs and ERUs that may be used by these installations as well as other features such as the size of the new entrants' reserve and the treatment of existing installations or the process of allocation (free allocation or auctioning).

New South Wales Greenhouse Gas Reduction Scheme (NSW GGAS): Operational since January 1, 2003 (to last at least until 2012), the NSW Greenhouse Gas Abatement Scheme aims at reducing GHG emissions from the power sector. NSW and ACT (since January 1, 2005) retailers and large electricity customers have thus to comply with mandatory (intensity) targets for reducing or offsetting the emissions of GHG arising from the production of electricity they supply or use. They can meet their targets by purchasing certificates (NSW Greenhouse Abatement Certificates or NGACs) that are generated through project activities.

New Zealand Emissions Trading Scheme (NZ ETS): The NZ ETS will progressively regulate emissions of the six Kyoto gases in all sectors of the economy by 2015. Forestry is covered since 2008, and by July 1, 2010, stationary energy, industrial processes, and liquid fossil fuel will be phased in. The government recently announced, however, that full implementation could be delayed if adequate progress is not made in establishing similar regulations in other developed countries.

Offsets: Offsets designate the emission reductions from project-based activities that can be used to meet compliance—or corporate citizenship—objectives vis-à-vis greenhouse gas mitigation.

Primary transaction: A transaction between the original owner (or issuer) of the carbon asset and a buyer.

Project Design Document (PDD): A central document of project-based mechanisms, the PDD notably describes the project activity (including environmental impacts and stakeholders consultations), the baseline methodology and how the project is additional as well as the monitoring plan.

Project Idea Note (PIN): A note prepared by a project proponent presenting briefly the project activity (e.g., sector, location, financials, estimated amount of ERs, etc.).

REDD plus: All activities that reduce emissions from deforestation and forest degradation, and contribute to conservation, sustainable management of forests, and enhancement of forest carbon stocks.

Regional Greenhouse Gas Initiative (RGGI): Under RGGI, 10 Northeast and Mid-Atlantic states aim to reduce power sector CO2 emissions by 10% below 2009 levels in 2019. Within this 10-year phase, there are three shorter compliance periods. During the first and second compliance periods (2009–2011 and 2012–2014) the cap on about 225 installations is set at 171 MtCO2e (or 188 M short ton CO2e). This is followed by a 2.5% per year decrease in cap during the third compliance period (2015–2018).

Reforestation: This process increases the capacity of the land to sequester carbon by replanting forest biomass in areas where forests have been previously harvested.

Registration: The formal acceptance by the CDM Executive Board of a validated project as a CDM project activity.

Removal unit (RMU): RMUs are issued by Parties to the Kyoto Protocol in respect of net removals by sinks from activities covered by Article 3(3) and Article 3(4) of the Kyoto Protocol.

Secondary transaction: A transaction where the seller is not the original owner (or issuer) of the carbon asset.

Supplementarity: Following the Marrakesh Accords, the use of the Kyoto mechanisms shall be supplemental to domestic action, which shall thus constitute a significant element of the effort made by each party to meet its commitment under the Kyoto Protocol. However, there is no quantitative limit to the utilization of such mechanisms. While assessing the NAPs, the European Commission considered that the use of CDM and JI credits could not exceed 50% of the effort by each member state to achieve its commitment. Supplementarity limits may thus affect the demand for some categories of offsets.

United Nations Framework Convention on Climate Change (UNFCCC): The international legal framework adopted in June 1992 at the Rio Earth Summit to address climate change. It commits the Parties to the UNFCCC to stabilize human-induced greenhouse gas emissions at levels that would prevent dangerous manmade interference with the climate system, following "common but differentiated responsibilities" based on "respective capabilities".

Validation: Validation is the process of independent evaluation of a project activity by a Designated Operational Entity (DOE) against the requirements of the CDM. The CDM requirements include the CDM modalities and procedures and subsequent decisions by the CMP and documents released by the CDM Executive Board.

Verified Emission Reductions (VERs): A unit of greenhouse gas emission reductions that has been verified by an independent auditor. Most often, this designates emission reductions units that are traded on the voluntary market.

Verification: Verification is the review and ex post determination by an independent third party of the monitored reductions in emissions generated by a registered CDM project, a determined JI project (or a project approved under another standard) during the verification period.

Voluntary market: The voluntary market caters for the needs of those entities that voluntarily decide to reduce their carbon footprint using offsets. The regulatory vacuum in some countries and the anticipation of imminent legislation on GHG emissions also motivate some pre-compliance activity.

Western Climate Initiative (WCI): The WCI covers a group of seven US states (Arizona, California, Montana, New Mexico, Oregon, Utah, and Washington) and four Canadian provinces (British Columbia, Manitoba, Ontario, and Quebec), with an aggregate emissions target of 15% below 2005 levels by 2020. Other US and Mexican states and Canadian provinces have joined as observers.

Source: Kossoy & Ambrosi (2010, pp. 71-75)

Appendix B Cap-and-Trade Policies

Table 7 Policy Overview (April 2009)

Venue	Current Status	Year Initiated	Operational Ever?	Gasses	Sectors	Regulatory Status
Australia	Design	2007	No	All Kyoto	Stationary energy; transport; fugitive; industrial processes; waste and forestry	Mandatory for some
BP	Inactive	1997	Yes	CO_2 and methane	Internal business units in four segments	Voluntary
California	Design	2005	No	All Kyoto	Electricity generation and large industrial facilities	Mandatory
Canada	Deliberation	1998	No	No data	Industry	No Data
CCX	Operational	2000	Yes	All Kyoto	Multiple	Voluntary (but binding)
Denmark	Inactive	1999	Yes	CO_2	Electricity generation	Mandatory
EU	Operational	1999	Yes	CO_2	Various (excludes electricity generation)	Mandatory
Florida	Deliberation	2007	No	All Kyoto	Electrical and possibly industrial stationary sources	Mandatory (prop being discussed)
Illinois	Inactive	2006	No	CO_2 and maybe others over time	Electricity generation units with a capacity of 25MW or higher, or emitting 25,000 metric tons of CO_2 annually at the start of the program. Other, smaller sources and gases would be included over time	No Data
Japan	Operational	2002	Yes	CO_2	Industrial (multiple sectors)	Voluntary
Korea	Design	2008	No	Discussions mostly on CO_2	Industry?	Mandatory/voluntary Debate
Kyoto Protocol	Design	1997	No	CO_2	Up to parties	Voluntary
Massachusetts	Inactive	2001	No	No data	No data	No Data
NAFTA-CEC	Deliberation	2001	No	No data	No data	No Data
NEG/ECP	Inactive	2001	No	No data	No data	No Data
New Mexico	Inactive	2005	No	No data	No data	No Data
New Zealand	Operational	2007	Yes	All Kyoto	Forestry, transport, energy, industry, agriculture, wastes	Mandatory for some
New Jersey	Inactive	1998	No	All Kyoto	Stationary and non-stationary sources (not differentiated by sector)	Voluntary

Table 7 Policy Overview (April 2009) (continued)

Venue	Current Status	Year Initiated	Operational Ever?	Gasses	Sectors	Regulatory Status
Norway	Inactive	1998	Yes	CO_2	Energy, mineral oil refining, iron/steel, cement, ceramic	Mandatory
NSW	Operational	1998	Yes	All Kyoto	Electricity retailers and large users	Mandatory
Oregon	Inactive	2004	No	No data	No data	No Data
PEMEX	Deliberation	2009	No	Unclear	PEMEX (oil), the Federal Electric Commission (power – in general) and cement makers, metals, chemicals and textiles are being considered as well	No Data
RGGI	Operational	2003	Yes	CO_2	Power	Mandatory
Shell	Inactive	1998	Yes	CO_2 and methane	Internal business units	Voluntary
Switzerland	Operational	2000	Yes	CO_2	Varied–businesses that want out of carbon tax	Voluntary (but binding once in)
UK	Inactive	1998	Yes	CO_2 or all Kyoto	Various (excludes electricity generation)	Voluntary (but binding)
US Congress	Deliberation	2003	No	No data	No data	No Data
WCI	Design	2004	No	All Kyoto	Economy-wide	Mandatory

Source: Betsill & Hoffmann (2009)

3. Sustainable Investing

Chapter Overview

3.1 Introduction

After discussions on financing the transition to sustainable energy (Chapter 1) and one of the primary public policy instruments to foster this transition, namely carbon trading (Chapter 2), this chapter focuses on sustainable investing. Sustainable investing is an investment approach that integrates long-term environmental, social, and governance (ESG) criteria into investment and ownership decision-making with the objective of generating superior risk-adjusted financial returns. These extra-financial criteria are used alongside traditional financial criteria such as cash flow and price-to-earnings ratios. Sustainable investing – as an investment approach – can be practised across all asset classes (e.g. equity and fixed-income investments in both listed and non-listed companies).

Section 3.2 explores the economic rationale for corporations to embed social, environmental and/or ethical factors into business strategies and operations. Section 3.3 explores the economic rationale for investors to include environmental, social, and governance factors in investment and ownership decision-making processes.

3.2 Sustainability and Value Creation – a Corporate Perspective

3.2.1 *Introduction*

The traditional definition of Corporate Social Responsibility (CSR) is linked to the idea that "business organizations have societal obligations which transcend economic functions of producing and distributing scarce goods and services and generating a satisfactory level of profits for their shareholders" (Epstein, 1989, p. 585). Nowadays, many companies embrace the concept of CSR not only from a responsibility perspective, but also from an economic (financial) perspective. Many corporations are convinced that by effectively integrating social, environmental, and/or ethical considerations into core business strategies and operations, they will be able to create more value for their stakeholders (e.g. customers, employees, local communities) while generating better risk-adjusted financial returns for their shareholders.

There is a myriad of definitions of CSR in both the academic literature and in practice.[1] This hinders the discussion of the link between CSR and corporate financial performance. In this book, the definition of Renneboog et al. (2007) is adopted, as it offers a helpful framework for categorizing the various (empirical) studies on the performance drivers and implications of CSR. Renneboog et al. (2007) define CSR as a combination of:

- Good corporate governance: protecting **shareholders**' interests;
- Environmental efficiency: protecting **environmental stakeholders**' interest; and
- Good stakeholder relations: protecting the interests of **stakeholders other** than shareholders and environmental stakeholders, including those of employees and the local community.

A fundamental question is whether there is a tradeoff between maximizing shareholder value and maximizing stakeholder value (Harold, Spitzer, & Emerson, 2007; Renneboog et al., 2007; Steger, 2004). One group of scholars – e.g., Friedman (1970) and Jensen (2002) – has argued that social responsibility detracts from a firm's financial performance: "[a]ny discretionary expenditures on social betterment unnecessarily raise a firm's costs, thereby putting it at an economic disadvantage in a competitive market" (Barnett & Salomon, 2006, p. 1102).

Another group of scholars has argued that a firm's social performance can enhance its ability to attract resources, obtain quality employees, market its products and services, and create unforeseen opportunities (Barnett & Salomon, 2006; Cochran & Wood, 1984; Crowther, 2000; Fombrun, Gardberg, & Barnett, 2000; Greening &

1. In addition, many different terms are being used for similar or affiliated concepts; for example, "corporate responsibility", "corporate sustainability", and "corporate citizenship". Although differences exist, all these concepts focus on addressing social, environmental, and/or ethical issues from a corporate perspective. Some companies address these issues mainly out of (longer-term) economic considerations, others mainly out of ethical considerations, and others out of both economic and ethical considerations.

Turban, 2000; Harold et al., 2007; Steger, 2004; Turban & Greening, 1997; Waddock & Graves, 1997).

According to the theory of Adam Smith (1776), both goals can be achieved without any conflicts of interest: in competitive and complete markets, when all firms maximize their own profits, the resource allocation is Pareto-optimal, and the social welfare is maximized. This would imply there is no trade-off between CSR and company performance. However, modern economic theory shows that with the existence of externalities, profit maximization does not necessarily imply social welfare maximization (Renneboog et al., 2007; Renneboog, Ter Horst, & Zhang, 2008b; Steger, 2004). The point of view by the authors directly challenging Friedman's approach – both on economic and ethical bases – seems to be gaining momentum (Harold et al., 2007). The focus of the remainder of this chapter is on economic/financial rather than ethical arguments for CSR.

3.2.2 *Measuring the Value of CSR*

A review of the academic literature on the business case for CSR reveals that it is very difficult to quantify the bottom-line impact of CSR activities. This has, for example, to do with the broad range of sustainability issues, the variation of relevant sustainability factors by industry, and due to measurement difficulties (of social and environmental factors). Steger (2004, p. 3), for example, concludes that "After about 450 interviews in 16 developed countries and a survey of over 1000 respondents, the bottom line [for CSR] is still not easy to draw [because] sustainability issues are extremely fragmented, uncertain, controversial and difficult to quantify".

To address the question regarding the business case for CSR, the finance literature mainly focuses on monetization of shareholder or stakeholder value.[2] This usually concerns either market prices (such as stock prices/returns) or other corporate finance ratios, such as return on equity or return on assets (Kim & Van Dam, 2003; Orlitzky, Schmidt, & Rynes, 2003; Peloza & Shang, 2010).[3]

Other, more indirect approaches exist as well. Godfrey et al. (2009), for instance, focus on the *preservation* of Corporate Financial Performance (CFP) through CSR rather than the *generation* of economic value. They argue that the goodwill or moral capital a firm builds up through CSR activities acts as 'insurance-like' protection (or

2. There are other perspectives to value CSR than just from a financial point of view. 'Doing things the right way' (or even altruism) might also provide value/utility to the individual company owner, manager or employee. However, this paper focuses on financial criteria.

3. UNEP (2006) mentions five valuation tools that have emerged in recent years: benchmarking, scenario analysis, proprietary valuation methodologies and case studies. They admit, however, that "further development [of valuation tools] is clearly desirable". Kim et al. (2003) suggest that the economic value and reputational value created by CSR should be measured using, respectively, Value-Based Management (VBM) and Economic Value Added (EVA) and the 'Reputation Quotient' (developed by the Reputation Institute).

value preservation) when negative events occur. Contrary to the economic value generation research angle, the insurance perspective is relatively underexposed, the authors note, in the current empirical literature.

Another approach is the 'customer/marketing outcome' of sustainability. CSR activities have been attributed to increased customer loyalty, a willingness to pay premium prices, a decreased blame attribution in the face of a product-harm or other crisis, and increased brand value (Creyer & Ross, 1996; Du, Bhattacharya, & Sen, 2007; Klein & Dawar, 2004; UNEP, 2006).[4] Barnett (2005) adopts a slightly wider perspective by arguing that the ability of CSR to create firm value lies in its ability to generate positive stakeholder relations (i.e., not just customer relations) for the firm.

3.2.3 *The Business Case for CSR*

The Value of Sustainable Companies

In general, the empirical literature concludes that CSR has the potential to enhance a company's financial performance (Godfrey et al., 2009; Hill, Ainscough, Shank, & Manullang, 2007; Renneboog et al., 2007, 2008b; Shank, Manullang, & Hill, 2005; UNEP, 2006).

Table 1 Environmental performance and company value

	Increase company value	Decrease company value
Direct **revenue** impact	- Green products and services that appeal to consumers	- Boycotts or decreased demand because of perception of negative environmental qualities
Indirect **revenue** impact	- Potential for regulatory advantage versus competitors - Improvement in employee morale and productivity	- Potential for regulatory disadvantage versus competitors
Direct **cost** impact	- Reduction in waste-disposal costs	- Commodity price variation
Indirect **cost** impact	- Decrease in staff turnover costs	- Higher insurance premiums - Legal fees - PR costs - Increase in costs due to long-term environmental change (e.g., climate)

Source: Adapted from Harold et al. (2007, p. 9)

4. Peloza & Shang (2010, pp. 9-11) provide an extensive overview of the empirical literature on the causality between CSR and marketing outcomes (generally customer-related).

In theory, the 'value drivers' that support the business case for CSR include operational efficiency opportunities, increased brand value and reputation, better risk management, attracting and retaining talented employees, and pre-empting regulatory intervention (Crowther, 2000; Steger, 2004). Harold et al. (2007) point out a similar theoretical linkage between environmental and financial performance (Table 1).

The empirical literature is diverse in its research angles. The remainder of this section is dedicated to studies on the empirical relationship between company value and CSR. Empirical findings are categorized according to the three 'pillars' of CSR that were introduced in section 3.2.1: (i) corporate governance (protecting shareholders' interests), (ii) environmental efficiency (protecting environmental stakeholders' interest), and (iii) stakeholder relations. Although diverse in its research questions and methodologies, the empirical literature generally points to a positive link between CSR and company performance.

Corporate Governance

The relationship between corporate governance, defined by Tirole (2001) as "the design of institutions that induce or force management to internalize the welfare of stakeholders", and the firm's subsequent value (e.g., measured by stock price or stock return) has been examined empirically by various authors.

Gompers et al. (2003) have shown a positive relation between effective corporate governance and stock returns. Based on a study of 1,500 companies, they conclude that by buying companies with the strongest shareholder rights and selling those with the weakest shareholder rights, an abnormal yearly return of 8.5% resulted in the 1990s.

Bauer et al. (2004) applied the same (GIM[5]) methodology to European companies and found that good corporate governance – they use the overall governance ratings from Deminor Corporate Governance Ratings, which are the aggregates of 300 criteria covering shareholder rights, takeover defense, information disclosure and board structure – leads to higher stock returns and higher firm value.

From their empirical analysis Godfrey et al. (2009) conclude that participation in *institutional* CSR activities (ICSRs), aimed at a firm's secondary stakeholders[6] or society at large, provides an 'insurance-like' benefit and thus creates value for shareholders. They focus on the preservation of a company's value through insurance-like protection (see also Section 3.2.2).

5. The *GIM methodology* refers to the empirical analysis by Gompers, Ishii and Metrick (2003).
6. *Primary* stakeholders make legitimate claims on the firm and its managers and have both urgency and power (utilitarian, coercive, or normative) to enforce those claims. *Secondary* stakeholders have legitimate claims on the firm, but lack both urgency and power to enforce those claims (Mitchell, Agle, & Wood, 1997).

Other studies pointing at a positive relation between corporate governance and a firm's value include La Porta et al. (2002) and Cremers & Nair (2005).

Environment

A growing body of empirical literature reports a positive relation between corporate environmental performance and firm value (Renneboog et al., 2007, 2008b).

Klassen & McLaughlin (1996) find statistically significant, positive, abnormal returns after a firm receives environmental performance awards, and significant negative returns after an environmental crisis. Dowell et al. (2000) find that US-based multinational enterprises adopting a stringent global environmental standard have much higher market values than firms with less stringent standards. Konar & Cohen (2001) conclude that poor environmental performance is negatively correlated with the intangible asset value.

Hamilton (1995) documented a statistically significant negative impact of the announcements of the release of information on the use of toxic chemicals on stock prices in the US. Ten years later, Gupta & Goldar (2005) studied the impact of public disclosure of environmental performance on the financial performance of firms, i.e. the impact of environmental rating of large pulp and paper, auto, and chlor-alkali firms in India on their stock prices. They also found that the market generally penalizes environmentally unfriendly behavior: the announcement of weak environmental performance by firms leads to negative abnormal returns of up to 30%.[7]

Halkos & Sepetis (2007) show that improved environmental management systems and environmental performance result in reductions in the firms' beta.[8] Firms making reference to their environmental policy in their annual financial reports and firms publishing an annual social report note a beta reduction in the period 2001-2004 compared to the period 1998-2001.

Nakao et al. (2007) claim that Japanese firm data show a two-way positive interaction between environmental performance and financial performance: a firm's environmental performance has a positive impact on its financial performance and vice versa. They used five years' worth of financial data from approximately 300 listed firms as well as the results of the Nikkei environmental management surveys.[9]

---

7. See Guenster et al. (2010) for a similar study.

8. The *beta* is a measure of the volatility of a firm's stock compared to the overall market (the market's beta is 1). The higher a firm's beta, the greater its systematic risk (Halkos & Sepetis, 2007).

9. Previous, somewhat dated studies finding similar relationships between financial and environmental performance include Annandale et al. (2001) and Dasgupta et al. (2002).

Stakeholder Relations

Empirical studies on the relationship between corporate performance and corporate stakeholder relations are scarce. Hillmann & Keim (2001) show that management focusing on *stakeholder value* (improving the relationships with primary stakeholders like employees, customers, suppliers and communities) also creates shareholder value, while *social issue participation* (e.g., a ban on nuclear energy and avoidance of 'sin' industries) often destroys shareholder value. Goergen & Renneboog (2002) analysed the relationship between control concentration (e.g., the existence of a major shareholder) and CSR (stakeholder management and social issue participation) but failed to find statistically significant results.

Implications for Investment and Investors

The cost of capital for any company is related to the perceived risk associated with investing in that company. This implies a direct correlation between the risk involved in an investment and the rewards which are expected to accrue from a successful investment. Companies with positive environmental records are rewarded with a lower cost of capital (at least in theory), since they are less risky for investors (Harold et al., 2007). Some empirical evidence has been found that the sustainability a firm demonstrates indeed influences its creditworthiness as part of its financial performance (Weber, Scholz, & Michalik, 2010).

Some authors also suggest that CSR is sometimes used to 'mislead' investors. Aras & Crowther (2009, p. 279) argue that the future effects of corporate activity upon its external environment can be obscured/clouded by environmental statements (e.g., an annual sustainability report) so that "the cost of capital for the firm is reduced as investors are misled into thinking that the level of risk involved in their investment is lower than it actually is". This obfuscation could be fuelled by a lack of a full understanding of what is meant by 'sustainability' and the fact that risk evaluation methodologies are often deficient in their evaluation of environmental risk (Aras & Crowther, 2009).

CSR and sustainable investing are closely related. As demonstrated in this section, CSR influences the corporate financial performance and thereby the company's intrinsic value. This is relevant information for investors as most of them aim to maximize risk-adjusted financial returns. Sustainable investing – as an investment approach – is discussed in section 3.3.

3.2.4 *Reporting Requirements*

CSR can also be driven (or 'imposed') by reporting requirements, either on a regulatory or voluntary basis. CSR-related legislation, however, is not widespread. In fact, Renneboog et al. (2008b, p. 1728) mention that "France is the first and so far the only country making social, environmental and ethical reporting mandatory for all listed companies". Since 2009, Denmark has been added to this short list.[10] Similarly, the Swedish government decided to make sustainability reporting statutory for all public companies. This law took effect on January 1, 2009 (Nilsson & Nilsson, 2010).

The reason for the lack of CSR regulation could lie in the general consideration that "CSR initiatives are voluntary and go beyond what is required by law" (van Dijken, 2007, p. 142), although whether self-regulation is sufficient to guarantee CSR is still a matter of debate.[11]

An important recent development that holds great promise to further drive CSR and sustainable business practices is the move towards integrated reporting (financial & sustainability). Traditionally, listed companies only/mainly publish their financial results (in their annual reports and quarterly statements). Since the 1990s, an increasing number of companies have started to publish CSR or sustainability reports as well. Integrated reporting aims to integrate financial and sustainability reporting. It refers to the integrated representation of a company's performance in terms of both financial and sustainability (environmental, social, governance) results. It provides a greater context for performance data, clarifies how sustainability fits into the operations of a business, and may help embed sustainability into company decision-making.

In August 2010 two of the leading initiatives to promote integrated reporting – Accounting for Sustainability (A4S) and the Global Reporting Initiative (GRI) – joined forces to launch the International Integrated Reporting Committee (integratedreporting.org). Its remit is to: "create a globally accepted framework for accounting for sustainability: a framework which brings together financial, environmental, social and governance information in a clear, concise, consistent and comparable format … The intention is to help with the development of more comprehensive and comprehensible information about an organization's total performance, prospective as well as retrospective, to meet the needs of the emerging, more sustainable, global economic model".

Integrated reporting[12] is likely to raise the profile of environmental, social, and governance (ESG) issues for investor relations and for investors, and it arms corporate executives with the information to communicate on ESG issues and their impact on the business.

10. See the website of the Danish Government Centre for CSR: www.csrgov.dk. CSR is not obligatory as such, but if a company has no policy, it must state its positioning on CSR in their annual financial report. This is similar to the comply-or-explain axiom underlying several corporate governance codes, *inter alia* the 'Tabaksblat Code' in The Netherlands (Akkermans et al., 2007).

11. For further discussion, see for instance UNRISD (Utting, 2004).

12. An interesting and comprehensive book on the topic of integrated reporting is Eccles & Krzus (2010).

3.2.5 *Conclusion*

In this section, a large variety of empirical studies and different financial aspects of CSR has been discussed. Most empirical research indicates that CSR has the potential to lead to better corporate financial performance. Additional research might be useful to explore how best to integrate CSR/sustainability considerations into core business strategies and operations.

Clearly, given the broad range of sustainability issues and differences between industries, companies that aim to optimize their corporate financial performance need to carefully assess which sustainability factors are financially most relevant to their business.

3.3 Sustainability and Value Creation – an Investor's Perspective

3.3.1 *Introduction*

There are many definitions in both the academic literature and business world of sustainable investing. In this book, a definition of a World Economic Forum report (2011)[13] on accelerating the transition towards sustainable investing is adopted. Sustainable investing is defined as an investment approach that integrates long-term environmental, social, and governance (ESG) criteria into investment and ownership decision-making with the objective of generating superior risk-adjusted financial returns. These extra-financial criteria are used alongside traditional financial criteria such as cash flow and price-to-earnings ratios.

The focus on superior risk-adjusted financial returns distinguishes sustainable investing from similar-sounding approaches such as "impact investing" or "ethical investing", in which lower financial returns may be accepted as a trade-off for meeting social or environmental goals. As defined in this book, sustainable investing is therefore consistent with the fiduciary duty of many institutional investors to maximize risk-adjusted financial returns.

An overview of some key definitions is provided below.

Table 2 Definition of some key investment approaches (as used in this book)

Investment approach	Definition
Sustainable investing	Investment approach that integrates long-term environmental, social, and governance (ESG) criteria into investment and ownership decision-making with the objective of generating superior risk-adjusted financial returns. These extra-financial criteria are used alongside traditional financial criteria such as cash flow and price-to-earnings ratios.
Responsible investing	Investment approach that integrates consideration of environmental, social and governance (ESG) issues into investment decision-making and ownership practices, and thereby improving long-term returns to beneficiaries. NB: This definition is derived from the UN-backed Principles for Responsible Investment. Please note that, in this book, the terms "sustainable investing" and "responsible investing" are used as synonyms.
Ethical investing	An investment philosophy guided by moral values, ethical codes or religious beliefs. Investment decisions include non-economic criteria. This practice has traditionally been associated with negative screening.
Impact investing	Investment approach that aims to proactively create positive social and environmental impact against an acceptable risk-adjusted financial return. This requires the management of social and environmental performance (in addition to financial risk and return). With impact investing, "impact" comes first, whereas with sustainable investing, "financial returns" come first.

13. One of the authors of this book, B.J. Sikken, is lead author of this World Economic Forum report.

Table 2 Definition of some key investment approaches (as used in this book)

Investment approach	Definition
SRI[14]	Generic term covering ethical investments, responsible investments, sustainable investments, and any other investment process that combines investors' financial objectives with their concerns about environmental, social and governance (ESG) issues.

Source: Adapted from Eurosif (2010), J.P. Morgan (2010), Mercer (2007), PRI (2011), World Economic Forum (2011)

In this book, SRI is considered the umbrella term for sustainable investing, responsible investing, ethical investing, and impact investing. This section especially focuses on the concept of sustainable investing and thus less on the other investment approaches[15]. The main reason is that many institutional investors have a fiduciary duty to maximize risk-adjusted financial returns. Therefore, like in section 3.2 on CSR, the main focus in this section is on the financial motives for embedding sustainability considerations into key decisions.

3.3.2 *Key Drivers of Sustainable Investing*

According to a 2010 Eurosif survey, the four main drivers for SRI[16] in the next three years will be:

1. Demand from institutional Investors
Many large asset owners and asset managers embrace the concept of sustainable investing. Although motivations vary, they typically include: improving risk-adjusted financial returns, demonstrating social responsibility, and helping safeguard the integrity of financial markets.

Many large institutional investors are also interested in sustainable investing from a universal ownership perspective. The universal owner hypothesis states that although a large long-term investor with a diverse investment portfolio can initially benefit from an investee company externalizing costs, the investor might ultimately experience a reduction in market and portfolio returns due to these externalities adversely affecting returns from other assets (Hawley & Williams, 2000). Universal owners therefore have an incentive to reduce negative externalities (e.g. pollution and cor-

14. Traditionally, the term "SRI" means "Socially Responsible Invesment". Eurosif (the European Sustainable Investment Forum; a pan-European network and think-tank whose mission is to develop sustainability through European financial markets) also uses the term "SRI" but has changed its direct meaning to "Sustainable and Responsible Investment" as an acronym encompassing all the subsets discussed above.

15. In this book, some broader SRI studies are discussed as well as – especially in older academic studies – in which the distinction between the various investment approaches (e.g. sustainable vs ethical investing) was made less clear.

16. Please note the focus on the broader concept of SRI, as opposed to just sustainable investing.

ruption) and increase positive externalities (e.g. sound corporate governance and human capital practices) across their investment portfolios (Thamotheram & Wildsmith, 2007).

2. *The uptake of voluntary initiatives such as the PRI*
In the past few years, several multistakeholder initiatives have emerged to help drive the transition towards sustainable investing. Examples include: the UN Principles for Responsible Investment (PRI), the Global Reporting Initiative (GRI), the Prince of Wales' Accounting for Sustainability Project, and the Carbon Disclosure Project. The PRI especially has raised awareness among large institutional investors: at the end of 2010 more than 850 investors had signed the Principles, representing approximately US$25 trillion in assets under management.

3. *External pressures (NGOs, media, unions)*
In a media age, investors are increasingly aware of their potential exposure when companies are implicated in environmental or social controversies.

4. *Demand from retail investors*
According to the Eurosif 2010 survey, demand from retail investors has increased significantly in a number of European countries – notably Germany, France and Belgium – in the past few years. Eurosif expects this trend to continue and also believes that demand from high net worth individuals (HNWIs) will expand significantly. At the end of 2009, approximately 11% of European HNWIs' portfolios represented SRI investments[17]; this is expected to increase to 15% in 2013.

The World Economic Forum report (2011) also mentions as key drivers: a *growing awareness* within the investment community that global mega trends such as demographic changes, climate change, and natural resource scarcity are becoming increasingly financially material[18], the growing momentum of *legislative initiatives* in many Western countries[19], and the *global financial crisis* that has increased the interest of investors in ESG factors.

Finally, another reason for incorporating sustainability information into investment decision-making processes is that it provides more information about a company, information that can be salient. For example, sound social and environmental performance might signal high managerial quality, which translates into favourable finan-

17. Ibid.

18. A recent study from UNEP FI and the PRI concludes that "environmental costs are becoming increasingly financially material. Annual environmental costs from global human activity amounted to US$6.6 trillion in 2008, equivalent to 11% of GDP." Source: UNEP FI, PRI,. (2010). *Universal Ownership – Why environmental externalities matter to institutional investors.*

19. Table 5 in Appendix A provides an overview of regulatory initiatives for investors to disclose environmental, social, and ethical factors and/or considerations.

cial performance (Renneboog, Ter Horst, & Zhang, 2008a; Renneboog et al., 2008b).[20].

3.3.3 *The Market Size and Growth of Sustainable Investing*

Eurosif (2010) estimates the global market for "sustainable and responsible investment" to be around 7 trillion euros (in 2009), of which Europe accounts for roughly 5 trillion. In Europe, for which the most recent figures are available, the market is estimated to have almost doubled between 2008 and 2010.

As the World Economic Forum (2011) report indicates, "these estimates should be taken cautiously, for two reasons. Firstly, the Eurosif figures cover not only sustainable investing, but also impact investing and ethical investing. Secondly, these figures are based on self-disclosure by asset managers; it is possible that the growing profile of sustainable investing may provide an incentive to overstate the reality of ESG integration. Nonetheless, while the numbers may be disputed, what can be said for certain is that – despite the financial crisis – the uptake of sustainable investing is continuing and looks set to deepen and widen."

Eurosif (2010) believes that the market for sustainable investing is "reaching a tipping point", but that accelerating this process will "require activity and commitment from major asset owners, governments and civil society".

3.3.4 *Sustainable Investing and Investment Performance*

In analyzing the performance of sustainable investment funds, it is important to keep the clear distinction with other more values-based investment approaches such as ethical investing in mind. As indicated in table 2, sustainable investing aims to maximize risk-adjusted financial returns, whereas ethical investing aims to apply specific ethical criteria to investment decisions. SRI, as defined in this book, is an umbrella term for investment processes that combine investors' financial objectives with their concerns about environmental, social and governance (ESG) issues (and thus encompasses sustainable investing, ethical investing, and impact investing).

Underlying Theory

Renneboog et al. (2007) suggest that there are three hypotheses regarding the relationship between SRI[21] screening and SRI fund performance:

1. SRI funds underperform compared to conventional funds;
2. SRI funds outperform conventional funds;

---

20. Renneboog et al. (2008a; 2008b) consider this signalling function as an argument for their 'outperforming SRI hypothesis'.

21. Please note the broader focus on SRI as opposed to sustainable investing. Still, many conclusions from the study of Renneboog apply to the narrower concept of sustainable investing as well.

3. SRI portfolios have different risk exposures than conventional funds.

The first two hypotheses are about risk-adjusted returns (sometimes referred to as 'alphas'), while the last hypothesis is about the risk exposures ('betas') of SRI portfolios.

The first hypothesis states that negative SRI screens imply a constraint on the investment universe (the exclusion of 'sin stocks') and therefore impose a limit on diversification possibilities. According to this hypothesis SRI funds should underperform conventional funds.

The first hypothesis correlates with the efficiency of optimizing risks and returns, i.e., whether it is possible to exclude or include stocks without loss of efficiency. Geczy et al. (2005, p. 3) argue that SRI constraints[22] can impose diversification costs, "in the sense that the constrained investors are less able to balance optimally their portfolios' exposures to factor-related risks and to eliminate risks that, on average, investors are not compensated to bear". They conclude that SRI constraints impose large costs on investors who rely heavily on individual funds' track records to predict future performance. See also Barnett et al. (2006), Bello (2005), Galema et al. (2008), Hoepner et al. (2009) and Renneboog et al. (2007; 2008b) for further reading on the diversification costs of investing in SRI funds.

The second hypothesis is that SRI portfolios outperform their conventional peers as information on corporate governance and environmental performance is underpriced by the stock markets: SRI screening generates value-relevant non-public information that helps fund managers to select securities and consequently generate better risk-adjusted returns than conventional mutual funds.

The second hypothesis thus implies that the screening process for SRI funds generates information which is normally not available for investors. This extra information can result in a better selection and hence generate better risk-adjusted returns. The underlying arguments are that sound social and environmental performance indicates good managerial quality which results in a higher financial performance. Also, screening based on social and environmental criteria reduces the potential costs during corporate social crises or environmental disasters (Renneboog et al., 2008b).

A key assumption underlying the 2nd hypothesis is that conventional portfolio managers do not use all value-relevant information, which is at odds with the market efficiency theory: some claim that, since SRI portfolios are based on public information such as CSR issues, they cannot generate a better return than 'normal' funds (Barnett & Salomon, 2006; Bollen, 2007; Halkos & Sepetis, 2007; Harold et al., 2007; Renneboog et al., 2008a, 2008b; Soppe, 2004). This *Efficient Market Hypothesis* (EMH) refers to "a market where, given the available information, actual prices at

22. In the sense of negative screens,

every point in time represent very good estimates of intrinsic values" (Fama, 1970, p. 90).[23]

The third hypothesis claims that SRI portfolios have different risk exposures and therefore different expected returns than conventional portfolios. For example, companies with sound environmental performance may have a lower book-to-market ratio than companies with poor environmental performance, which results in SRI portfolios having a lower risk exposure to the book-to-market factor in the *Fama-French Pricing Model* than a conventional portfolio (Dowell et al., 2000).[24]

Meta-Studies on the Relationship between ESG Factors and Investment Performance

In order to answer the question of to what extent does the inclusion of ESG factors into investment and ownership decision-making processes lead to better risk-adjusted investment returns, it is useful to explore meta-studies. Meta-studies compare the results of many individual studies in a specific domain. They provide an overarching view, and the conclusions are thus less dependent on the specific methodologies or time series used.

In this section, three meta-studies on the performance of SRI funds are presented:

1. Renneboog, L., Ter Horst, J., & Zhang, C. (2008b). Socially responsible investments: Institutional aspects, performance, and investor behavior. *Journal of Banking & Finance*, 32(9), 1723-1742.
2. Mercer, UNEP Finance Initiative. (2007). Demystifying Responsible Investment Performance
3. Mercer. (2009). Shedding light on responsible investment: Approaches, returns and impacts

It is important to note that, until 2 to 3 years ago, empirical research on the (relative) performance of SRI funds was dominated by mutual fund studies that measure the performance of a SRI portfolio using a single index model and/or compare the performance of SRI funds with that of a reference group identified by a matched-pair analysis, in which SRI funds are matched to conventional mutual funds with similar investment objectives and fund sizes (Renneboog et al., 2007, p. 25, 2008b, p. 1739).

---

23. Usually a taxonomy of three EMHs are distinguished (Fama, 1991): the *weak* form of efficiency (the information set includes only the history of prices), the *semi-strong* form of efficiency (the information set includes all information known to all market participants; i.e., all publicly available information) and the *strong* form of efficiency (the information set includes all information known to any market participant, including private information).

24. The Fama-French *pricing* (or *three-factor*) *model* (1993) evaluates fund performance. It consists of the capital asset pricing model (CAPM) plus two additional factors: the market capitalization factor (SMB) and the book-to-market factor (HML).

Most of these mutual fund studies are unable to conclude that SRI underperform or outperform conventional funds, as most research brings forward statistically insignificant results (Benson, Brailsford, & Humphrey, 2006; Benson & Humphrey, 2008; Harold et al., 2007; Mulder, 2007; Plinke, 2008; Renneboog et al., 2007, 2008b). This conclusion can also be drawn from the meta-study by Renneboog et al. (2008b) on the performance of SRI funds/portfolios.[25] Table 3 provides an overview of the results of this study.

Table 3 Overview of SRI performance studies (sorted by publication date)[26]

Study	Country	Outcome	Comments
Luther et al. (1992)	UK	NSD	The Jensen's alphas of ethical funds have a mean of 0.03% per month (**not significantly different from 0**). Ethical funds have relatively high portfolio weights on small-cap companies.
Luther & Matatko (1994)	UK	NSD	The Jensen's alphas of ethical funds are measured against the FT. All share index or against a small-cap index. R-squared is higher in the first regression than the second one, which implies that the SRI portfolio is biased towards small-caps. The average alphas measured both ways are **not significantly different from zero**.
Hamilton et al. (1993)	US	NSD	For 17 SRI funds established before 1985, the average alpha is 0.06% per month, which is higher than the average monthly alpha (0.14%) of 170 non-SRI funds (the **difference is not significant**). Meanwhile for the 15 SRI funds with a shorter history, i.e. established after 1985, the average alpha is 0.28% per month, which is worse than the average monthly alpha (0.04%) of the corresponding 150 non-SRI funds.
Mallin et al. (1995)	UK	NSD	The monthly alphas of ethical funds range from 0.28% to 1.21%, while 22 out of the 29 alphas are positive. Alphas of non-ethical funds, 23 of which are positive, range from 0.41% to 1.56% per month (difference is **not statistically different**).
Gregory et al. (1997)	UK	Mixed	The alphas of ethical funds range from 0.71% to 0.24% per month (almost all are not significant). In a regression with both ethical and non-ethical funds, the ethical fund dummy does not have a significant impact on fund performance after controlling for fund age, size, and the market risk. Most of the ethical funds have a significant exposure to the small-cap factor.

25. Although not explicitly defined, it seems the study applies the broader, SRI-based, definition as selection criterion.

26. The quality of financial data used in SRI studies is subject to some debate. This is a research area in its own right, and first and foremost the expertise of methodologists. Therefore, it is beyond the scope of this paper. A good starting point for further reading on the subject of date quality is Chatterji & Levine (2005) and Hoepner & McMillan (2009).

Study	Country	Outcome	Comments
Goldreyer et al. (1999)	US	NSD	The average Jensen's alpha of 29 SRI equity funds is 0.49% per annum, whereas that of 20 non-SRI equity funds is 2.78%. The **difference is not significant**. SRI funds using positive screens outperform the SRI funds that do not (the average monthly alphas are 0.11% and 0.81%, respectively, and the difference between them is statistically significant).
Statman (2000)	US	NSD	The average monthly alpha is 0.42% for SRI funds and 0.62% for non-SRI funds; the **difference is not significant** (t-statistics = 1.84). The DSI 400 index has a higher Sharpe ratio than the S&P 500 index (0.97 vs. 0.92).
Schroder (2004)	Germany, Switzerland, and US	NSD	The monthly alphas range from 2.06% to 0.87%. Of the 46 alphas 38 are negative; only 4 of them are significant at the 0.05 level. SRI funds **do not significantly underperform** the benchmark portfolio consisting of both large stocks and small stocks. Note that 11 of the 16 German and Swiss funds have higher exposures to the small-cap index than to the large-cap index. Only 5 of the 46 funds have positive timing ability, while 7 fund managers time the market in the wrong direction.
Kreander et al. (2005)	Europe	NSD	The average Jensen's alphas of SRI and non-SRI funds are 0.20% and 0.12% per month, respectively (difference is **statistically insignificant**). In addition, the market timing coefficients are similar for the two types of funds (0.29 vs. 0.28), and each of them is significant at the 95% level. However, the signs of the timing coefficients are negative, which implies that both SRI and non-SRI fund managers time the market in the wrong direction.
Bauer et al. (2005)	Germany, UK, and US	US: mixed UK: OP DE: mixed	Ethical funds have a smaller size and higher expense ratio than conventional funds. The average monthly alphas of SRI funds are 0.29%, 0.09% and 0.05% for Germany, UK domestic and US domestic funds, respectively. The **US domestic ethical funds significantly underperform** conventional domestic funds, while for **US international funds** the difference in returns between ethical and conventional funds is **insignificant**. The **UK ethical funds**, both domestic and international, **significantly outperform** conventional funds. The difference in average alphas between **German** SRI and non-SRI funds is **insignificant**. Overall, there is little evidence of **significant differences in risk-adjusted returns** between SRI and non-SRI funds For German and US ethical funds: after significant underperformance in the early 1990s, they match conventional fund performance over 1998-2001. Older ethical funds (launched before 1998) outperform younger ethical funds. German and UK ethical funds are heavily exposed to small-cap stocks while US funds are less so. All SRI funds are more growth- than value-oriented.

Study	Country	Outcome	Comments
Renneboog et al. (2005)	Worldwide		Ethical money chases past returns. In contrast to conventional funds' investors, SRI investors care less about the funds' risks and fees. Funds characterized by shareholder activism and by in-house SRI research attract more stable investors. Membership of a large SRI fund family creates higher flow volatility due to the lower fees to reallocate money within the fund family. SRI funds receiving most of the money -inflows perform worse in the future, which is consistent with theories of decreasing returns to scale in the mutual fund industry. Finally, the money -flows and the flow -past performance relationship crucially depend on the types and intensities of SRI screening activities
Geczy et al. (2005)	US	NSD	The average expense ratio of SRI funds is higher than that of non-SRI funds (1.33% vs. 1.10%), whereas the average annual turnover of SRI funds is much lower than that of non-SRI funds (81.5% vs. 175.4%). The SRI funds have a much smaller size than non-SRI funds: the average asset under management (across time and across funds) is $149 million and $257 million, respectively. The monthly alpha of the SRI portfolio is higher than that of the non-SRI portfolio (0.21% vs. 0.08%), but the **difference is insignificant**. Meanwhile, the risk exposure of the SRI portfolio to the size factor (SMB factor) is higher than that of the non-SRI portfolio (0.20 vs. 0.16). To a market index investor the financial cost of the SRI constraint is 5 basis points per month. The SRI constraint imposes large costs, more than 1.5% per month, on investors whose beliefs allow selection skill. Moreover, further restricting the SRI universe to the funds that screen out "sin" stocks (e.g. alcohol, tobacco or gambling) increases the monthly cost of the SRI constraint by 10 basis points or more.
Bauer et al. (2006)	Australia	NSD	Domestic ethical funds underperform domestic conventional funds by 1.56% per year. International ethical funds outperform their conventional peers by 3.31% per year. **None of these differences are significant**.
Bauer et al. (2007)	Canada	NSD	The difference in average alphas is **insignificant** between the SRI funds and non-SRI funds (0.21% vs. 0.18% per month).
Barnett & Salomon (2006)	US		When the number of social screens used by an SRI fund increases, the fund's annual return declines at first, but rebounds as the number of screens reaches a maximum.

Study	Country	Outcome	Comments
Renneboog et al. (submitted for publication)	Worldwide	UP	Consistent with investors paying a price for ethics, SRI funds in many European and Asia-Pacific countries strongly underperform domestic benchmark portfolios. For instance, the risk-adjusted returns of the average SRI funds in Belgium, France, Ireland, Japan, Norway, Singapore, and Sweden are on average less than 5% per annum. SRI investors are unable to identify the funds that will outperform in the future, whereas they show some fund-selection ability in identifying ethical funds that will perform poorly in the future. Finally, the screening activities of SRI funds have a significant impact on the funds' risk-adjusted returns and loadings on risk factors.

NSD = Differences between funds are not statistically different
OP = SRI-fund outperformed conventional fund
UP = SRI-fund underperformed conventional fund
Source: Adapted from Renneboog et al. (2008b)

Plinke (2008) offers a similar synopsis. This can be found in Table 6 of the appendix to this chapter.

Two other meta-studies on the relationship between ESG factors and investment performance have been conducted by Mercer (Mercer, UNEP Finance Initiative, 2007; Mercer, 2009) and offer a more positive view on the relationship.[27] Considering these two reports together, a total of 36 studies examining the link between ESG factors and investment performance have been reviewed. Of these, twenty show evidence of a positive relationship between ESG factors and financial performance, and only three show evidence of a fully negative relationship.

Table 4 Outcome of two meta-studies conducted by Mercer on the link between ESG factors and investment performance

	2009 Mercer study	2007 Mercer / UNEP FI study	Total
Studies showing positive impact	10	10	20
Studies showing neutral to positive impact	0	2	2
Studies showing neutral impact	4	4	8
Studies showing neutral to negative impact	2	1	3
Studies showing negative impact	0	3	3

Source: Mercer, 2009; Mercer & UNEP FI, 2007

27. Here, the focus seems to be more on sustainable investing (as defined in this book), instead of the broader definition of SRI, Still, challenges to explicitly differentiate between investment funds in terms of underlying goals remain. Some studies analyzed as part of the Renneboog meta-study are also included in the meta-studies by Mercer.

Mercer indicates that the academic studies' results vary in part due to differing research methods and sample periods. Variations also exist due to a focus on different ESG inclusion approaches like screening, ESG integration, and engagement.

Multifactor Models

In recent years, a series of authors have focused on the marginal effect of ESG-related variables, thereby trying to disentangle the effect of ESG screens from other portfolio management decisions. This latter wave of studies uses multifactor models, which are more sophisticated econometric models than the single factor mutual fund studies discussed in the previous section, in order to incorporate non-quantifiable fund aspects. A detailed discussion of underlying econometric methodologies is beyond the scope of this review. Of relevance here is that these studies – compared to single factor mutual funds studies – generally reach a more positive verdict on the question of whether SRI funds outperform conventional funds.

The primary advantage of multifactor models is that they control for non-quantifiable aspects such as momentum effects, management skill and mutual fund style (Bauer et al., 2005, p. 1765; Derwall, Guenster, Bauer, & Koedijk, 2005, p. 52; Kempf & Osthoff, 2007, p. 913, 2008; Renneboog et al., 2007, p. 25). Bauer et al. (2007, p. 112) argue that "not using a multifactor model to evaluate ethical funds can lead to an erroneous assessment of mutual fund performance [since without] multifactor models, we cannot separate returns associated with social investment policies from the returns on common investment styles that do not incorporate those policies".

Derwall et al. (2005), for instance, measure the performance of portfolios that are selected by means of positive screening (based on environmental performance criteria).[28] Portfolios comprising shares with a positive sustainability rating outperform a portfolio with companies with low environmental scores by 6% per annum, over the period 1997-2003. The authors conclude that financial institutions can improve their profitability by taking into account the environmental information of a portfolio.

Kempf et al. (2007) perform a similar portfolio analysis, comparing 10% of companies with the best CSR ratings with 10% of companies with the worst CSR ratings, using a 4-factor financial model and socially responsible ratings from KLD Research & Analytics. A strategy of buying stocks with high socially responsible ratings and selling stocks with low socially responsible ratings leads to high abnormal returns of up to 8.7% per year. In other words, portfolios with a negative sustainability rating produced a weaker performance than portfolios with a positive sustainability rating, even after taking into account reasonable transaction costs.

---

28. They compare 30% of US companies with the best CSR ratings with 30% of companies with the worst CSR ratings, using Innovest ratings.

Edmans (2010) analyzes the relationship between employee satisfaction and long-run stock returns. He finds that a portfolio of the "100 Best Companies to Work for in America" (companies with a good working environment) exhibits significantly higher returns than the (adjusted) market portfolio.[29] This leads him to conclude that the stock market does not fully value intangibles, and that certain ESG screens may improve investment returns.

Conclusion on Investment Performance

Despite the differences between the various studies, and the fact that not all single-factor studies show significant results, what can be concluded is that there is considerable empirical evidence that indicates that by including environmental, social, and governance information in investment and ownership decision-making processes, there is at least the potential to generate a better risk-adjusted financial return.

3.3.5 *Accelerating the Transition towards Sustainable Investing*

Given the upside potential of sustainable investing (in terms of risk-adjusted financial returns for investors and in terms of promoting more sustainable business practices), it is interesting to explore what are the major pathways for investors, corporations and other key stakeholders in the investment value chain to accelerate the transition towards sustainable investing.

The World Economic Forum (2011) highlights some of the key barriers that currently inhibit the transition towards sustainable investing as a mainstream investment approach:

- Key barriers for investors include: restrictions in conventional valuation models, lack of ESG expertise, lack of awareness and/or scepticism regarding the investment case
- Key barriers for corporations include: insufficient integration of sustainability factors into core business strategies, lack of a formal approach in setting ESG targets and holding senior staff accountable
- Key barriers for investor-corporation interaction include: lack of clarity on which ESG factors are financially material and over which time frame, insufficient communication of link between ESG and corporate financial performance
- Key barriers at system-wide level include: disproportionate focus on short-term performance and issues with a near-term impact, and the fact that many negative externalities are underpriced.

The World Economic Forum report also describes some key strategic options for investors, corporations and other key stakeholder to accelerate the transition towards sustainable investing. The report highlights four broad action areas:

29. The portfolio comprising companies with a good working environment earned an annual alpha of 3.5% from 1984-2009, and 2.1% above industry benchmarks.

1. Improve information: Make sure that financially material ESG information is widely shared between corporations and investors, and that ESG and financial information are communicated in an integrated way.
2. Strengthen competencies: Make sure that both investors and corporate executives have the skill set to assess ESG factors from an economic value creation perspective.
3. Modify incentives: Link incentives in the investment value chain more to long-term, risk-adjusted financial performance. (The authors note that "this doesn't imply that all incentives in the financial system need to be long-term oriented. We recognize there is also a need for investing that is short-term in horizons and/or holding periods".)
4. Enhance governance: Strengthen the governance relationship between corporations' owners – that is, shareholders – and management teams. This relationship is two-way and based on a mutual interest in optimizing shareholder value creation over the long run.

An overview of more detailed ideas (by action area and key stakeholder) is provided in table 5 (on the next two pages).

3.3.6 *Conclusion*

As indicated at the beginning of Section 3.3, SRI is a generic term for investment approaches that incorporate environmental, social and governance (ESG) issues into fund management. It covers ethical investments, responsible investments, sustainable investments, and any other investment process that combines investors' financial objectives with their concerns about environmental, social and governance (ESG) issues.

This section especially focused on the concept of sustainable investing: an investment approach that integrates long-term environmental, social, and governance (ESG) criteria into investment and ownership decision-making with the objective of generating superior risk-adjusted financial returns.[30]

Empirical evidence indicates that by including environmental, social, and governance information into investment and ownership-decision making processes, there is at least the potential to generate a better risk-adjusted financial return.

Additional research is needed, for example, on determining the financial materiality of ESG factors per industry. Other areas for further research include: the impact of CSR on the cost of capital, and how to best integrate ESG factors into investment decisions (both equity and fixed-income investing).

---

30. An important reason for this specific focus is that many institutional investors have a fiduciary duty to maximize risk-adjusted financial returns.

Table 5 Ideas to accelerate the transition towards sustainable investing (by action area and stakeholder)

Key Stakeholders	A. Improve Information	B. Strengthen Competencies	C. Modify Incentives	D. Enhance Governance
Asset owners, e.g. public and corporate pension funds, sovereign wealth funds, insurance firms, family offices, endowments, foundations	A1. Increase disclosure on ESG factors in investment portfolio A2. Assess materiality of ESG factors at macroeconomic and industry level	B1. Increase the capacity of pension fund trustees to exercise independent judgement in the long-term interest of beneficiaries (including ESG awareness training) *See B2, B3*	C1. Develop performance measurement systems for in-house and external fund managers that balance fostering a long-term perspective with short-term accountability C2. Implement compensation systems that better align stakeholders with the long-term mandate C3. Encourage the analysis of financially material ESG factors via mandates to asset managers	D1. Demonstrate more active ownership through engagement, shareholder resolutions and/or proxy voting D2. Rationalize number of portfolio holdings in order to increase capacities as active owner (and consider potential trade-offs in terms of portfolio diversification)
Asset managers, e.g. mutual funds, private equity firms, hedge funds, asset management divisions of banks	*See A1* A3. Buy- and sell-side analysts determine – together with corporate executives – the financially material KPIs at the sector and/or company level A4. Communicate results of materiality assessments by investor to portfolio companies	B2. Increase ESG awareness and analytical skills through – for example – ongoing training and making ESG data available to all staff B3. Strengthen the interaction between financial and ESG analysts and integrate those skills further	C4. Negotiate with asset owners a fund management compensation arrangement linked to superior long-term performance	*See D1, D2*

Key Stakeholders	A. Improve Information	B. Strengthen Competencies	C. Modify Incentives	D. Enhance Governance
Corporations (listed and non-listed)	A5. Corporate executives communicate better to investors which ESG factors are financially material and in what timeframe A6. Focus corporate-investor communication around long-term metrics A7. Publish an integrated report as opposed to a separate financial report and a separate CSR report	B4. Further develop the understanding of senior executives and investment relations officers (IROs) of the link between social & environmental performance, financial performance, and stock market valuations	C5. Link the remuneration of corporate executives not only to short-term financial results, but also to longer-term financial and non-financial performance	D3. Create structured, regular dialogue between senior executives and investors on ESG issues D4. Fully integrate ESG factors into the corporate strategy development process D5. Integrate ESG criteria into corporate capital allocation decisions D6. Strengthen the interaction between CSR specialists, operational management, and investor relations officers to inform the dialogue with investors
Accounting bodies	A8. Develop standards for ESG disclosure A9. Stimulate integrated reporting			
Others, e.g. public authorities, investment advisors, ESG research firms, stock exchanges, business schools	A10. Public authorities encourage the disclosure of ESG information A11. Incorporate ESG disclosure requirements in listing rules (IPOs and ongoing) stock exchanges and corporate governance standards A12. Mainstream data providers make ESG data broadly accessible for investors	B5. Business schools increase emphasis on ESG issues B6. Incorporate ESG training into industry and corporate training schemes	C6. Investment advisors raise the awareness of clients (e.g. corporate and public pension funds) to integrate ESG factors into investment analysis	

Source: World Economic Forum (2011)

References

Akkermans, D., Van Ees, H., Hermes, N., Hooghiemstra, R., Van der Laan, G., Postma, T., et al. (2007). Corporate Governance in the Netherlands: an overview of the application of the Tabaksblat Code in 2004. *Corporate Governance: An International Review, 15*(6), 1106-1118.

Annandale, D., Bailey, J., Ouano, E., Evans, W., & King, P. (2001). The potential role of strategic environmental assessment in the activities of multi-lateral development banks. *Environmental Impact Assessment Review, 21*(5), 407-429.

Aras, G., & Crowther, D. (2009). Corporate sustainability reporting: a study in disingenuity? *Journal of Business Ethics, 87*, 279-288.

Barnett, M. L. (2005). Stakeholder influence capacity and the variability of financial returns to corporate social responsibility. *Academy of Management Review.*

Barnett, M. L., & Salomon, R. M. (2006). Beyond dichotomy: the curvilinear relationship between social responsibility and financial performance. *Strategic Management Journal, 27* (11), 1101-1122.

Bauer, R., Derwall, J., & Otten, R. (2007). The ethical mutual fund performance debate: New evidence from Canada. *Journal of Business Ethics, 70*(2), 111-124.

Bauer, R., Guenster, N., & Otten, R. (2004). Empirical evidence on corporate governance in Europe: The effect on stock returns, firm value and performance. *Journal of Asset Management, 5*(2), 91-104.

Bauer, R., Koedijk, K., & Otten, R. (2005). International evidence on ethical mutual fund performance and investment style. *Journal of Banking & Finance, 29*(7), 1751-1767.

Bauer, R., Otten, R., & Rad, A. T. (2006). Ethical investing in Australia: Is there a financial penalty? *Pacific-Basin Finance Journal, 14*(1), 33-48.

Bello, Z. Y. (2005). Socially responsible investing and portfolio diversification. *Journal of Financial Research, 28*(1), 41-57.

Benson, K., Brailsford, T., & Humphrey, J. (2006). Do Socially Responsible Fund Managers Really Invest Differently? *Journal of Business Ethics, 65*(4), 337-357.

Benson, K., & Humphrey, J. (2008). Socially responsible investment funds: Investor reaction to current and past returns. *Journal of Banking & Finance, 32*(9), 1850-1859.

Biermans, M., Grand, H. l., Kerste, M., & Weda, J. (2009). *De kapitaalmarkt voor duurzame projecten: De regels van het spel zijn het zelfde maar het spel verloopt anders*. Amsterdam: SEO Economisch Onderzoek.

Bollen, N. P. B. (2007). Mutual Fund Attributes and Investor Behavior. *Journal of Financial and Quantitative Analysis, 42*(03), 683-708.

Chatterji, A., & Levine, D. (2005). Breaking down the wall of codes: evaluating non-financial performance measurement.

Cochran, P. L., & Wood, R. A. (1984). Corporate social responsibility and financial performance. *Academy of Management Journal, 27*(1), 42-56.

Cremers, K. J. M., & Nair, V. B. (2005). Governance mechanisms and equity prices. *The Journal of Finance, 60*(6), 2859-2894.

Creyer, E. H., & Ross, W. T. (1996). The impact of corporate behavior on perceived product value. *Marketing Letters, 7*(2), 173-185.

Crowther, D. (2000). *Social and environmental accounting*. London, New York, Tokyo: Financial Times Prentice Hall.

Dasgupta, S., Laplante, B., Wang, H., & Wheeler, D. (2002). Confronting the environmental Kuznets curve. *Journal of Economic Perspectives*, 147-168.

Derwall, J., Guenster, N., Bauer, R., & Koedijk, K. (2005). The eco-efficiency premium puzzle. *Financial Analysts Journal, 61*(2), 51-63.

Dowell, G., Hart, S., & Yeung, B. (2000). Do corporate global environmental standards create or destroy market value? *Management Science, 46*(8), 1059-1074.

Du, S., Bhattacharya, C. B., & Sen, S. (2007). Reaping relational rewards from corporate social responsibility: The role of competitive positioning. *International Journal of Research in Marketing, 24*(3), 224-241.

Dijken, F. van (2007). Corporate social responsibility: market regulation and the evidence. *Managerial Law, 49*(4), 141-184.

Eccles, R. G., & Krzus, M. (2010). *One report: Integrated Reporting for a Sustainable Strategy*: Wiley.

Edmans, A. (2010). Does the stock market fully value intangibles? Employee satisfaction and equity prices. University of Pennsylvania.

Epstein, E. M. (1989). Business ethics, corporate good citizenship and the corporate social policy process: A view from the United States. *Journal of Business Ethics, 8*(8), 583-595.

Eurosif. (2010). *European SRI Study 2010 Revised Edition*. Paris: Eurosif.

Fama, E. F. (1970). Efficient capital markets: A review of theory and empirical work. *Journal of Finance, 25*(2), 383-417.

Fama, E. F. (1991). Efficient capital markets: II. *Journal of Finance*, 1575-1617.

Fama, E. F., & French, K. R. (1993). Common risk factors in the returns on stocks and bonds *Journal of Financial Economics, 33*(1), 3-56.

Fombrun, C. J., Gardberg, N. A., & Barnett, M. L. (2000). Opportunity platforms and safety nets: Corporate citizenship and reputational risk. *Business and Society Review, 105*(1), 85-106.

Friedman, M. (1970). The social responsibility of business is to increase its profits. *New York Times Magazine,* pp. 32–33.

Galema, R., Plantinga, A., & Scholtens, B. (2008). The stocks at stake: Return and risk in socially responsible investment. *Journal of Banking & Finance, 32*(12), 2646-2654.

Geczy, C., Stambaugh, R. F., & Levin, D. (2005). Investing in socially responsible mutual funds.

Gil-Bazo, J., Ruiz-Verdú, P., & Santos, A. (2010). The Performance of Socially Responsible Mutual Funds: The Role of Fees and Management Companies. *Journal of Business Ethics, 94*(2), 243-263.

Godfrey, P. C., Merrill, C. B., & Hansen, J. M. (2009). The relationship between corporate social responsibility and shareholder value: an empirical test of the risk management hypothesis. *Strategic Management Journal, 30*(4), 425-445.

Goergen, M., & Renneboog, L. (2002). The social responsibility of major shareholders. Sheffield University.

Goldreyer, E. F., & Diltz, J. D. (1999). The performance of socially responsible mutual funds: incorporating sociopolitical information in portfolio selection. *Managerial Finance, 25*(1), 23-36.

Gompers, P., Ishii, J., & Metrick, A. (2003). Corporate governance and equity prices. *Quarterly Journal of Economics, 118*(1), 107-155.

Greening, D. W., & Turban, D. B. (2000). Corporate social performance as a competitive advantage in attracting a quality workforce. *Business & Society, 39*(3), 254.

Gregory, A., Matatko, J., & Luther, R. (1997). Ethical unit trust financial performance: small company effects and fund size effects. *Journal of Business Finance & Accounting, 24*(5), 705-725.

Guenster, N., Bauer, R., Derwall, J., & Koedijk, K. (2010). The Economic Value of Corporate Eco-Efficiency. *European Financial Management*, 1-26.

Gupta, S., & Goldar, B. (2005). Do stock markets penalize environment-unfriendly behaviour? Evidence from India. *Ecological Economics, 52*(1), 81-95.

Halkos, G., & Sepetis, A. (2007). Can capital markets respond to environmental policy of firms? Evidence from Greece. *Ecological Economics, 63*(2-3), 578-587.

Hamilton, J. (1995). Pollution as news: Media and stock market reactions to the Toxics Release Inventory data. *Journal of Environmental Economics and Management, 28*(1), 98-113.

Hamilton, S., Jo, H., & Statman, M. (1993). Doing well while doing good? The investment performance of socially responsible mutual funds. *Financial Analysts Journal, 49*(6), 62-66.

Harold, J., Spitzer, J., & Emerson, J. (2007). *Blended Value Investing: Integrating Environmental Risks And Opportunities Into Securities Valuation*. Oxford: Saïd Business School.

Hawley, J. P., & Williams, A. T. (2000). *The rise of fiduciary capitalism: How institutional investors can make corporate America more democratic*. Philadelphia, Pennsylvania: University of Pennsylvania Press.

Hill, R. P., Ainscough, T., Shank, T., & Manullang, D. (2007). Corporate social responsibility and socially responsible investing: A global perspective. *Journal of Business Ethics, 70*(2), 165-174.

Hillman, A. J., & Keim, G. D. (2001). Shareholder value, stakeholder management, and social issues: what's the bottom line? *Strategic Management Journal, 22*(2), 125-139.

Hoepner, A. G. F., & McMillan, D. G. (2009). *Research on 'Responsible Investment': An Influential Literature Analysis Comprising a Rating, Characterisation, Categorisation and Investigation*. St. Andrews: University of St. Andrews.

Jensen, M. C. (2002). Value Maximization, Stakeholder Theory, and the Corporate Objective Function. *Business Ethics Quarterly, 12*, 235-256.

Kempf, A., & Osthoff, P. (2007). The effect of socially responsible investing on portfolio performance. *European Financial Management, 13*(5), 908-922.

Kempf, A., & Osthoff, P. (2008). SRI Funds: Nomen est Omen. *Journal of Business Finance & Accounting, 35*(9-10), 1276-1294.

Kim, R., & Van Dam, E. (2003). *The added value of corporate social responsibility*. Leeuwarden: Netherlands Initiative for Sustainable Development (NIDO).

Klassen, R. D., & McLaughlin, C. P. (1996). The impact of environmental management on firm performance. *Management Science, 42*(8), 1199-1214.

Klein, J., & Dawar, N. (2004). Corporate social responsibility and consumers' attributions and brand evaluations in a product-harm crisis. *International Journal of research in Marketing, 21*(3), 203-217.

Kolk, A., van der Veen, M., Pinkse, J., & Fortanier, F. (2005). *KPMG International Survey of Corporate Responsibility Reporting 2005*. Amsterdam: University of Amsterdam/KPMG Global Sustainability Services.

Konar, S., & Cohen, M. A. (2001). Does the market value environmental performance? *Review of Economics and Statistics, 83*(2), 281-289.

Kreander, N., Gray, G., Power, D. M., & Sinclair, C. D. (2005). Evaluating the performance of Ethical and Non-SRI funds: a matched pair analysis. *Journal of Business, Finance and Accounting, 32*(7), 1465-1493.

La Porta, R., Lopez-de-Silanes, F., Shleifer, A., & Vishny, R. (2002). Investor protection and corporate valuation. *The Journal of Finance, 57*(3).

Luther, R. G., & Matatko, J. (1994). The performance of ethical unit trusts: choosing an appropriate benchmark. *The British Accounting Review, 26*(1), 77-89.

Luther, R. G., Matatko, J., & Corner, D. C. (1992). The Investment Performance of UK 'Ethical' Unit Trusts.

Lydenberg, G. (2008). *Innovations in social and environmental disclosure outside the United States*. New York.

Mallin, C. A., Saadouni, B., & Briston, R. J. (1995). The financial performance of ethical investment funds. *Journal of Business Finance & Accounting, 22*(4), 483-496.

Mercer. (2009). *Shedding Light on Responsible Investment: Approaches, Returns, and Impacts*. Toronto: Mercer Investment Consulting.

Mercer, & UNEPFI. (2007). *Responsible Investment Performance: A review of key academic and broker research on ESG factors*.

Mitchell, R. K., Agle, B. R., & Wood, D. J. (1997). Toward a theory of stakeholder identification and salience: Defining the principle of who and what really counts. *Academy of Management Review, 22*(4), 853-886.

Mulder, I. (2007). *Biodiversity, the Next Challenge for Financial Institutions: A scoping study to assess exposure of financial institutions to biodiversity business risks and identifying options for business opportunities*. Gland, Switzerland: The World Conservation Union (IUCN), Alterra, FSD.

Nakao, Y., Amano, A., Matsumura, K., Genba, K., & Nakano, M. (2007). Relationship between environmental performance and financial performance: an empirical analysis of Japanese corporations. *Business Strategy and the Environment, 16*(2), 106-118.

Nilsson, J., & Nilsson, Å. (2010). *Global Reporting Initiative: Hallbarhetsredovisningens externa tranparens i statliga företag*. Lulea: Lulea tekniska universitet.

Orlitzky, M., Schmidt, F. L., & Rynes, S. L. (2003). Corporate social and financial performance: A meta-analysis. *Organization Studies, 24*(3), 403.

Peloza, J., & Shang, J. (2010). How can corporate social responsibility activities create value for stakeholders? A systematic review. *Journal of the Academy of Marketing Science*, 1-19.

Plinke, E. (2008). *Sustainability and share performance – a long-running debate revisited*. Basel: Bank Sarasin & Co. Ltd.

Renneboog, L., Ter Horst, J., & Zhang, C. (2007). Socially responsible investments: Methodology, risk exposure and performance. *Discussion Paper*.

Renneboog, L., Ter Horst, J., & Zhang, C. (2008a). The price of ethics and stakeholder governance: The performance of socially responsible mutual funds. *Journal of Corporate Finance, 14*(3), 302-322.

Renneboog, L., Ter Horst, J., & Zhang, C. (2008b). Socially responsible investments: Institutional aspects, performance, and investor behavior. *Journal of Banking & Finance, 32*(9), 1723-1742.

Richardson, B. (2007). *Financing Sustainability: The New Transnational Governance of Socially Responsible Investment*. New York: Oxford University Press.

Schröder, M. (2004). The performance of socially responsible investments: investment funds and indices. *Financial Markets and Portfolio Management, 18*(2), 122-142.

Shank, T., Manullang, D., & Hill, R. (2005). Doing Well While Doing Good' Revisited: A Study of Socially Responsible Firms' Short-Term versus Long-term Performance. *Managerial Finance, 31*(8), 33-46.

Smith, A. (1776). *An Inquiry into the Nature and Causes of the Wealth of Nations*. Chicago, IL: The University of Chicago Press.

Soppe, A. (2004). Sustainable corporate finance. *Journal of Business Ethics, 53*(1), 213-224.

Statman, M. (2000). Socially Responsible Mutual Funds. *Financial Analysts Journal, 56*(3), 30-39.

Statman, M., & Glushkov, D. (2008). The wages of social responsibility. Unpublished Working Paper. Santa Clara University.

Steger, U. (2004). What is the business case for corporate sustainability, *IMD Perspectives for Managers* (pp. 2-4).

Thamotheram, R., & Wildsmith, H. (2007). Increasing Long Term Market Returns: realising the potential of collective pension fund action. *Corporate Governance: An International Review, 15*(3), 438-454.

Tirole. (2001). Corporate governance. *Econometrica, 69*, 1–35.

Turban, D. B., & Greening, D. W. (1997). Corporate social performance and organizational attractiveness to prospective employees. *Academy of Management Journal, 40*(3), 658-672.

UNEP. (2006). *Show Me The Money: Linking Environmental, Social and Governance Issues to Company Value*. Geneva: UNEP Finance Initiative.

Utting, P. (2004). Corporate Social Responsibility and Business Regulation. *UNRISD Research and Policy Brief, 1*.

Waddock, S. A., & Graves, S. B. (1997). The corporate social performance-financial performance link. *Strategic Management Journal, 18*(4), 303-319.

Weber, O., Scholz, R., W., & Michalik, G. (2010). Incorporating sustainability criteria into credit risk management. *Business Strategy and the Environment, 19*(1), 39-50.

World Economic Forum. (2011). *Accelerating the Transition towards Sustainable Investing: Strategic Options for Investors, Corporations and other Key Stakeholders*.

Willis, A. (2003). The role of the Global Reporting Initiative's Sustainability Reporting Guidelines in the social screening of investments. *Journal of Business Ethics, 43*(3), 233-237.

Appendix

Table 6 SRI fund performance: a research review

Study	Content	Conclusion
Edmans, A.: Does the Stock Market Fully Value Intangibles? Employee Satisfaction and Equity Prices; University of Pennsylvania – The Wharton School; 2008	Portfolio analysis ("100 Best Companies to Work for" vs. market; correction of sector distortions) with a 4-factor financial model. Sustainability ratings: limited to quality of the workplace. Approx. 100 US companies; timeframe 1984-2006	Significantly higher return from the portfolio comprising companies with a good working environment versus the (adjusted) market portfolio
Kempf, A.; Osthoff. P.: The Effect of Socially Responsible Investing on Portfolio Performance, European Financial Management 13 (5), 908-920, 2007	Portfolio analysis (10% of companies with the best CSR ratings versus 10% of companies with the worst CSR ratings; correction of sector distortions) with a 4-factor financial model. Sustainability ratings of KLD (limited thematic spectrum), 700 – 3000 US companies; variable over the period 1992-2004	No reduction in the performance of the portfolio with a positive sustainability rating; portfolio with a negative sustainability rating produced a weaker performance
Bauer, R., J. Derwall, and R. Otten: The Ethical Mutual Fund Performance Debate: New Evidence from Canada, Journal of Business Ethics 70, 111-124, 2007	Portfolio analysis of 8 sustainability funds (compared with the market or benchmark) with a 4-factor financial model. Sustainability ratings: different (depending on funds), 8 Canadian funds with global components; timeframe 1994-2003	No difference in the performance of sustainability funds and the benchmark/market
Guenster, N., J. Derwall, R. Bauer, and K. Koedijk: The Economic Value of Corporate Eco-Efficiency, RSM Erasmus University Rotterdam, 2006.	Econometric analysis of the link between sustainability ratings and enterprise value ("Tobin Q") (at company level). Sustainability ratings: limited to environmental protection, in accordance with Innovest, 150 – 410 US companies, variable over the period 1996-2002	No reduction in the performance of companies with a positive sustainability rating; companies with a negative sustainability rating gave a weaker performance
Derwall, D.; Guenster, N.; Bauer, R.; Koedijk, K.: The Eco-Efficiency Premium Puzzle; Financial Analysts Journal; Vol. 61; No. 2; 2005	Portfolio analysis (30% of companies with the best CSR ratings versus 30% of companies with the worst CSR ratings), different financial models (incl. correction of sector distortions). Sustainability ratings: limited to the environment (Innovest), 180 – 450 US companies; time frame 1995 – 2003	Substantially higher average return on the portfolio comprising shares with a positive sustainability rating versus portfolios comprising stocks with a negative sustainability rating
Schröder, M.: Is there a Difference? The Performance Characteristics of SRI Equity Indexes, Journal of Business Finance and Accounting 34 (1) & (2), 331-348; 2007	Portfolio analysis of 29 sustainability indexes (comparison with market or benchmark) with 1-factor and 3-factor financial models. Sustainability ratings: different (no use of rating, but ready-made indexes), 29 indexes with global components; timeframe: from inception up to y/e 2003	No difference in the performance of sustainability indexes, and the benchmark/market

Source: Adapted from Plinke (2008, p. 14)

Table 7 SRI screens

Screens	Definitions	Type
Tobacco	Avoid manufacturers of tobacco products	-
Alcohol	Avoid firms that produce, market, or otherwise promote the consumption of alcoholic beverages	-
Gambling	Avoid casinos and suppliers of gambling equipment	-
Defense/weapons	Avoid firms producing weapons for domestic or foreign militaries, or firearms for personal use	-
Nuclear power	Avoid manufacturers of nuclear reactors or related equipment and companies that operate nuclear power plants	-
Irresponsible foreign operations	Avoid firms with investments in government-controlled or private firms located in oppressive regimes such as Burma or China, or firms which mistreat the indigenous peoples of developing countries	-
Pornography/ adult entertainment	Avoid publishers of pornographic magazines; production studios that produce offensive video and audio tapes; companies that are major sponsors of graphic sex and violence on television	-
Abortion/birth control	Avoid providers of abortion; manufacturers of abortion drugs and birth control products; insurance companies that pay for elective abortions (where not mandated by law); companies that provide financial support to Planned Parenthood	-
Labor relations and workplace conditions	Seek firms with strong union relationships, employee empowerment, and/or employee profit sharing	+
	Avoid firms exploiting their workforce and sweatshops	—
Environment	Seek firms with proactive involvement in recycling, waste reduction, and environmental cleanup	+
	Avoid firms producing toxic products, and contributing to global warming	—
Corporate governance	Seek companies demonstrating "best practices" related to board independence and elections, auditor independence, executive compensation, expensing of options, voting rights and/or other governance issues	+
	Avoid firms with antitrust violations, consumer fraud, and marketing scandals	—
Business practice	Seek companies committed to sustainability through investments in R&D, quality assurance, product safety	+
Employment diversity	Seek firms pursuing an active policy related to the employment of minorities, women, gays/lesbians, and/ or disabled persons who ought to be represented amongst senior management	+
Human rights	Seek firms promoting human rights standards	+
	Avoid firms which are complicit in human rights violations	—
Animal testing	Seek firms promoting the respectful treatment of animals	+
	Avoid firms with animal testing and firms producing hunting/trapping equipment or using animals in end products	—
Renewable energy	Seek firms producing power derived from renewable energy sources	+
Biotechnology	Seek firms that support sustainable agriculture, biodiversity, local farmers, and industrial applications of biotechnology	+
	Avoid firms involved in the promotion or development of genetic engineering for agricultural applications	—

Community involvement	Seek firms with proactive investments in the local community by sponsoring charitable donations, employee volunteerism, and/or housing and educational programs	+
Shareholder activism	The SRI funds that attempt to influence company actions through direct dialogue with management and/ or voting at annual general meetings	+
Non-married	Avoid insurance companies that give coverage to non-married couples	-
Healthcare/pharmaceuticals	Avoid healthcare industries (used by funds targeting the "Christian Scientist" religious group)	-
Interest-based financial institutions	Avoid financial institutions that derive a significant portion of their income from interest earnings (on loans or fixed income securities). (Used by funds managed according to Islamic principles)	-
Pork producers	Avoid companies that derive a significant portion of their income from the manufacturing or marketing of pork products. (Used by funds managed according to Islamic principles)	-

Source: Adapted from Renneboog et al. (2008b, p. 1729)

Table 8 Regulatory SRI initiatives taken by national government in Western countries[31]

Country	SRI-related regulations
Australia	- In a 2001 bill it is stated that all investment firms' product disclosure statements should include a description of "the extent to which labor standards or environmental, social or ethical considerations are taken into account". Since 2001, all listed companies on the Australian Stock Exchange are required to make an annual social responsibility report.
Belgium	- In 2001, Belgium passed the 'Vandebroucke' law, which requires pension funds to report the degree to which their investments take into account social, ethical and environmental aspects.
France	- In May 2001, the legislation "New Economic Regulations" came into force requiring listed companies to publish social and environmental information in their annual reports. - Since February 2001 managers of the Employee Savings Plans are required to consider social, environmental or ethical considerations when buying and selling shares.
Germany	- Since 1991, the Renewable Energy Act gives a tax advantage to closed-end funds to invest in wind energy. - Since January 2002, certified private pension schemes and occupational pension schemes 'must inform the members in writing, whether and in what form ethical, social, or ecological aspects are taken into consideration when investing the paid-in contributions'.
Italy	- Since September 2004 pension funds are required to disclose non-financial factors (including social, environmental and ethical factors) influencing their investment decisions.
Netherlands	- In 1995, the Dutch Tax Office introduced a 'Green Savings and Investment Plan', which applies a tax deduction for green investments, such as wind and solar energy, and organic farming.
Sweden	- Since January 2002, Swedish national pension funds are obliged to incorporate environmental and ethical aspects in their investment policies.
UK	- In July 2000, the Amendment to 1995 Pensions Act came into force, requiring trustees of occupational pension funds in the UK to disclose in the Statement of Investment Principles "the extent (if at all) to which social, environmental and ethical considerations are taken into account in the selection, retention and realization of investments". - The Trustee Act 2000 came into force in February 2001. Charity trustees must ensure that investments are suitable to a charity's stated aims, including applying ethical considerations to investments. - In 2002, The Cabinet Office in the UK published the Review of Charity Law in 2002, which proposed that all charities with an annual income of over £1 m should report on the extent to which social, environmental and ethical issues are taken into account in their investment policy. The Home Office accepted these recommendations in 2003. - The Association of British Insurers (ABI) published a disclosure guideline in 2001, asking listed companies to report on material social, environmental and ethical risks relevant to their business activities.
US	- Section 406 of the Sarbanes-Oxley Act, which came into effect in July 2002, requires companies to disclose a written code of ethics adopted by their CEO, chief financial officer and chief accountant.

Source: Adapted from Renneboog et al. (2007, pp. 5-6; 2008b, p. 1727)

31. For an overview of the mandatory environmental and social disclosure in countries not mentioned in Table 8, see the research by the Social Investment Forum (Lydenberg, 2008). This paper provides models for similar regulatory action by agencies or stock exchanges in the United States to promote transparency and efficiency.

Table 9 Voluntary Codes of Conduct Relevant to SRI[32]

Code of Conduct	Principal Sponsor
CERES Principles	Coalition for Environmentally Responsible Economies
Collevecchio Declaration	Coalition of Non-Governmental Organizations
Global Sullivan Principles	Reverend Leon Sullivan
London Principles of Sustainable Finance	UK Department of Environment and Corporation of London
UN Global Compact	United Nations
UN Principles for Responsible Investment (UNPRI)	UN Environment Program Finance Initiative (UNEP FI)
UN Statement by Financial Institutions on the Environment and Sustainable Development	UN Environment Program Finance Initiative (UNEP FI)
UN Norms on the Responsibilities of Transnational Corporations	UN Sub-Commission on Promotion and Protection of Human Rights

Source: Adapted from Richardson (2007, p. 81)

32. See Richardson (2007, pp. 82-88) for an elaboration of these codes of conduct.

4. Innovations in Financing Environmental and Social Sustainability

Chapter Overview

4.1 Introduction

Chapter 1 discussed how to finance the transition towards sustainable energy, while Chapter 3 zoomed in on the business case for private parties to invest in sustainable development. The focus was primarily on traditional funding sources and existing public policy instruments to increase investments in sustainable development to required levels. The enormous challenge ahead, however, asks for innovative ways to increase funding, by both the private (financial) sector and governmental institutions. As an example that can already be regarded as an important pillar of market-based public policy, Chapter 2 provided more detail on one such instrument – carbon trading.

In view of the importance of innovative ways to increase funding, this chapter highlights the leading literature and empirical research on 'innovations in financing environmental and social sustainability'. Even more so than for the main topics addressed in the other three chapters, academic interest in this topic is fairly young. So far, an academic consensus on how to assess innovative finance instruments is lacking – and this at a time when concerns about social and environmental development are taken more and more seriously, and new funding ideas seem to emerge every day. The first part of this chapter provides a literature overview of the relevant innovative finance landscape and defines a general framework based on it to describe and analyze innovative finance instruments. The second part does just that for a sample of instruments, namely green bonds, index-linked carbon bonds, payment for environmental services, and peer-to-peer lending.

4.2 Innovative Finance

4.2.1 *Definition and Scope*

Innovative financing (IF)[1] is often used in the context of the Millennium Development Goals[2], as being aimed at finding alternative sources of Official Development Assistance (ODA) to finance their achievement. During the International Conference on Financing for Development in 2002, the international community explicitly recognized the value of exploring innovative sources of finance.

As yet, there is no internationally agreed definition of IF (Sandor, Scott, &Benn, 2009). Definitions by authorities in the field include:

- World Bank Group (2010, p. 1) defines IF as financing approaches that "[g]enerate additional development funds by tapping new funding sources … or by engaging new partners …", that "[e]nhance the efficiency of financial flows, by reducing delivery time and/or costs …" or that "[m]ake financial flows more results-oriented";
- Girishankar (2009, pp. 3-4) defines IF as non-traditional applications of mechanisms that "(i) support fundraising by tapping new sources and engaging investors beyond the financial dimension of transactions, as partners and stakeholders in development; or (ii) deliver financial solutions to development problems on the ground";
- In its Issue Brief on IF, OECD (Sandor et al., 2009, p. 3) considers IF to comprise "mechanisms of raising funds or stimulating actions in support of international development that go beyond traditional spending approaches by either the official or private sectors" but excludes "innovative uses of traditional development finance, such as counter-cyclical lending, debt swaps..." as well as "innovative delivery mechanisms, such as results-based aid".

Although not explicitly addressed in the definitions as such, all three focus on IF aimed at aiding developing countries ('development'). Because many elements in terms of social and environmental sustainability can be of importance in developed countries as well, this book does not preclude these countries from the IF definition. In addition, all three definitions seem primarily focused on mobilizing or deploying official flows (primarily ODA) in one way or the other. This does not mean private flows are not of importance nor that the literature does not cover purely private initiatives.[3] They are therefore not precluded from the IF definition in this book.

---

1. Also referred to as: Innovative financing for development.
2. "In September 2000, building upon a decade of major United Nations conferences and summits, world leaders came together at United Nations Headquarters in New York to adopt the United Nations Millennium Declaration, committing their nations to a new global partnership to reduce extreme poverty and setting out a series of time-bound targets – with a deadline of 2015 – that have become known as the Millennium Development Goals". See www.un.org/millenniumgoals.
3. See for instance the vast literature on (commercial) microfinance.

4.2.2 *Classification of the IF landscape*

In order to improve understanding of the vast amount of IF initiatives, their background, development, interrelations and (most importantly) their success, some kind of a structure is needed.

Many sources use either the type of underlying financial instrument or the objective as the starting point to categorize IF. For example: WEF (2006) discusses innovations in debt financing, credit guarantees and private equity investing; World Bank Group (2010) distinguishes three areas of IF: generating additional funds, enhancing the efficiency of financial flows, and linking financial flows to results. Sandor et al. (2009) report examples divided into IF Agencies and IF Mechanisms, the latter further subdivided into revenue raising, bonds, voluntary contributions and guarantees. Like most other papers on the subject, these papers do not aim to provide a structure for IF as such, but rather to categorize the examples they intend to discuss in a logical manner.

De Ferranti (2006), on the other hand, explicitly tries to "make sense of [the] heterogeneous multitude of proposals". The author considers the use of the underlying objectives to structure IF, defining objectives in terms of (i) the problem being addressed (e.g., a disease or the effect of natural disasters) and (ii) the related financing opportunity (e.g., a debt to be repaid in the case of debt buy-downs, or the terms of lending in the case of local currency lending). In addition, the author proposes looking at the sources and destinations of the financial flows. He defines IF options within a matrix of sources and destinations (e.g., public sector, financial sector, and corporate sector). For example, funds from the public sector to civil society (NGO and the like) might be channelled via Debt Buy-downs. According to the author, this exercise is mainly of importance for the attention it draws to the tendency to "focus on one's own backyard", that is channelling funds from public to public, from corporate to corporate, etc.

Meijerink et al. (2008)[4] divide IF mechanisms into four categories, based on the source of funding (private or public) and the mechanism (market-based or non-market-based):

- Self-organized private market arrangements;
- Voluntary private, non-market funding mechanisms;
- Government-supported market creation;
- Government-run financing mechanisms but also the creation of an enabling environment.

4. Based on Emerton et al. (2006).

Figure 1 shows examples of mechanisms per category. Although illustrative, it is evident that the use of market- versus non-market-based mechanisms does not provide a clear distinction in instruments.

Figure 1 Innovative finance mechanisms: (non-)market versus (non-)private

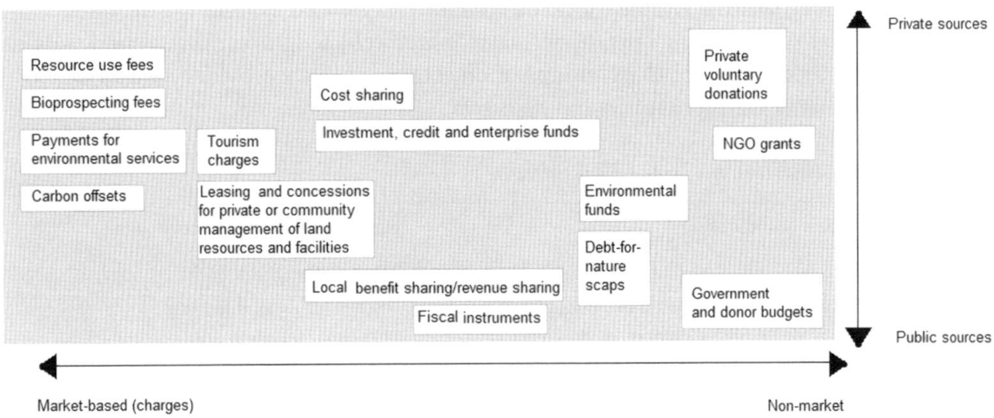

Source: Emerton et al. (2006)

The idea of structuring IF by means of sources and destinations, as suggested by De Ferranti, is further expanded by Girishankar (2009). An important part of the author's definition of IF (see above) is the identification of innovative mechanisms, based on the sources of funding (whether to mobilise public or to leverage private sources) and the uses they support (whether public or private). Figure 2 shows the four resulting mechanisms: Public-Private Partnerships (PPP), Pure Private, Solidarity and Catalytic.[5]

Figure 2 Innovative finance mechanisms: sources versus uses

SOURCES OF FUNDING	USES OF FUNDING: *Public*	USES OF FUNDING: *Private*
Leverage private	**Public-Private Partnerships (PPP)** *Private finance for public service delivery and other public functions*	**Pure Private** *Private initiative in the market and in civil society*
Mobilize public	**Solidarity** *Public-to-public transfers using concessional flows (ODA)*	**Catalytic** *Public support for market creation and development or for promoting private entry into existing markets*

Source: Girishankar (2009)

5. Importantly, the author does not include Pure Private mechanisms in his definition of IF.

Innovation takes place within each mechanism using financial instruments, products and services (hereafter: financial instruments or instruments).[6] IF instruments could include, but are not limited to, cash instruments (such as grants, loans, and securities), risk mitigation instruments (such as guarantees, swaps, hedging products, and derivatives) and advisory services (Girishankar, 2009).[7]

These mechanisms and instruments are either organized as fund-raising efforts or as financial solutions for operational development challenges 'on the ground' – which can be seen as two primary groups of objectives.[8] Table 1 provides an overview of IF instruments per mechanism and objective.

Table 1 Instruments in the IF landscape

Objective mechanism	Fund-raising	Financial solution ('on the ground')
Solidarity	- ODA financed by budget outlays from emerging sovereign donors - Global solidarity levies (such as airline ticket tax, adaptation fund) - National lotteries - Stolen asset recovery	- Counter-cyclical lending - Debt swaps for results
PPS	- Joint financing with private donors - New bonds (those in local currencies or those targeting sustainable investors) - Sovereign catastrophe risk (incl. derivatives, currency swaps) - Frontloading ODA	- Private participation in social sectors and infrastructure (incl. through guarantees, OBA) - Sovereign catastrophe risk finance (through derivative and hedging, deferred draw-down options or DDOs)
Catalytic	- Carbon funds	- Leveraging private investment in the financial and productive sectors (through local currency lending, guarantees, risk-sharing facilities) - Creating private insurance markets (through insurance pools and DDOs) - Advance market commitments - Co-payment schemes

Source: SEO Economic Research, based on Girishankar (2009)

6. A financial instrument is any contract that gives rise to a financial asset of one entity and a financial liability or equity instrument of another entity (IASC Foundation, IAS 32).

7. The inclusion of advisory services points to a somewhat broader scope for financial instruments than in the IASC definition.

8. For example: an airline ticket tax is evidently aimed at *raising funds*. Because it mobilizes *public* funds to be used for *public* functions of government it is a *Solidarity mechanism*. Guarantees provided by governments are a *financial solution* aimed at decreasing risks which pose barriers to funding 'on the ground'. Because it mobilizes *public* funds to promote *private* funding, it is a *Catalytic mechanism*. The author does not specify financial solutions 'on the ground'. Here, it will be interpreted as referring to solutions for the (process of) funding actual projects, activities and companies, in comparison with activities to spur the required development fund-flow which could eventually be used to do this (i.e., fund-raising).

Here, the definition of IF mechanisms, instruments and objectives as used by Girishankar (2009) is followed. Most definitions (see Section 4.2.1) and classifications of IF implicitly or explicitly focus on IF instruments aimed at developing countries and official flows. As said, both are included in the scope of this book. This means classification of IF, as interpreted here, should also include the difference between IF instruments aimed at developing and developed countries and the difference between purely private initiatives and initiatives requiring some sort of public support.

In addition, two elements not directly encountered in the described classifications are worth mentioning. First, a large part of IF instruments focuses on internalizing positive and/or negative externalities.[9] IF instruments might be aimed at compensating for these benefits (make the beneficiary pay) or costs (make the 'polluter' pay). Here, these instruments will be referred to as 'compensation schemes'.[10] Second, the funds raised or the financial solutions targeted – to stick to Girishankar's terminology – may be earmarked (or: ring fenced) for specific purposes. Whether it is clear to which end funds will be used may impact on the success of obtaining funding. These schemes will be referred to as 'hypothecated finance'. These two classification characteristics are taken into account in addition to the IF mechanism discussed above.[11]

4.2.3 *Measuring Funds Generated by IF Instruments*

Measuring the impact of IF in terms of financial flows is not an easy task. Macro-data is generally focused on IF to developing countries. The OECD's Development Assistance Committee (DAC), for instance, collects and publishes statistics on aid flow. Even in terms of funds to developing countries, they can only provide a partial picture of innovative financing, for instance because they only record official, and not private, contributions and measure flows on a cash basis, thereby neglecting pledges and guarantees (Sandor et al., 2009).

The most recent and extensive overview is provided by Girishankar (2009). Table 2 and Table 3 provide a quick scan of the development funds generated globally via fund-raising and to support financial solutions 'on the ground', respectively, both per IF mechanism as defined in section 4.2.2.

---

9. Benefits and costs resulting from transactions which are not internalized in decision-making.

10. Various terms are used in this regard. A large number of these instruments is aimed at decreasing the negative impact on ecosystems. Therefore, 'Payment for Environmental Services' (PES) is often used as the overall term, or 'Conservation Finance'. This seems somewhat out of tune with the broad scope often applied, including instruments varying from Carbon Trading to Revenue from tourism. The writers of this book are of the opinion that 'compensation schemes' is appropriate as an overall term as it focuses on the mechanism – compensating positive or negative externalities – and not on a specific (though key) objective. See for instance WWF (2009) for an overview of instruments. Payment for Ecosystem Services is discussed in section 4.5.

11. In the opinion of the authors of this book, these two classification characteristics are of specific importance. Evidently, many other classification characteristics are possible, and experience and further research will have to determine which characteristics have the greatest value in assessing IF instruments.

Table 2 IF volume generated via fund-raising (US$million)

Mechanism	2000-2005	2006	2007	2008	Total
Solidarity	7,080	3,045	1,104	485	11,713
Catalytic	112	154	681	668	1,615
PPP	14,390	7,034	10,977	11,352	43,754
Total	**21,582**	**10,233**	**12,763**	**12,505**	**57,082**

Table 3 IF volume generated to support financial solutions 'on the ground' (US$million)

Mechanism	2000-2005	2006	2007	2008	Unspecified	Total
Solidarity	74		66			140
Catalytic	23,602	5,734	7,138	1,192	1,688	39,355
PPP	7,745	761	1,067	464	3,190	13,227
Total	**31,423**	**6,495**	**8,271**	**1,656**	**4,879**	**52,723**

Source: SEO Economic Research, adapted from Girishankar (2009); figures refer to (international) official flows to developing countries and exclude flows from Purely Private IF instruments[12]

Girishankar (2009) estimates that for the period 2000-2008, international efforts in innovative fund-raising generated around US$57 billion, while international efforts to support innovative financial solutions on the ground generated around US$53 billion. To put these figures in perspective, they amount to 4.5% and 5.7%, respectively, of total official flows to development countries over the period 2000-2008 Girishankar (2009).

These figures do not include the proceeds from purely private IF instruments, like commercial microfinance, nor do they include flows towards developed countries, like from emission reduction projects as part of EU ETS.[13] More work is needed to complete the picture of the flows resulting from IF.

4.2.4 Choosing and Evaluating IF Mechanisms

The number of IF mechanisms is enormous. New ideas are generated every day. This merits the questions of which IF mechanisms are interesting enough to analyse (and possibly implement) and how they should be judged. A logical starting point is the objective: without a clear objective, judgement is impossible. Additional variables to

12. For data sources and methods, see Girishankar (2009, pp. 38-39).

13. The proceeds stemming from emission reduction projects in developing countries as part of EU ETS – the value of Certified Emission Rights – *are* included in the figures.

assess when choosing between projects include public and private costs and benefits, what would happen if no action is taken, institutional and political feasibility, and the time and supporting actions required for the mechanism to become effective (De Ferranti, 2006). According to Girishankar (2009, pp. 4-5) innovative fund-raising mechanisms should be evaluated in terms of the "ability to mobilize adequate and predictable resources from a given source at the minimum cost and risk", while financial solutions 'on the ground' should be evaluated in terms of the "ability to efficiently and effectively deliver development results or maximize net development benefit". The risk profile should be taken into account when assessing both types of schemes.

In terms of finance, the (potential) importance and success of an instrument are primarily determined by the money (investment) flow it establishes towards the stated objective, in absolute terms and in terms of leveraging effects. The World Bank (2010, p. 3) concludes "compared to [ODA] and traditional private-capital flows to developing countries, the funding from IF instruments is as yet very small".

4.2.5 *Experience so far: Lessons Learned*

Many innovative finance instruments have not been implemented for very long as yet or are even still in their design phase. Assessment of the experience so far, in general and certainly within (the academic) literature, is still in its infancy. Below some lessons drawn by the literature to date are described.

The International Conference on Financing for Development in 2002, the 'political' start of the international search for IF mechanisms and instruments seemed to have come at a perfect moment. Interest rate premiums were low, banks leveraged their equity capital as never before, and credit volume grew beyond imagination between 2003 and 2007. A favourable time to fund investments, and also for development flows. As a result, development countries experienced an investment boom (The World Bank, 2010). The financial crisis ended this development and highlighted the importance of timely and predictable development resources and the challenge for "healthy aid levels in [an] uncertain environment" (The World Bank, 2010). This might point at a risk of dependency on private capital – which did not end up being very predictable. At the same time, as De Ferranti (2006, pp. 2-3) notes, official flows are expected to drift downward rather than upward. This causes the author to ask "whether private flows can somehow evolve in directions that can be of more help to development".

An interesting set of innovations in this regard revolves around levies on private (or sometimes public) purchases, like air ticket levy schemes. The risk with private investment capital for development is that it might change quite rapidly from great highs, like before the financial crisis, to great lows as was evidenced during the crisis. Although levies will also be impacted by the economic cycle, because purchases fluctuate with market development, they will do so in a less drastic way. It is therefore no coincidence that the financial crisis has increased interest in levy-based schemes (Sandor et al., 2009).

International conferences, like the G8 in 2009, repeatedly point to the importance of exploring the potential for new IF mechanisms, and, indeed, many new innovations are emerging (Sandor et al., 2009). This development of striving for new instruments, however, comes with a risk. The aim should be to implement those instruments that are most effective and efficient. It does not seem plausible that more instruments will always result in more funds for social and environmental development. In this regard, Girishankar (2009) points to the necessity to employ instruments selectively.

Lessons should be learned from instruments that have already been implemented. With the first IF instruments focused on combining public and private sources to meet health challenges, this could be an area for specific attention. Fryatt et al. (2010) summarise the key challenges faced by the High Level Taskforce on Innovative International Financing for Health System, created in 2008. Aside from health-specific conclusions, the paper points to the need for (i) research on where investments have the biggest impact; (ii) combining the many ideas on new ways to raise and using funding with more research on what works in different situations; (iii) more impartial assessments among governments which invested in their own innovations; (iv) long-term predictability of funds; (v) improved accountability from governments and donors to stakeholders. Improvements in the health sector, like increasing predictability through the International Finance Facility for Immunisation (IFFIm)[14], might be used for other development areas.

Meijerink et al. (2008) point to an effective governance regime and a well-functioning institutional environment as pre-conditions for innovative finance mechanisms. This is especially true for funding of ecosystem services, i.e., the benefits people obtain from the ecosystem (Engel, Pagiola, &Wunder, 2008), where it is vital that property right structures, laws on ecosystem protection and definitions of rights and responsibilities are clear and can be legally enforced. In addition, transaction costs are an important, albeit frequently overlooked, factor in assessing IF instruments.

With a focus on developing countries, Girishankar (2009) describes various lessons based on the experience so far. First, the author concludes IF instruments can help increase development effectiveness. Without having to increase public funds as such, multilateral development banks could provide risk management services (e.g. customizing risk-decreasing instruments in areas like country and currency risk to the specific needs of developing countries, which they are in grave need of[15]), and official flows could be channelled more systematically through Catalytic and PPP mechanisms to leverage funds. Another point is that expectations of the potential for addi-

14. For more on the role of IF for improving health aid predictability, see for instance Lane et al. (2008).

15. See for instance: UNEP et al. (2009).

tional development flows through fund-raising IF instruments should be more realistic. They should be viewed as a complement – rather than a substitute – to traditional efforts. New instruments, such as debt offerings in local currency, show potential but are modest compared to traditional efforts. This also strengthens the importance of the first point. Finally, and maybe most importantly, more in-depth information is required to assess the net benefits of IF instruments. The author (p.36) concludes "[i] nnovations need to be tested and evaluated to determine their value-added".[16]

4.2.6 *Describing and Analyzing IF Instruments*

The remainder of this section describes and analyzes a sample of IF instruments. Based on the literature on IF and related instruments discussed in this section, a high-level and transparent 5-step framework has been designed. Each instrument is described and analyzed in identical steps in order to structure the different angles and approaches used by the literature to cover the various types of instruments and to provide a framework for further research:

1. Underlying problem and objectives
   The 5-step framework assumes that for individual IF instruments to be effective, they must target clear problems and objectives. A description of objectives would facilitate measuring and assessing effectiveness. Moreover, those instruments targeting identical problems could be compared: are they complementary, or does the sum equal less than one alone?

2. Structure
   In addition, the 5-step framework assumes that the structure of an instrument, i.e., how it works, determines to a large extent how the underlying problem is challenged and whether objectives are met. Instruments with identical objectives might have a different structure in order to approach the underlying problem in a different manner. Insight into the structure might explain differences in success and thereby facilitate identification of critical success factors.

3. Place in IF landscape
   Classification of instruments facilitates understanding and comparison of the vast number of IF instruments. Together with the objective, it provides a simplified way to characterize an instrument. The typology in IF mechanisms based on Girishankar (2009) described in section 4.2.2 will be used as a guideline for classification. Other classification variables that will be taken into account are: (i) is the instrument aimed at environmental or social sustainability? (ii) is or can the instrument be used for funding in developed and/or developing countries? (iii) is the instrument part of 'compensation schemes' or 'hypothecated finance'?

16. In this regard, Girishankar (2009) sees an important role for agencies like the World Bank Group: they should monitor the impact of innovative financing and determine success factors; and this information should be shared.

4. Business Case Assessment
   The first step towards implementation is assessing whether the proposed IF instrument is expected to be effective and efficient and why (and when not), which potential challenges may be encountered, etc. Relevant questions include: Is the structure really designed to target the underlying problem and meet the defined objectives? What are the costs and benefits (financial and social)? What will happen if the instrument is not implemented? Does it interfere with other instruments, and are these other instruments expected to deliver higher or lower net benefits?

5. Impact and Lessons Learned
   For instruments that have been implemented, the impact should be measured and assessed. The main question is whether objectives are actually being met and why or why not. The analysis should focus on lessons learned, for both the instrument being analysed and other instruments.

The following instruments will be discussed and analysed based on the above 5-step approach: green bonds, index-linked carbon bonds, payment for environmental services, and peer-to-peer lending.[17] Strictly based on the existing literature and limited to a relatively low number of IF instruments, this will primarily be a first step to gain further insights into the critical success factors of IF instruments, provide starting points for lessons learned and for further research.

Box 1 Some other authors discussing a sample of IF instruments

- World Bank Group (2010) shortly discusses, amongst other instruments, the Adaptation Fund, the International Financing Facility for Immunization, local currency bonds, the advance market commitments, results-based financing
- kethar et al. (2009) are editors of a book discussing future-flow securitization, diaspora bonds, GDP-indexed bonds, partial guarantees provided by multilateral agencies, and the International Financing Facility for Immunization.
- Girishankar (2009) provides an extensive overview of IF instruments with a short description of and related literature for each.
- WWF (2009) discusses various conservation finance innovations.
- Meijerink et al. (2008) discuss several instruments aimed at sustainable ecosystem management.
- De Ferranti (2006) discusses results-based sequencing of loans and grants, global development bonds and investing in grassroots business organizations.

17. Choosing from the vast number of implemented IF instruments, and those still in their early days of design and development, this relatively small sample attempts to cover a broad scope of instrument types.

4.3 Green Bonds

This section, and each of the following sections, describes an IF instrument based on the 5-step framework defined in section 4.2.6:

- Step 1 – Underlying problems and objectives: introduces the problem(s) the instrument aims to solve and summarizes its objectives;
- Step 2 – Structure: defines the instrument and explains how it works;
- Step 3 – Place in the IF landscape: categorizes the instrument based on a fixed set of characteristics;
- Step 4 – Business Case Assessment: assesses whether and why the instrument is (or might not be) expected to be effective and/or efficient;
- Step 5 – Impact and Lessons learned: evaluates experience if the instrument has been implemented and identifies what lessons can be learned.

4.3.1 Underlying Problem and Objectives

> *Step 1 – introduce the problem(s) the instrument aims to solve and summarize its objectives*

The concept of green bonds starts from the notion that climate change is too great a challenge to be covered by government resources alone. The vast amount of finance needed to fund required investments will have to come, for the most part, from private sources. More specifically, given the scale of funds needed, funds will have to be generated from global markets and institutional investors in particular. So far, however, private funding is far from sufficient.[18] Equity from private parties – that is: private equity and equity from public markets – has characteristics that prevent it from being exploited in sufficiently large volumes to fund sustainable energy investments. Private equity lacks liquidity and requires high upfront, due-diligence costs, while public equity market activity is focused on big companies (not so much on a sector comprised of many business opportunities, like SE) and is especially challenging in times of economic recession. Based on this conclusion, IF instruments could be designed to offer the right financial incentives to attract private debt, preferably from institutional investors, while using public credit efficiently (Reichelt, 2010).

At the same time, borrowers face a high-risk premium in interest rates due to the (perceived) high-risk character of most low-carbon technologies. This might prevent them from borrowing money to invest in these types of assets or projects and focus on traditional fossil-fuel technologies (or other investments) instead (Fine, Madison, Paddon, Sniderman, &Rand, 2009). In order to persuade them to invest in low-carbon technologies, IF instruments might be designed to decrease the cost of debt.

---

18. As was discussed in chapter 1, *Financing the Transition to Sustainable Energy.*

Green bonds (GB)[19] are aimed at increasing funding resources for low-carbon investments by creating a financial instrument that appeals to the debt market, especially institutional investors, and at increasing low-carbon investments by decreasing debt-risk premiums for this type of project and activities.

4.3.2 *Structure*

Step 2 – define the instrument and explain how it works

There is no single definition for the structure of GB. Ideas on GB and actually issued GB do share some common characteristics:

- a conventional, simple structure, comparable with other 'plain vanilla' bonds;
- fixed income to investors in the bond[20];
- obtained funds are ring fenced to (be lent to) specified low-carbon projects and/or assets, whether or not via a specific fund;
- bond obligations are guaranteed (partly), lowering credit risk;
- lending is done based on favourable terms, with a margin covering overhead and an interest rate reflecting the low risk of the bonds.

A structure of a GB includes many other characteristics, which might differ between individual issuances. Examples include: the creation of a separate institution to issue and manage the bond (like a Green Bank), the role and responsibilities of fund management versus the guarantor (governance), the guaranteeing party and the level of the guarantee, and the targeted investors (only institutional investors or also retail).[21]

Box 2 provides three examples of GB issued by the World Bank.

---

19. Green bonds are also referred to as climate bonds, although some authors mean different things with these two terms. On Climatebonds.net the following definitions are provided: green bonds are issued to raise the finance for an environmental project; climate bonds are issued to raise finance for investments in emission reduction or climate change adaption.

20. Fine et al. (2009) propose a variable rate of return, noting that "[t]he reason for the variable upper rate is to attract large institutional investors". In the presented case study, however, a fixed interest rate is applied. Reichelt (2010) seems to exclude bond schemes from her definition of green bonds if they do not apply to the fixed income criterion (for instance Eco Notes and Cool Bonds, issued by the World Bank in 2007 and 2008, respectively). The reason is that these are "not designed for institutional investors' fixed-income allocations". In Cameron et al. (2009) and Holmes et al. (2009), a fixed interest rate is also seen as a required design element.

21. Fine et al. (2009) presents a proposal for a Canadian Green Bond, including an extensive description of design elements to be taken into account.

Box 2 Examples of Green Bonds issued by the World Bank

Eco notes
total USDeq 390 million, in three transactions: September and December 2007,and February 2008
Eco notes are six-year euro-denominated notes with a coupon of 3%, plus a potential additional return linked to an ABN-Amro index of "green" equities. The notes raised funds for International Bank for Reconstruction and Development (IBRD)* at attractive rates, while raising awareness for funding "green" activities, at the same time that the hedging activities of IBRD's swap counterparties also supported capital available to companies in the index. ABN-Amro and Fortis Bank distributed the notes in the Netherlands, Switzerland, and Belgium, primarily to retail investors. Proceeds were used in the general operations of IBRD.

Cool bonds
total USDeq 31.5 million to date in two transactions, June and September 2008
Cool bonds are five-year, USD-denominated notes paying a coupon of 3% for an initial period, and a variable coupon amount for the remaining maturity of the note-tied CERs generated by specified greenhouse gas (GHG)-reducing projects in China and Malaysia. Hedging exposure to CERs by IBRD counterparties contributes to expansion of this market as well. Daiwa Securities and Mitsubishi UFJ Securities distributed the notes to Japanese investors. Proceeds were used in the general operations of IBRD.

World Bank Green bonds
USDeq 350 million, October 2008
World Bank Green bonds are 6-year, Swedish kronor notes paying investors a 3.5% annual interest rate and raising funds at a spread of 0.25% over comparable maturity Swedish government paper. They enabled IBRD to raise funds at an attractive cost despite the challenging market environment. Skandinaviska Enskilda Banken (SEB) underwrote the issue and distributed mainly to Scandinavian institutional investors, who were attracted to the investment because the proceeds would be credited to a special account at IBRD that supports World Bank loan disbursements on qualifying climate change mitigation and adaptation projects.

*The IBRD aims to reduce poverty in middle-income and creditworthy poorer countries by promoting sustainable development through loans, guarantees, risk management products, and analytical and advisory services (www.worldbank.org)
Source: Girishankar (2009), based on IBRD

4.3.3 *Place in IF Landscape*

Step 3 – categorize the instrument based on a fixed set of characteristics [22]

Girishankar (2009) includes GB in the category of fund-raising *public-private partnerships*. Bonds, guaranteed by government (partly) and aimed at obtaining loans from private parties, are issued by private financial institutions or multilateral agencies in order to finance (country-level) development efforts. In other words, private sources are leveraged by means of public instruments (guarantees) to support public service delivery. This point of view seems mostly focused on the objective to increase the level of debt (from institutional investors), which indeed points to fund-raising efforts. The objective to reduce borrowing rates seems to point more in the direction of a financial solution 'on the ground'.

GB are aimed at financing *environmental development*. Proceeds are ring fenced, and the instrument is therefore a *hypothecated finance* scheme. The ring fencing refers to the type of project that is to be funded – low-carbon project – and not to the region. Proceeds can be used for investments in both *developed and developing countries.*

4.3.4 *Business Case Assessment*

Step 4 – assess whether and why the instrument is (or might not be) expected to be effective and/or efficient

The issue of attracting institutional investors is indeed seen as an important, albeit challenging, opportunity to increase investments in low-carbon activities (UNEP, 2009; WEF, 2009). Green bonds target this type of investor via bonds combined with a guarantee and fixed income to reduce risks and comply with institutional investors' preferences. According to Reichelt (2010) this would have benefits over using equity instruments (as discussed in section 4.3.1). The London School of Economics (LSE, 2009) and World Economic Forum (WEF, 2009), however, point to two other instruments – low-carbon challenge funds and low-carbon cornerstone funds – aimed at the same objective: targeting institutional investors to increase scale.[23] These instruments do not focus on debt, but combine equity, leveraging debt and the use of a set of public finance mechanisms to address specific barriers.[24] In addition to targeting equity instead of only debt, an important difference is that barriers preventing institutional investors from investing in low-carbon activities are more specifically addressed. Green bonds depend on guaranteeing bond obligations as a mechanism to

22. For definitions, see Section 4.2.2.

23. For a full description of these two instruments, see London School of Economics (LSE, 2009) and World Economic Forum (WEF, 2009). These papers focus on funding to developing countries.

24. Public finance mechanisms are defined as "financial commitments made by the public sector which alter the risk-reward balance of private sector investments" (UNEP, 2009). They include for instance grants, risk mitigation instruments, governmental loans and (subordinated) equity positions. The guarantee included in GBs from the issuer, which could be a government but also a multilateral development bank like the World Bank, can essentially be seen as a public finance mechanism.

decrease risks. But different kinds of risk could call for different kinds of mechanisms. Risks of a specific set of activities might more effectively be decreased via a country-risk cover or a subordinated equity position than a guarantee – making the GB a less effective instrument. Although no direct comparison is made with GBs, it seems there are other instruments aiming at the same objective offering potential added value. More research is necessary on the effectiveness of GBs compared to other instruments, on whether these instruments are complementary to GBs, etc.

According to Fine et al. (2009), private parties should control and manage the proceeds of the bond (or: the fund). Incentives in the private sector, contrary to those in the public sector, will be aimed at efficient management of the fund. Moreover, the private sector has ample experience in performing the required due diligences to chose projects to be funded, while this experience is mostly not available within governmental institutions. These arguments are in line with minimizing operational or default costs of the instrument.

4.3.5 *Impact and Lessons Learned*

> *Step 5 – evaluate experience if the instrument has been implemented and identify what lessons can be learned*

The World Bank played an important role in the development and uptake of the GB instrument. It issued its first GB in 2007 and 2008 – 'Eco Notes' and 'Cool Bonds', respectively. Investors were interested in the bonds, but the amounts raised were relatively low. The schemes were targeted at individual investors (retail investors) and not so much at institutional investors (Reichelt, 2010).[25] Thereafter, it issued several GBs aimed at institutional investors. Buyers of the bonds included a Swedish life insurance provider and the California State Teachers' Retirement System. One bond issue was totally absorbed by the State of California. Other examples of bonds issued are presented in Table 4.

Recently, GBs have been mentioned by the UK government as a means of funding for the Green Investment Bank initiative (Green Investment Bank Commission, 2010). Many other institutions are advocating the use of GBs, including the Climate Change Capital (advocating bonds to be issued by the OECD) and the influential Canadian group PowerUP Canada (advocating bonds to be issued by Canada). Still, Reichelt (2010) concludes, "funds generated from green bonds so far are small, relative to the estimated amounts needed to fill the climate change funding gap". The author does imply room for improvement, whether in the exact form of GBs or another fixed-income debt instrument. An important point for improvement is to design the bonds in a standardized way that helps index providers to include them in

25. See also: http://climatebonds.net/.

the 'Green Index', so that index-investors automatically include the bonds in their investment portfolios.[26]

Expected amounts to be raised via low-carbon challenge funds and low-carbon cornerstone funds, instruments with identical objectives to GBs (see Section 4.3.4), amount to US$10 billion and US$50-75 billion, respectively (WEF, 2009).[27] This greatly exceeds the amounts mentioned in the table above. First, they are expected amounts, and second, they include leverage potential. More research is needed to compare the instruments.

Table 4 Examples of Issued Green Bonds

Issued by	Year	Interest	Amount
World Bank	2007-2008 (in 3 tranches)	Index-linked	$390mio
	2008 (in 2 tranches)	Fixed + coupon linked to CER price	$31.5mio
	2008	Fixed	$350mio
	2009	Fixed	
	2009	Floating	$300mio
	2009	Fixed	$130mio
European Investment Bank	2007	Zero coupon	€600mio
US government	2009	Paid in tax credits	$2.2billion

Source: Climate Bonds25

26. The research for this book has not resulted in a clear picture of the regional focus of the proceeds: developed or developing countries. This could be an interesting subject for further research. The outcome might impact, for instance, the risk profile of projects and therefore the costs of the guarantee and possibly the appeal to both issuers and investors.

27. The instruments are focused on regions. The amounts are per region and for a three-year period (WEF, 2009).

4.4 Index Linked Carbon Bonds

4.4.1 *Underlying Problem and Objectives*

Step 1 – introduce the problem(s) the instrument aims to solve and summarize its objectives

In order for low-carbon investments to become financially attractive, public policy aims to influence returns and risks and to decrease potential funding barriers (see chapter 1). With investor return depending for a large part on public policy, regulatory risk is an important factor in business case decisions. The lower the confidence in governments keeping their promises, the higher the risk premium factored into the cost of capital. Regulatory risk can therefore be a major obstacle for low-carbon investments.

Index-linked carbon bonds (ILCB) are aimed at increasing low-carbon investments by decreasing regulatory risk.

4.4.2 *Structure*

Step 2 – define the instrument and explain how it works

Index-linked carbon bonds (ILCB) are government-issued bonds, with interest payments linked to the measurable outcome of public policy. ILCB in its simplest form links the return of the bond to the actual greenhouse gas (GHG) emissions of the issuing country against published targets, with higher GHG emissions resulting in a higher interest rate to be paid by the issuing country. By linking the return of the bond to the extent governments keep their promises on low-carbon policies – e.g. the promise to decrease GHG emissions to a certain level – ILCB create a hedge for regulatory risk (Mainelli, Onstwedder, Parker, &Fischer, 2009; Onstwedder &Mainelli, 2010).

The primary design elements of ILCB are:

- bonds issued by governments (or multilateral agencies);
- the interest rate depends on a specific (published) index which reflects whether the issuing government keeps certain environmental promises, for example an index of the:
  - level of GHG emissions;
  - level of feed-in-tariffs for renewable energy;
  - percentage of renewable energy in overall energy supply;
  - price of emission reduction certificates in a trading system;
  - level of taxes on fossil fuels or fossil fuel end-user price (Onstwedder &Mainelli, 2010).
- the investor receives an excess return if the chosen index of the issuing government exceeds a predetermined level.

In practical terms: an investor buys a government bond – the ILCB – *and* invests in a low-carbon project of choice. The financial return of the low-carbon project will depend on the government keeping its promise on e.g., the level of the feed-in tariff. If the government fails to do so, the return of the project will decrease, but the interest received on the bond will increase.

If and when these bonds are actively traded, financial markets could provide further elements to the scheme, increasing its effectiveness. For example, derivatives would allow the possibility to hedge risk without actually having to buy the bond.[28]

4.4.3 *Place in IF Landscape*

> *Step 3 – categorize the instrument based on a fixed set of characteristics* [29]

ILCB can be grouped under *Catalytic* financial solutions.[30] Although seemingly in the same field as GBs (classified under PPP), the proceeds of ILCB will not necessarily be used to finance development efforts (at country-level) as is the case for GBs. It is the characteristics of the ILCB (see further below) that turns it into a hedging instrument for the private investor. Therefore, it mobilizes public sources (in terms of a risk instrument) to promote private entry into existing markets.

ILCB are aimed at financing *environmental development*. The instrument catalyzes funding in the region in which the linked index (reflecting regulation risk) is applicable; this might be a region of *developed and developing* countries. Although the instrument is obviously aimed at a specific objective, increasing funds to low-carbon investments, the proceeds of the instrument are not earmarked. They can be used by the issuing party for whatever cause seems fit.[31]

4.4.4 *Business Case Assessment*

> *Step 4 – assess whether and why the instrument is (or might not be) expected to be effective and/or efficient*

ILCB provide a hedge against regulatory risk, one of *the* risk categories posing a barrier for low-carbon investments. They facilitate hedging against various kinds of regulatory risk by means of different indexes, thereby providing hedges for different

28. For the background on this and other options, see Mainelli et al (2009) and Onstwedder et al. (2010).

29. For definitions, see Section 4.2.2.

30. Girishankar (2009) does not include ILCB in its overview of instruments, most probably because these instruments are not specifically focused on developing countries.

31. Although not specifically addressed by the literature on the structure of ILCB, the possibility of ring fencing the proceeds for the issuer to low-carbon projects does not seem attractive for the issuer as it would add to the risk. If regulatory promises are not met, not only would the issuer have to pay a higher interest rate, it would also face default risk because the underlying projects will suffer from the deviation from regulatory promises.

kinds of projects. Still, some limits to the number of underlying indexes would facilitate standardisation and market liquidity, which are important for further development.

By providing a hedge against regulatory risk, investors will become more inclined to fund low-carbon projects and activities. Importantly, though, it would require investors to buy a bond – the ILCB. The funds used to buy the bond cannot be used for other investments. Assuming that an investment budget has limits, the money available for low-carbon projects decreases. Moreover, it impacts on the total project return profile: the return on government bonds is low compared to the required return for low-carbon projects.[32] This issue is partly mitigated by the fact that the project does not have to be hedged on a 1 to 1 basis, i.e. an investment of, say, $1million does not require buying ILCB for the same amount. This 'hedge ratio' is primarily determined by the dependence of the project's return on the specific regulatory risk – for example, the carbon price – but also on the level of trust in government promises (City of London, The London Accord, &CEAG Ltd, 2009). The higher the impact of the risk and the lower the level of trust, the higher the required hedge ratio.

Box 3
Business Case Index-linked Carbon Bond

For example, consider a complex, long-term investment in a tidal barrage scheme. Such schemes have characteristically huge capital costs, low costs of operation once installed, and long lifetimes (around 200 years). This means they are difficult to value using conventional, discounted cash flow methods.

Let us assume that a 4 km barrage costing €1.5bn producing 2.75 terawatt hours of electricity per year needs carbon prices of €40/tonne CO_2e to give a payback period of around 80 years and a price of €60/tonne for a payback of 30 years. The effect of a high carbon price is to raise the wholesale costs of electricity produced by conventional means. These costs are passed on to the consumer thereby raising electricity prices, including the price that can be charged by the barrage scheme generator, which does not have to buy carbon allowances in order to generate. If the price of carbon is low, the barrage generator will lose this competitive advantage over fossil fuel generators.

The investor may buy a bond with the following characteristics:

- The base yield is 4% per annum;

32. Of course, the risk of government bonds is also lower. But many investors have general minimum return targets or even internal guidelines specifically excluding low-risk/government bonds from the investment opportunities. On the other hand, exactly this element might appeal to institutional investors like pension funds, who want to invest in renewable projects/funds. A part of their funds is invested in government bonds anyway. With ILCB they can invest in bonds which at the same time facilitate investing in 'green' projects.

- The base yield is indexed to a carbon price of €60/tonne, and the bond is slightly leveraged:
  - above €60, the interest rate falls by 1% for every €20 increase in carbon;
  - below €60 the interest rate increases by 1% for every €5 decrease in the carbon price; and,
  - below €40 the rate increases by 1% for every €2.50 decrease.

The impact of such an instrument is to significantly reduce the investors' carbon price risk. When the carbon price is low, the barrage generator receives additional interest from the bond to compensate it for the loss of competitive advantage.

The investor does not have to hedge the entire capital sum of €1.5 ($2.2) billion. Buying bonds of 10% of the project capital (€150million), i.e. a 'hedge ratio' of 10%, is sufficient in this case to hedge against a fall in the carbon price to €30/tonne. Without the bond, the payback period for the project at this €30 price is 450 years (longer than its expected lifetime), while with the bond, its payback is 70 years.

Source: City of London et al. (2009)

City of London et al. (2009) point to other instruments to hedge regulatory risks. Regulatory risks depending on actively traded indexes, such as the price of European Unit Allowances, might preferably be hedged on one of the relevant markets.[33] Still, there remain ample examples of regulatory risk which are not hedgeable by conventional financial instruments.

The primary objective of ILCB is to provide a hedge for investors facing regulatory risk. The issuing government provides the market with a hedge instrument *and* receives the proceeds of the bonds as is the case for a regular government bond. Part of the appeal of this instrument, however, is that it has some beneficial side-effects for the issuing government. For one, they will pay low interest rates on their bonds if they meet their stated objectives. Moreover, they will have a way to differentiate their bond issues in an overcrowded bond market[34], targeting specific investor groups. At the same time, governments can signal their commitment to environmental regulation, providing trust to the market.

Academics from the London School of Economics (LSE, 2009) conclude ILCB are "emerging as one of the most promising instruments for raising finance on the capital markets, since they provide for genuine government commitment that directly addresses the primary concern of private sector investors".

33. EUA is the trading unit within the EU ETS.
34. The crisis has, generally, resulted in high government debt.

4.4.5 *Impact and Lessons Learned*

> *Step 5 – evaluate experience if the instrument has been implemented and identify what lessons can be learned*

So far, Index-Linked Carbon Bonds have not yet been issued. The idea of index-linked carbon bonds emerged from discussions with participants in the London Accord community. It was presented to the World Bank in 2009 and discussed with government debt offices and treasuries. According to sources from within or close by the London Accord community, governments as well as investors have shown interest. As a next step, further market research on supply and demand is required (Mainelli et al., 2009). In terms of financial flow potential, City of London et al. (2009, p. 19) note, "[t]he scale of the potential market in [ILCB] is limited only by government deficits and borrowing needs". This seems rather optimistic, as it will also depend on uptake by investors – and the type of investors that will be attracted.

4.5 Payment for Environmental Services

4.5.1 *Underlying Problem and Objectives*

Step 1 – introduce the problem(s) the instrument aims to solve and summarize its objectives

Deforestation and use of land for pasture imply *benefits* for the land users and *costs* to other. As ecosystems provide benefits to 'outsiders' (e.g., water services and biodiversity), the use of land (e.g. deforestation) provides a cost. The benefits of ecosystems for 'outsiders' are called positive externalities and – mirrored – the costs of land use are called negative externalities. The land use benefits typically outweigh the benefits of land conservation because neither the negative nor the positive externalities are taken into account in the decision-making process by land users/owners. All in all, there are incentives for deforestation and use of land for pasture, and there is a lack of incentives for land conservation (Mayrand &Paquin, 2004; Pagiola, 2003).

As a result, environmental (or ecosystem) services (ES) are becoming increasingly threatened. Since 1961, tropical countries have lost over 500 million hectares of forest cover, the consumption of forest products has risen by 50% worldwide, and nearly two-thirds of global ecosystem services are in decline (Engel et al., 2008; Mayrand &Paquin, 2004). This leads to the loss of environmental services such as carbon sequestration and storage, biodiversity protection, watershed protection, and landscape/scenic beauty.

Payments for Environmental Services try to correct these market failures.

4.5.2 *Structure*

Step 2 – define the instrument and explain how it works

Payments for Environmental Services (hereafter: PES) intend to correct market failures by bridging the interests of landowners and outsiders. They seek to reconcile conflicting interests through compensation; PES schemes are intended "to support positive environmental externalities through the transfer of financial resources from beneficiaries of certain environmental services to those who provide these services or are fiduciaries of environmental resources" (Mayrand &Paquin, 2004). The goal of PES programs is to make privately unprofitable but socially desirable practices profitable to individual land users, thus encouraging them to adopt them (Engel et al., 2008).

The principle behind PES is that the users of resources and the communities that are in a position to provide ES should be compensated for the costs of their provision, and that those who benefit from these services should pay for them, thereby internalizing these benefits and offering incentives to farmers or landowners to provide ES in exchange for managing their land (Figure 3). In other words, it is based on the 'beneficiary-pays principle' (rather than the 'polluter-pays principle', as is the case in, for example, carbon trading), thereby making it attractive in settings where ES providers are poor, marginalized landholders or powerful groups of actors (Engel et al., 2008; Mayrand &Paquin, 2004; USAID PES Sourcebook, 2007).

Figure 3 The logic of payment for environmental services (PES)

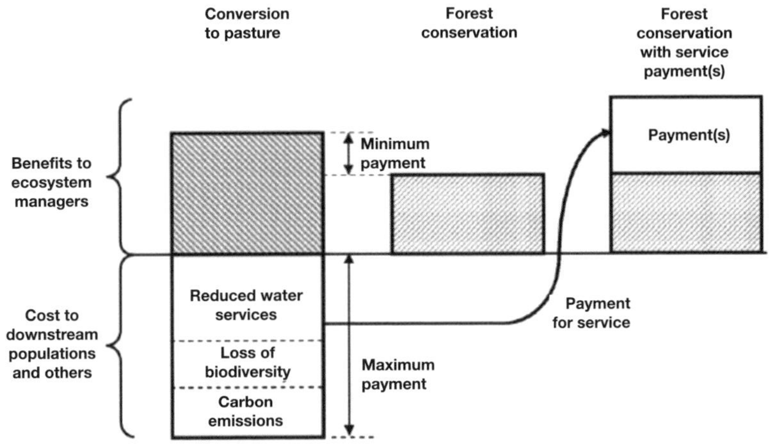

Source: Engel et al. (2008, p. 665)

In short, a PES is (Wunder, 2005):

1. a *voluntary* transaction where
2. a *well-defined* ES (or a land use likely to secure that service)
3. is being 'bought' by an ES *buyer* (minimum of one)
4. from an ES *provider* (minimum of one)
5. if and only if the ES provider secures ES provision (*conditionality*).

There is a great diversity of existing PES models (and therefore a great variation of what is regarded as being 'PES'), though they all "share the objective of providing environmental services that are undersupplied due to the lack of a compensatory mechanism, and to provide a mechanism by which services can be provided in a cost-efficient manner over the long run" (Mayrand &Paquin, 2004, p. 6).

In a 'user-financed' PES program, the ES *buyers* are the actual users (e.g., a hydroelectric power producer pays upstream land users to conserve the watershed above its plant). In a 'government-financed' PES program, the ES *buyers* are a third party acting on behalf of service users, typically a government agency. ES *sellers* are those who are in a position to safeguard the delivery of the ES. This generally means that the potential sellers are landholders, and the vast majority of PES programs is aimed at private landholders (Engel et al., 2008).

Illustrations of PES schemes include (Wunder, 2005):

- Carbon sequestration and storage: a Western electricity company paying farmers in the tropics for planting and maintaining additional trees;
- Biodiversity protection: conservation donors paying local people for setting aside or naturally restoring areas to create a biological corridor;
- Watershed protection: downstream water users paying upstream farmers for adopting land uses that limit deforestation, soil erosion, flooding risks, etc.;
- Landscape/scenic beauty: a tourism operator paying a local community not to hunt in a forest being used for tourists' wildlife viewing.

4.5.3 *Place in IF Landscape*

Step 3 – categorize the instrument based on a fixed set of characteristics[35]

There are many forms of PES schemes. As the instrument targets a market imperfection, it would seem highly likely that the government has to perform a catalyzing role. Still, there are examples of self-regulation – like the example given of the Western electricity company paying farmers for planting additional trees. The instrument therefore seems to fit within *Catalytic or Pure Private* mechanisms.

PES is aimed at financing *environmental development*, i.e., to fund (the preservation of) environmental services by making users pay for them.[36] More and more, however, attention is being put on the possibility to use PES to finance *social development* (i.e., benefiting the poor) as evidenced by the increasing (empirical) literature on this option (see Section 4.5.5). Especially PES aimed at environmental development can be used in both developed and developing countries, although the literature seems to *focus on developing countries*. The latter is especially true for PES aimed at decreasing poverty. PES is clearly a *Compensation scheme*. As payments are directly made for environmental services, the proceeds are earmarked, and the instrument can be categorized as a *Hypothecated Finance scheme*.

4.5.4 *Business Case Assessment*

Step 4 – assess whether and why the instrument is (or might not be) expected to be effective and/or efficient

Success Drivers

In theory, PES works best when the value of ES (i.e., the positive externality) is high and the costs of providing ES is low. The high value of the ES implies a high willingness to pay for it. The relatively low cost of providing the ES tilts the cost-benefit scale for landowners in the direction of environmental conservation (Mayrand &Paquin, 2004).

There are various success drivers for PES schemes. They tend to work best when (Mayrand &Paquin, 2004):

- they are based on clear and consensual scientific evidence linking land uses to the provision of services;
- they clearly define the environmental services to be provided;
- their contracts and payments are flexible, ongoing and open-ended;
- their transaction costs do not exceed potential benefits;

---

35. For definitions, see Section 4.2.2.

36. For complete clarity: PES is not a funding instrument in the sense of a direct provision of equity or loans.

- they rely on multiple sources of revenues delivering money flows that are sufficient and sustainable over time;
- compliance, land use changes, and the provision of services are closely monitored; and
- they are flexible enough to allow adjustments to improve their effectiveness and efficiency and to adapt to changing conditions.

Furthermore, success depends greatly on pre-existing conditions: PES systems work best when services are visible and beneficiaries are well organized (reducing transaction costs), and when land-user communities are well structured, have clear and secure property rights, strong legal frameworks, and are relatively wealthy or have access to resources.

According to Mayrand &Paquin (2004), there also appears to be a trade-off between cost efficiency and effectiveness. Cost efficiency is highest when transaction costs are lowest, and thus PES schemes seek to minimize those costs. On the other hand, payments under PES schemes are more effective when they are targeted and involve detailed management requirements, which entails higher transaction costs.

Income Distribution Implications of PES

Although PES was primarily intended to improve the efficiency of natural resource management, many have assumed that PES will contribute to poverty reduction by making payments to poor land users. Of course, the potential distributional impacts of PES programs will only be experienced by those who participate.

There are two major obstacles for 'pro-poor PES'. The first is insecure land tenure – PES is easier to implement when land is securely held by the ES providers, and thus, by definition, it is less applicable to land held communally or without a legal title. Second, pro-poor PES implies dealing with a large number of poor people each delivering a small service, entailing high transaction costs (e.g., search and information costs, contracting costs and monitoring costs). Buyers therefore prefer to deal with single providers representing large bundles of resources rather than many poor people (Thuy, Ha, & Campbell, 2008).

Until recently, there was little empirical verification of the pro-poor PES hypothesis, and available evidence on participation of the poor was said to be mixed (Engel et al., 2008). More recent empirical data seems to point to a positive impact, as discussed in the next section.

4.5.5 *Impact and Lessons Learned*

Step 5 – evaluate experience if the instrument has been implemented and identify what lessons can be learned

Measuring PES Impact

There are several ways to measure the success of PES schemes. Mayrand &Paquin (2004) suggest the following success indicators:

- number of participants (both beneficiaries and land users);
- land area that is included under the PES scheme;
- extent to which PES scheme is generating land-use changes;
- net additional revenues that a PES scheme brings to land users;
- distributional impacts of PES schemes (e.g., impact on poor or traditional communities);
- long-run financial sustainability of the system;
- extent to which the system is generating environmental services;
- transfer efficiency of the system (net percentage of revenues that end up as net income gains for land users); and
- cost-effectiveness of PES schemes compared to alternatives.

USAID (USAID PES Sourcebook, 2007) proposes a treatment versus control group type of measurement, comparing PES programs with otherwise comparable non-PES projects. They do not, however, provide empirical application of this themselves. A similar approach is the use of counterfactual ES baselines, whereby one considers what would hypothetically happen without the PES scheme (Wunder, 2005). Both methodologies (treatment-control group and a baseline approach) use a counterfactual to evaluate PES effectiveness and efficiency. They provide an interesting venue for further research.

Empirical Findings

Few PES mechanisms have been carefully documented (Engel et al., 2008), many impact studies are either anecdotal or based on a small sample size, and studies that only include PES participants in their sample tend to suffer from selection bias (USAID PES Sourcebook, 2007). Or as Wunder (2008, p. 293) puts it: "empirical evidence on welfare impacts of PES in developing countries remains sketchy, both because many schemes are still young and because little systematic 'with and without PES' welfare data have been gathered". Moreover, more recent empirical studies tend to evaluate PES schemes only at a very detailed level, making it impossible to reach generalized conclusions.[37]

37. See, for instance, Bulte et al. (2008), Graff-Zivin &Lipper (2008), Horan et al. (2008)

Much of the more recent empirical literature is focused on the linkage to poor people's benefits of PES programs:

- Wunder (2008) concludes that poor people can widely participate in PES schemes and that this participation usually makes them better off – albeit seldom yielding huge gains.
- Antle &Stoorvogel (2008) offer three case studies (in Kenya, Peru, and Senegal) and find that carbon payments (payments for agricultural soil carbon sequestration) could have a positive impact on the sustainability of production systems while also reducing poverty.
- Alix-Garcia et al. (2008) conclude that capped flat PES payments are more egalitarian than risk-targeted payments and that risk-weighted schemes result in more payments to poor communities.
- Pagiola et al. (2008) show that poorer households are in fact able to participate, and that – by some measures – they participated to a greater extent than better-off households.

4.6 Peer-to-Peer Lending

4.6.1 *Underlying Problem and Objectives*

Step 1 – introduce the problem(s) the IF instrument aims to solve and summarize its objectives

Equity and corporate debt are primarily accessible for large-scale, mature borrowers. Microfinance, as a solution for smaller companies and entrepreneurs, has grown considerably, with annual growth at 30% since the early 1970s. Still, "the vast majority of the poor are still underserved. Moreover, most of them are being served at interest rates significantly over commercial lending rates, owing to small loan sizes leading to high transaction costs" (Ashta &Assadi, 2009, p. 3). The authors conclude that peer-to-peer (P2P) online lending could provide a solution.

This section focuses on Kiva, which is an organization providing (non-commercial) P2P lending aimed at providing funds to small firms and entrepreneurs, in both developing and developed countries. Taking Kiva as an example facilitates zooming in on one specific type of P2P lending, namely non-commercial P2P lending.

4.6.2 *Structure*

Step 2 – define the instrument and explain how it works

Started by Matt Flannery, his wife and Moses Onyango in 2005, Kiva is an online lending platform that allows individuals to loan to small businesspeople. As a P2P lending mechanism, it aims to directly link borrower and lender. As the primary difference with commercial P2P, Kiva offers zero interest to the lender. It is a non-profit organisation, with lenders donating money. They can get their money back at the end of the loan term (but often invest it in a new project) but do not receive interest on their loan.

Lenders chose a borrower from the site to provide a loan to. Kiva arranges that money is directed to the borrower via microfinance institutions (MFIs) in more than 40 countries. The MFI, also called 'field-partners', channel the funds from lenders to borrowers.

Initially, a loan was directly channelled from a lender to a borrower. As Kiva grew, it began to work with larger MFIs and larger fund flows – and thus more borrowers would have to go through the screening and administrative processes – which caused MFIs to sometimes pre-disburse funds to borrowers. Instead of telling the borrower to wait, pending on lenders choosing them as a borrower, MFIs provided the funding in anticipation of this happening. Although this was addressed on the Kiva site, it was not very clear to all lenders. During the course of 2009 this resulted in a public discussion, with extensive media coverage, on the lack of transparency of Kiva. In reaction, Kiva promised more clarity on the site. Surprisingly, this discussion on a potentially sensitive subject has not caused much damage to the image, nor to the fund flow – on the contrary.[38]

On the website the borrowers and the project, business or activity to be funded are presented, most times including pictures and other background information. In addition, MFIs are categorized based on a risk-rating system. Riskier MFI are generally smaller and newer. In this way, lenders can chose borrowers via MFI corresponding to their risk tolerance and other preferences.

Kiva has local staff to perform due diligences on the MFI. In addition, it teams up with external companies, like Ernst and Young, to use their expertise in the evaluation process.

At the start, the mechanism facilitated funds from developed countries to developing countries. Since 2009 the site was opened to borrowers from the USA. Kiva CEO Premal Shah summarized the vision behind this decision, criticized by some, as follows "[m]ore than 10 million US business owners face difficulty obtaining capital – even before the credit crisis and economic slowdown which made lending tight … [t]here is nothing wrong with giving US lenders the opportunity to boost entrepreneurship at home, especially at a time where jobs created by small business can help lift the economy out of a recession" (Rao, 2010).[39]

4.6.3 Place in IF Landscape

Step 3 – categorize the instrument based on a fixed set of characteristics[40]

Kiva leverages private sources to private initiatives, providing a market-based solution for a market imperfection in the financial sector – the negligence of small borrowers by financial intermediaries. It is therefore a *Pure Private* instrument aimed at financial solutions 'on the ground'.

Kiva is aimed at *financing social development*. It falls within the range of *Hypothecated Finance*, as it ring fences lender funds to low-income entrepreneurs, mostly referring to small-sized companies or projects. Although started as an initiative focused on borrowers in *developing countries*, with the inclusion of the US market, the developed world has entered the scope as well.

38. See Roodman's blog page (http://blogs.cgdev.org/open_book/2009/10/kiva-is-not-quite-what-it-seems.php), including Flannery's reaction, and for instance *Confusion on where money lent via Kiva goes*, *New York Times*, November 9, 2009.

39. Critics claim that Kiva deviates from its core, "small impactful contributions to entrepreneurs in impoverished situations in developing countries" (Rao, 2010).

40. For definitions, see Section 4.2.2.

4.6.4 Business Case Assessment

Step 4 – assess whether and why the instrument is (or might not be) expected to be effective and/or efficient

Pope et al. (2010, p. 1) define P2P as "an alternative credit market that allows individual borrowers and lenders to engage in credit transactions without traditional banking intermediaries … [while they] aggregate small amounts of money provided by a number of individual lenders to create moderately-sized, uncollateralized loans to individual borrowers". Web-based P2P lending markets have grown excessively, with e.g., the well-known P2P company Prosper having provided funding amounting to $179 million between 2006 and 2009 (Hartley, 2010). The uncollateralized nature of P2P is an important element for its success: it offers debt opportunities for small borrowers without collateral.[41] This is especially important in times of a tightening credit market, like with the recent credit crunch. Banks are more critical in lending money, especially hitting smaller borrowers hard. "To fill this financing gap, an increasing number of borrowers are turning to 'peer-to-peer' networks that connect individual borrowers directly to lenders, cutting out the banking middleman" (Fisman, 2009). According to Ashta et al. (2009) P2P lending has added value compared to traditional microfinance as it facilitates even smaller participation levels – there is practically no minimal lending amount. Moreover, borrowing participation might also increase as internet lending implies smaller transaction costs and thus potentially lower interest rates. Finally, the authors state P2P provides "an increased outreach to people living in isolated rural areas. This increased outreach would further reduce both transaction costs from economies of scale and financing costs through larger loan negotiations".

A large part of P2P initiatives is commercial in nature and designed as an alternative to other investments: it provides for investments with interest rates to investors' liking, while allowing them to provide funding to borrowers in need. Companies like Prosper and LendingClub are commercial and facilitate a specific type of investment, i.e., ones with a social character.

Kiva's aims to "connect people through lending for the sake of alleviating poverty".[42] This is in line with the benefits commercial P2P aim to offer. The difference between Kiva and this type of company lies mainly in the lack of commercial incentives – Kiva is a non-profit, and lenders are essentially donors.[43,44] A first advantage which comes to mind is that the lack of interest to lenders implies lower interest rates offered to

41. Based on e.g. Stiglitz and Weiss (1981) and Ang et al. (1995, 1998), Iyer et al. (2009) conclude that there is ample theoretical and empirical evidence that banks rely strongly on collateral when funding small companies, thereby limiting possibilities for otherwise creditworthy borrowers.

42. See www.kiva.org.

43. In terms of not receiving interest on their loans.

44. For literature on charitable giving, see for instance Andreoni et al. (2006) and Rose-Ackerman (1996).

borrowers. This appears not to be the case. Ashta et al. (2007) conclude, "It is found that the second intermediary, the local MFI, has new transaction costs with this type of financing, which are the costs of writing and uploading biographies of poor people onto websites. These costs compensate for the interest-free loans that they get from Kiva. As a result, no extra lowering of interest cost goes to the borrower". But they offer some relief as "[t]he social surplus lost by the Kiva lender (who lends interest free) is captured by the MFI or the people who are freelance writers. Therefore, to some extent, employment may go up in a poor country".

Kiva founder Matt Flannery points out "[t]he main constraint to our growth is user lending" (Flannery, 2009, p. 32), implying that number of lenders (and the amounts lent) might pose a limitation to further growth and not so much the availability of projects and entrepreneurs seeking funds. At the same time, the benefit of Kiva might well be found (at least partly) on this side of the equation, the lender side. More specifically, the 'donor' character might attract a different type of lender compared to commercial microfinance, thereby increasing the lending base.[45] More research is necessary in this field.

4.6.5 Impact and Lessons Learned

> *Step 5 – evaluate experience if the instrument has been implemented and identify what lessons can be learned*

Kiva is generally seen as a success. It has received lots of media attention and has thereby drawn attention to the importance of this type of finance and fighting poverty in general. Between 2007 and 2009 cumulative volume has grown from $6 million to $60 million (Flannery, 2009). The only problems it appears to have faced so far has been the criticism on pre-disbursement and lack of transparency (as discussed above). This did not have grave consequences, however.

In 2008 $36 million were lent to low-income entrepreneurs via Kiva (Flannery, 2009). Whether this is 'high', 'good' or even 'good enough' is hard to assess. Comparing it with the funding between 2006 and 2008 by Prosper of $179 million, this seems at least not bad for a donor-based mechanism – which would normally attract less funding than an investor-based principle. Compared to required needs, it might never be enough. More research is required to assess whether the potential is being met and whether altruistic P2P microfinance schemes like Kiva have a specific impact on fighting poverty – compared to, e.g., mainstream microfinance.

Kiva itself uses two measures for its 'sustainability rate' (Flannery, 2009). First, it measures income to costs, or 'Operational Self-Sufficiency' (OSS). Income refers to revenues to cover Kiva's overhead – so not including the loans provided by lenders.

---

45. No literature was found on this point.

The primary source of revenue is voluntary transaction fees.[46] Lenders are asked to donate an additional 10% on top of their loan for Kiva to cover its overhead. In 2008 OSS amounted to 67%, down from 100% in the early years. The deficit is covered by grants from several foundations. The difficulty with the OSS ratio is that it is more a reflection of strategy than performance as such. More specifically, the ratio reflects the extent to which the organization chooses to depend on grants. The lower the ratio, the higher the gap between Cost and Income, and more grants will be needed to cover that gap. But success in obtaining these grants is not known upfront, and dependence therefore implies a 'business' risk. On the other hand, eliminating this risk by setting an OSS goal of 100% – every dollar spent on overhead must be covered by a dollar in revenues – may limit loan provision because a growing loan base would require a higher overhead, thereby lowering OSS.

A second measure is the leverage ratio, which is defined as the money sent to low-income entrepreneurs as a factor of costs. This measures how much overhead is needed to achieve the company's goal and is thus an indication of efficiency. Kiva's leverage ratio has never been below eight – every dollar spent by Kiva on its organization and operational activities results in a minimum of eight dollars worth of loans – causing Flannery (2009, p. 40) to conclude that "a donation to Kiva's operational expenses generates real returns in the form of dollars being spent on the poor". This, however, would technically be true for any value above one. The question remains whether altruistic P2P microfinance, as an IF mechanism, adds value in terms of cost and benefits compared to alternatives and whether the concept could be improved further. Although Kiva is usually discussed in a microfinance or P2P context, assessment of these kinds of performance indicators could most probably benefit from comparison with charity organizations.

Essentially, lenders decide who gets their money. This might be based on a variety of variables, not necessarily including the 'business quality' or risk of the borrower, potentially undermining the effectiveness of the mechanism. Also, discrimination – e.g., in terms of gender, age or appearance – might be a potential risk. Ly et al. (2010) find that the first hypothesis is not true for Kiva lenders. Their empirical results suggest rational variables such as the likelihood of repayment, the constraints faced by borrowers, and the borrowers' needs (e.g., education or health projects) are taken into account when choosing borrowers. The authors conclude that "the selection criteria of individual lenders are partly aligned with the broader goals of poverty alleviation and financial sustainability advanced by the microfinance sector". In terms of discrimination, Ravina (2008) and Pope et al. (2010) find evidence that variables such as race and beauty do influence lenders' decisions. Although this is not based on Kiva data, but on data from Prosper.com, it might indicate that discrimination influences lenders' decisions.

46. As explained, Kiva does not charge interest to lenders.

References

Alix-Garcia, J., De Janvry, A., &Sadoulet, E. (2008). The role of deforestation risk and calibrated compensation in designing payments for environmental services. *Environment and Development Economics, 13*(03), 375-394.

Andreoni, J., &Serge-Christophe Kolm and Jean Mercier, Y. (2006). Chapter 18 Philanthropy. In *Handbook on the Economics of Giving, Reciprocity and Altruism* (Vol. Volume 2, pp. 1201-1269): Elsevier.

Antle, J. M., &Stoorvogel, J. J. (2008). Agricultural carbon sequestration, poverty, and sustainability. *Environment and Development Economics, 13*(03), 327-352.

Ashta, A., &Assadi, D. (2009). An Analysis of European Online micro-lending Websites. *Cahiers du CEREN, 29*, 147-160.

Bulte, E. H., Boone, R. B., Stringer, R., &Thornton, P. K. (2008). Elephants or onions? Paying for nature in Amboseli, Kenya. *Environment and Development Economics, 13*(03), 395-414.

Cameron, J., &Holmes, I. (2009). *Accelerating green infrastructure investment with green bonds*. London: Green Alliance.

City of London, The London Accord, &CEAG Ltd. (2009). *Delivering Copenhagen: The Role of the City's Financial Services Sector in Supporting Action on Climate Change*. London: CEAG Ltd.

De Ferranti, D. (2006). Innovative Financing Options and the Fight Against Global Poverty: What's New and What's Next. In L. Brainard (Ed.), *Transforming the Development Landscape*.

Emerton, L., Bishop, J., &Thomas, L. (2006). *Sustainable Financing of Protected Areas: A global review of challenges and options*: World Conservation Union.

Engel, S., Pagiola, S., &Wunder, S. (2008). Designing payments for environmental services in theory and practice: An overview of the issues. *Ecological Economics, 65*(4), 663-674.

Fine, B., Madison, O., Paddon, E., Sniderman, A., &Rand, T. (2009). *Green Bonds: A Public Policy Proposal*: Action Canada, Mimeo.

Fisman, R. (2009). It's Like eBay Meets Match.com: Does peer-to-peer lending work? .

Flannery, M. (2009). Kiva at Four (Innovations Case Narrative: Kiva). *Innovations: Technology, Governance, Globalization, 4*(2), 29-48.

Fryatt, R., Mills, A., &Nordstrom, A. (2010). Financing of health systems to achieve the health Millennium Development Goals in low-income countries. *The Lancet, 375*(9712), 419-426.

Girishankar, N. (2009). *Innovating Development Finance: From Financing Sources to Financial Solutions*. Washington, DC: The World Bank.

Graff-Zivin, J., &Lipper, L. (2008). Poverty, risk, and the supply of soil carbon sequestration. *Environment and Development Economics, 13*(03), 353-373.

Green Investment Bank Commission. (2010). *Unlocking Investment to Deliver Britain's Low Carbon Future*.

Hartley, S. (2010). Kiva.org: Crowd-Sourced Microfinance &Cooperation in Group Lending.

Holmes, I., &Mabey, N. (2009). *Accelerating Green Infrastructure Financing: Outline proposals for UK green bonds and infrastructure bank*. London: Climate Change Capital.

Horan, R. D., Shogren, J. F., &Gramig, B. M. (2008). Wildlife conservation payments to address habitat fragmentation and disease risks. *Environment and Development Economics, 13*(03), 415-439.

Iyer, R., Khwaja, A. I., Luttmer, E. F. P., &Shue, K. (2009). *Screening in New Credit Markets: Can Individual Lenders Infer Borrower Creditworthiness in Peer-to-Peer Lending?*

Lane, C., &Glassman, A. (2008). Smooth and Predictable Aid for Health: A Role for Innovative Financing. *Brookings Global Economy and Development, Washington DC http://www.brookings. edu/~/media/Files/rc/papers/2008/08_global_health_glassman/o 8_global_-health_glassman. pdf.*

LSE. (2009). *Meeting the Climate Challenge: Using Public Funds to Leverage Private Investment in Developing Countries.* London: London School of Economics and Political Science.

Mainelli, M., Onstwedder, J.-P., Parker, K., &Fischer, W. (2009). *Index-Linked Carbon Bonds - Gilty Green Government.* London: Z/Yen Group.

Mayrand, K., &Paquin, M. (2004). *Payments for environmental services: a survey and assessment of current schemes.* Montreal, Canada: Unisfera International Centre.

Meijerink, G., Diemont, H., Schrijver, R. A. M., Verhagen, A., &Wageningen, U. R. (2008). *Innovative Financing Mechanisms for Sustainable Ecosystem Management.* Wageningen: Wageningen UR.

Onstwedder, J.-P., &Mainelli, M. (2010). Living Up To Their Promises. *Environmental Finance,* 17.

Pagiola, S. (2003). *Can Programs of Payments for Environmental Services Help Preserve Wildlife?* Washington, DC: The World Bank.

Pagiola, S., Rios, A. R., &Arcenas, A. (2008). Can the poor participate in payments for environmental services? Lessons from the Silvopastoral Project in Nicaragua. *Environment and Development Economics,* 13(03), 299-325.

Pope, D., &Sydnor, J. (2010). What's in a Picture? Evidence of Discrimination from Prosper. com. *Journal of Human Resources.*

Rao, L. (2010, Jul 3, 2009). The Inevitable Anti-US Backlash has Started on Kiva. *TechCrunch.*

Ravina, E. (2008). *Love &Loans: The Effect of Beauty and Personal Characteristics in Credit Markets.*

Reichelt, H. (2010). Green bonds: a model to mobilise private capital to fund climate change mitigation and adaptation projects. In *The EuroMoney Environmental Finance Handbook 2010* (pp. 1-7): WestLB.

Rose-Ackerman, S. (1996). Altruism, nonprofits, and economic theory. *Journal of Economic Literature,* 34(2), 701-728.

Sandor, E., Scott, S., &Benn, J. (2009). *Innovative financing to fund development: Progress and prospects.* Paris: OECD.

The World Bank. (2010). *Innovative Finance for Development Solutions: Initiatives of the World Bank Group.* Washington, DC: The World Bank.

Thuy, P. T., Ha, H. M., &Campbell, B. M. (2008). Pro-poor payments for environmental services: Challenges for the government and administrative agencies in Vietnam. *Public Administration and Development,* 28(5), 363-373.

UNEP. (2009). *Catalysing low-carbon growth in developing economies: Public Finance Mechanisms to scale up private sector investment in climate solutions.* Paris: UNEP.

USAID PES Sourcebook. (2007). *Lessons And Best Practices For Pro-Poor Payment For Ecosystem Services*: USAID.

WEF. (2006). *Blended Value Investing: Capital Opportunities for Social and Environmental Impact.* Cologny/Geneva: World Economic Forum.

WEF. (2009). *Task force on low-carbon prosperity: Summary of Recommendations.* Cologny/Geneva: World Economic Forum.

Wunder, S. (2005). *Payments for environmental services: some nuts and bolts*: Center for International Forestry Research, Bogor.

Wunder, S. (2008). Payments for environmental services and the poor: concepts and preliminary evidence. *Environment and Development Economics,* 13(03), 279-297.

Afterword

Finance plays a pivotal role in accelerating the transition towards sustainable economies and societies. By providing an overview of key insights from academic studies, this book aimed to provide investors, corporate executives, and policymakers with a more thorough understanding of the opportunities that financing sustainability offers, as well as the related risks.

Besides underlining that financing sustainability is an emerging and dynamic field of interest for investors, policymakers and academics alike, this book also points out the necessity for further research in order to fully grasp the potential that financing sustainability provides. In this closing chapter, an overview is provided of some key (business and policy relevant) research questions for further exploration. This list is by no means exhaustive, but should offer a starting point for further research.

1. Financing the Transition to Sustainable Energy – Subjects for Further Research
   - What is the impact of sustainable energy insurance products on risks (perceived and actual) and on cost of capital?
   - How can risk considerations be incorporated in the net cost approach (i.e., the 'abatement cost curve')?
   - What is the potential role of innovative financial solutions – as compared to the focus on the role of regulation – to reap the fruits of investment potential by focusing on the specific barriers faced by sustainable energy investment (per stage in the life cycle)?
   - How can Public Finance Mechanisms (PFM) be used in innovative ways to leverage private investment towards developing countries?

2. Carbon Trading – Subjects for Further Research
   - How to improve the determination of cap levels in order to guarantee permit scarcity in a changing economic and political environment?
   - What are the costs and other consequences of the failure to signal clear international reduction targets? Can instruments be designed to prevent these costs?
   - How to measure the additionality of Green Investment Schemes under the JI mechanism? What can be learned from standards already used in assessing the additionality of CDM?

3. Sustainable Investing – Subjects for Further Research
   - How can the direction of causality between CSR and higher shareholder value be determined?
   - How does CSR influence the cost of capital of firms and their investment decisions?

   - Which ESG factors (by industry) are financially material and in what timeframe?
   - Do financial institutions that apply sustainability principles perform better or worse than otherwise comparable financial institutions?
   - How best to fully integrate ESG factors into investment decisions, both equity and fixed-income investments?

4. Innovations in Financing Environmental and Social Sustainability – Subjects for Further Research
   - What lessons can be drawn from past issues of Green Bonds?
   - What is the market potential for Index-Linked Carbon Bonds (ILCB)?
   - How effective and efficient are Payment for Ecosystem Services (PES)?
   - What is the impact of altruistic Peer-to-Peer Finance on fighting poverty compared to, e.g., conventional microfinance?

Finally, as indicated in the Introduction, 'sustainability' is not only a societal challenge, it is also an inspirational vision, a business opportunity, and a way of thinking. In this regard, we would like to close with the words of Sir Winston Churchill:

> *A pessimist sees the difficulty in every opportunity;*
> *an optimist sees the opportunity in every difficulty.*

We, the authors, hope that this book has provided you, the reader, with new insights into the opportunities that financing sustainability provides.

About the Authors

Marco Kerste is specialized in research on financial solutions to address key societal and business challenges – such as financing sustainability. He is Senior Researcher finance at SEO Economic Research and previously worked for Fortis and the Dutch Central Bank. He holds a master's degree in financial economics.

Nicole Rosenboom is primarily active in the field of competition and regulation, with a special interest in the financial sector. She is Researcher at SEO Economic Research and holds a master's degree in competition and regulation.

Bernd Jan Sikken is specialized in developing sustainable business and finance strategies. He is Programme Director Finance & Sustainability at Duisenberg school of finance and worked for the World Economic Forum, PwC, and ING Investment Management. He holds master's degrees in economics (cum laude) and leadership.

Jarst Weda focuses on energy-related studies, including subjects like renewable energy projects and the economic viability of energy efficiency measures. He is Researcher at SEO Economic Research and holds a master's degree in economics.

Further Information

For further information about the finance & sustainability activities at Duisenberg school of finance (www.dsf.nl), Holland Financial Centre (www.hollandfinancialcentre.com), and/or SEO Economic Research (www.seo.nl), please contact:

Bernd Jan Sikken at bernd.jan.sikken@dsf.nl
Gerard van Baar at vanbaar@hollandfinancialcentre.nl
Marco Kerste at m.kerste@seo.nl